# HOW TO WRITE BETTER LAW ESSAYS

## Tools and techniques for success in exams and assignments

**Steve Foster**
Principal Lecturer in Law
Coventry Law School,
Coventry University

**PEARSON**
Longman

An imprint of **Pearson Education**
Harlow, England · London · New York · Boston · San Francisco · Toronto
Sydney · Tokyo · Singapore · Hong Kong · Seoul · Taipei · New Delhi
Cape Town · Madrid · Mexico City · Amsterdam · Munich · Paris · Milan

**Pearson Education Limited**

Edinburgh Gate
Harlow
Essex CM20 2JE
England

and Associated Companies throughout the world

*Visit us on the World Wide Web at:*
www.pearsoned.co.uk

**First published 2007**

© Pearson Education Ltd 2007

ISBN: 978-1-4058-2200-8

British Library Cataloguing-in-Publication Data
A catalogue record for this book is available from the British Library

Library of Congress Cataloging-in-Publication Data

Foster, Steve, 1955-
How to write better law essays / Steve Foster.
   p. cm.
Includes index.
ISBN-13: 978-1-4058-2200-8 (alk. paper)
ISBN-10: 1-4058-2200-7 (alk. paper)
1. Legal composition–Great Britain. 2. Law examinations–Great Britain. I. Title.
KD404.F67 2007
808'.06634–dc22

                                               2006018361

10 9 8 7 6 5 4 3 2
10  09  08  07

Typeset in 9/12 Interstate Light by 72
Printed and bound by Henry Ling Limited, at the Dorset Press, Dorchester, DT1 1HD

*The publisher's policy is to use paper manufactured from sustainable forests.*

# Contents

## Supporting resources

Visit **www.pearsoned.co.uk/foster** to find valuable online resources

**Companion Website for students**
- Practice exercises for each chapter to test your writing skills
- 'You be the marker' exercises, allowing student to assess sample work

For more information please contact your local Pearson Education sales representative or **www.pearsoned.co.uk/foster**

# Preface

Many students find the transition between A level and undergraduate study quite daunting. In particular, they find the demands of undergraduate assessment quite different from those encountered in their previous study. They are now expected to write with greater clarity and precision, to employ sounder grammatical and writing skills, to research and refer to a variety of primary and secondary sources and to be critical and analytical in their work. Furthermore, as law undergraduates, students are expected to write with an air of legal professionalism, to support their arguments with legal authority and to employ solid referencing and citation skills. In practice, it is these aspects of undergraduate study, rather than the greater substantive content on undergraduate courses, that pose the greatest test to students.

The main aim of this book is to identify good research and writing skills, particularly in the preparation and submission of assessments in law. Throughout the book, the author identifies the key characteristics of good (and bad) techniques in the writing of law assessments and prepares students for the submission of their law assignments. The text is related to many legal skills and method courses, and students are referred to the skills taught on such modules, such as using a (law) library, reference and citation skills and other general and specific study skills.

In particular, the text offers clear and simple advice to those students who find the handling of legal materials difficult, and who find the task of preparing and writing law assignments daunting. The text takes the student through the entire process of researching, writing and presenting law assignments, from the early stages of research and planning to the presentation of the work itself. It provides practical advice to students on how to make the best of lectures, seminars and textbooks during their programme, thus enhancing their chance of success in assessments. It also shows them how to research and plan their assessments; how to write clearly, simply and in an appropriate legal style; how to cite and use legal authorities; how to avoid plagiarism; how to explain and apply legal principles and materials; and how to compile proper and appropriate bibliographies. Students can access the companion website (www.pearsoned.co.uk/foster) to carry out skills exercises and to view examples of advanced assessments.

The text is aimed at all levels of students, including those on undergraduate courses (particularly those at 'new' universities), those on joint law courses (e.g., Law and Business, Law and Economics, Law and Politics), those on professional courses such as CPE and ILEX, and those studying A level and GSCE law. In addition, postgraduate law students, particularly those whose first degree is not in law and who will need some assistance in preparing and writing law assessments, may also use the text.

I would like to thank everyone at Pearson for their help during the writing of this book and their assistance on the layout of the text. Special thanks go to my wife, Angela, who allowed me to reproduce some of her postgraduate coursework. The book is dedicated to her and to our three children – Tom, Ben and Ella.

*Steve Foster*

# Introduction

## How to Use This Book

This book is intended to assist with your law studies, particularly in relation to the research, planning and presentation of your assessments. **Chapters 1 and 2** on essay techniques and the use of legal material in writing law assessments will help you come to terms with the sort of skills you need to display when undertaking an undergraduate course and when writing assignments for such courses. These chapters, therefore, should be read as soon as possible into your course because the content will help you reflect on the expectations of a law course and of your teachers. They will also help you identify any particular weakness or concern that you might have at this early stage of your study.

**Chapters 3 and 4 -** dealing, respectively, with good and bad technique in writing assessments and answering problem questions - can be consulted at an early stage of your study, but will be particularly useful when you receive your first assignment, whether it is in the form of an essay or problem question. These chapters give examples of good and bad essays and give specific guidance on how - and how not - to answer questions, highlighting common mistakes made by students and providing examples of poor and inappropriate presentation. These chapters should be fully digested before you submit your first essay or problem-based assignment and then should be revisited after you have received feedback from your marked script.

**Chapter 5** gives guidance on preparing for and writing examinations in law. The chapter will be of most use during the run up to and the period of the examinations; however, it should be consulted as soon as possible into your studies. This will give you an indication of the skills that you will need to complete law examinations; and most importantly, it will show that succeeding in examinations is tied to good practice in your law study and your other assessments.

Finally, **Chapter 6** explores the skills required for more advanced assessments, including work at level 2 and 3 of your degree, dissertations and assessment at postgraduate level. These chapters should be consulted at the appropriate stage of your studies, but they may be looked at during the early stages of your study to give you an idea of the standard of skills expected later on in your course and to allow you to practice and display these advanced skills as soon as possible. The chapter may be particularly useful to first-year students who have been given an extended essay to submit; generally, though, the chapter will be of most use in your second and third years of your undergraduate course (especially if you are required to submit a dissertation) and in your postgraduate study if you go on to enrol on an LLM or other Master's programme.

# 1 Preparing and Writing Law Assignments

## ● Introduction

This chapter addresses basic essay writing skills and how to prepare and present law assignments. It begins by addressing basic matters such as time management, engaging with the legal area, the module and the module leader, and taking a pride in the module and the work that you have been set.

Specifically, the chapter gives advice on and covers the following matters:

- what to do when you get the assessment;
- the presentation of assessments including guidance on writing style and avoiding grammatical, spelling and typographical errors;
- avoiding plagiarism;
- how to address and show understanding of the question.

All these areas are illustrated by examples of good and poor skills and common errors made by students in the presentation of their work and their study patterns. The underlying point stressed in this chapter is that good students who engage in good study practices produce good essays, and that poor essays are generally the product of poor student practices such as poor time management, absence from lectures and seminars, lack of preparation and planning and a general failure to engage with their studies.

## ● Writing Law Assessments on Undergraduate Courses

Many students find it difficult to make the transition between A level (and other sub-degree courses) and undergraduate study. In particular they find that different and more enhanced skills are needed for the preparation and writing of assessments.

- You may be writing academic essays for the first time.
- Alternatively, you may have some experience in this area, but may have not written essays of any substantial length (essays on undergraduate courses range from 1,250 words to 4,000 words, with 1,500 to 2,000 words being the norm).
- You may have little or no experience in answering problem questions and applying legal principles to hypothetical scenarios.
- Lecturers on undergraduate courses expect you to employ sound essay writing skills including good grammar and spelling.
- You are expected to undertake individual research and to read beyond your lecture notes and basic textbook.
- The secondary sources are more advanced than those you encountered at A level and adopt a more academic style.

- You are required to use legal materials in an appropriate and confident manner.
- The questions tend to be more analytical and less descriptive and often ask you to take a critical approach.
- Lecturers give little guidance on how to answer the question – you will be expected to find out the answer yourself.
- Lecturers do not generally allow you to bring drafts of your essay for correction before submission.

The above-listed points reflect the nature and level of undergraduate study. Many students find the experience of submitting coursework at this level quite different and often quite daunting. These skills can be acquired, or refined, quite quickly, although they are mostly learnt by practise and will not be perfectly honed until the final years of study. Although you are not totally on your own, you will be expected to show an element of independence that you might not have been asked to display previously.

- Learn to be independent in your research.
- Ensure that you read as much legal material as you can, including books, articles, cases, and legal newspaper reports.
- Take your legal skills/method courses very seriously. They are the key to your success on the law programme, particularly with respect to law assessments.

## ● Some Common Complaints

Lecturers have many common complaints regarding the standard and style of student work. It is important that you do not give the lecturer the opportunity to identify these errors and shortcomings in your work because you will invariably lose marks or risk failure.

- Students write in an inappropriate and casual style, not suitable for the submission of law answers: 'I think Frank might have a good chance of winning his case,' rather than 'Given the existing case law in this area, the possibility of Frank succeeding in his action appears strong.'
- Students do not check their work thoroughly before submission for spelling and typographical errors and for poor grammar. Some sentences do not make sense and need re-phrasing before submission.
- Students make lists of relevant points, rather than writing in prose.
- Students do not cite cases or other legal sources properly, referring, for example, to 'the Carlill case' or 'it's in the Theft Act that . . . .'
- Students do not explain cases properly, and do not explain the significance of the case. Instead they cite cases for the sake of it, regardless of whether it is relevant to the point they are making or the facts they are applying it to.
- Students do not include a bibliography, or cannot construct their bibliography in an appropriate manner.
- Students do not credit their sources.

This chapter and subsequent chapters address these issues giving advice on how, and how not, to present your work and to how avoid these criticisms.

Most of the following advice applies to writing assessments in coursework and in examinations. However, some of the skills expected in coursework, such as referencing and layout, are not expected in examinations. As well, you will need to display further and different skills in examinations. This matter is referred to again throughout this and subsequent chapters, and specific guidance on examination questions is given in Chapter 5.

## ● Some Basic Points

Let us start by identifying some basic points with respect to essay writing. Some of these points may seem obvious to you, particularly if you are studying at undergraduate level, but nevertheless they should not be discarded. In my experience, students at all levels ignore these rules to their detriment; whatever level you are studying at, the lecturer and marker will expect you to have displayed these basic skills. This chapter stresses the importance of these basics in the context of writing law assessments and highlights the disadvantages of ignoring them.

### Time Management

You have been warned all through your school days and college life not to leave the research and presentation of your assessment until the last minute. Such advice is still relevant to your undergraduate and postgraduate studies, as is advice on basic time management. Although it is quite usual, and to some extent acceptable, to type up your essays close to the submission date, what is unacceptable is to leave the research and planning to the last minute. In that case you will not leave yourself time to acquire the relevant materials and will find yourself attempting to learn the law whilst you are writing the assessment – a sure way to write confused and unstructured essays.

Provided you have done the necessary research, planned your answer and written out an appropriate draft it is acceptable to write it up shortly before you submit it – this not only reflects human nature, but also allows you to modify your answer in line with information acquired since you started your original research. However, this approach is subject to one important proviso – always leave yourself enough time to check over your work and to account for things such as computer failure; few courses accept this as a reason for handing in late.

### Respect for the Module and the Module Leader, Engaging With the Module and Taking a Pride in the Work That You Have Been Set

Teaching staff expect you to be as engrossed in the subject area as they are. They may be deluded in this respect, but they do not take kindly to students who approach the subject in a casual manner and who do not show pride in the work. This will be reflected in the marking, for they believe that sloppily presented essays with countless grammatical and legal errors are a product of indifference towards the subject and their module.

More specifically, teaching staff expect you to have learnt the information and skills that they have taken time teaching you – nothing infuriates the law teacher more than when a student ignores the advice and information that has been presented in lectures and seminars. For example, a student who omits a recent case or other development that the lecturer has drawn the student's attention to incurs the wrath of the marker. More generally, the lecturer will be annoyed that the student has not even demonstrated the ability to repeat basic information presented in class.

The staff teaching you normally set and mark your work. Show them that you have attended and listened to their classes and that you have appreciated, even enjoyed, what you have been taught and what you have managed to discover by your research. All these efforts will be rewarded by the lecturer, who will recognise that you have made an effort to engage with the subject, to conduct thorough research, and to take care with the presentation of your work.

## Getting on the Module Leader's 'Wavelength,' and at Least Tuning in to the Area of Law Being Studied

The module leader will expect you to display in the assessment the basic knowledge and skills which he or she has spent time giving you. More specifically, the module leader will expect you to approach the subject in much the same manner as he or she delivers it. Module leaders have their own styles, their own way of presenting things and their own views regarding the law and its efficiency and possible reform. It is not necessary that you agree with the module leader in all respects, but it is advisable that you are at least aware of and appreciate his or her views and style. Regular attendance at lectures and seminars gives you an insight into these matters and, it is hoped, makes the law easier to digest and understand – the purpose of lectures and seminars is to highlight the main issues of the law and its difficulties, and the module leader is trying to help you with these matters.

You do not want to make a mistake in an essay that the module leader has warned you about, and you do not want to miss something that he or she has taken an effort to relay to you. By making these mistakes, you are giving the impression that you have not attended or listened.

---

**Note**

**Essay writing skills are related to other study skills – organising your studies, attending and making the most of lectures, effective note taking, and seminar preparation. Most poor essays are a result of poor technique in the aforementioned skills. In addition, writing an essay is really hard work if you do not take an interest in the subject.**

---

## What Should I Do When I Get an Assignment?

It is essential that you receive the work the moment it is distributed – many inadequate essays are written by students who were not in the class when it was given to the other students, and who do not obtain the assignment in time to conduct proper research and planning. Although you may not write the essay until perhaps much later, you need to be aware of the deadline and the subject matter of the essay. This allows you to:

- conduct proper library and other research;
- discuss the subject area and question with other students;
- identify whether the subject matter or the question is particularly difficult, or whether it requires special research; and
- take in relevant information given in lectures and seminars which is relevant to the subject area and the question.

## Early Preparation and Research

It is essential that you do not leave your research and planning to the last minute. You should identify the subject matter of the essay and be thinking of the plan for it almost the moment you receive the work.

Specifically, if you leave your research to the last moment, you will miss out on the most relevant and appropriate sources. The better-organised student will have gone to the library and taken the most useful books, leaving the badly organised student with out-of-date or inappropriate texts and other sources. Even if you can find appropriate texts, you will have little time to digest the information and apply it to the set question. Conduct your research in the library and on the Internet as soon as you can, and photocopy relevant sources in preparation for the time that you begin to plan your answer.

## Get to Know the Area Involved in the Question

Although you must display sound essay writing skills to succeed, good assessments are written by students who know the relevant law, and poor ones are written by students who are not knowledgeable about the law. A sound knowledge of the legal principles and sources is a prerequisite of success.

If you are already conversant with the relevant legal area before you begin researching and writing the piece, it is much easier to tackle the question. This allows you to concentrate on the specific task in hand (whether that is analysing an essay question or solving a problem question), and your knowledge and confidence with the subject matter are reflected throughout your answer.

If the area is one that is to be, or already has been, covered in lectures and seminars, ensure that you attend those sessions, or get notes from any missed sessions. Those sessions not only cover the relevant material, but also may provide you with reading lists and other references to relevant cases and other materials. In addition, it is not uncommon for an assessment to be set on a topic specifically covered in seminars, and for the students to be given a 'rehearsal' for the actual assessment. If that is the case, ensure that you prepare for, attend, and contribute to the seminar.

If the area is not one covered in class – many staff like to set such assessments to test research skills – then ensure that you research the area well in advance of typing up the assessment. As you do not have the benefit of lectures and seminars in the area, you are responsible for finding the relevant information (the lecturer may have given you a reading list, in which case obtain the texts and read the relevant information as soon as possible). In any case, you need to ensure that you fully understand the area. Conducting research and discussing the area with fellow students will help you achieve this.

## Listening Carefully (Lecturers Often Drop Hints)

The assessment has been set by your lecturer, who knows the answer and who expects you to cover specific issues (although the question rarely admits of one specific answer). Although your lecturer is not likely to tell you how to answer the question, some lecturers give general guidance on what skills should be employed and what general points should be covered. Attending lectures and seminars (on a regular basis) in the relevant area and listening to the lecturer has the following advantages:

- The lecturer gives his or her views on relevant legal issues – the importance of a case, why it was decided in that way, whether a case was correctly decided, why an Act of Parliament was passed or amended.
- The lecturer gives his or her views on the morality of the law – this also gives you a good indication of whether, and the extent to which, the lecturer is asking for a 'black letter' or critical/analytical approach to the question.
- The lecture on the relevant area may follow a pattern similar to the one required to answer the question, or at least cover the most essential cases and principles in that area. In other words, the lecturer shows you how the subject 'fits together.'
- The lecturer can explain difficult concepts and legal issues that are required to answer the question. For example, if the question asks, 'To what extent is the British Constitution consistent with constitututionalism?' the lecturer may be able to explain what constitutionalism is and may give examples of the British Constitution, which can be used in answering the question.

## Researching for Assessments

Chapter 2 provides more detailed information and advice on how to research law assessments including what books, articles and other legal materials to use. For present purposes we provide some basic advice on how to research your assessments including the timing of your research.

- The first thing you should do is to look at the title as soon as possible after distribution and find out whether it is on an area covered, or to be covered, on the course (see earlier under 'What Should I Do When I Get the Assignment?').
- Read the question carefully to identify its scope, and thus the scope of your research.
- If the area has been covered on the course ensure that you have all the handouts and lecture or seminar notes on the area. If you haven't, chase them up immediately.
- If the area is to be covered in lectures and seminars, ensure that you attend and prepare for those sessions and listen carefully to the lecturer for any hints and guidance (see earlier).
- If the area is not to be covered on the course, or will not be covered before submission, get to know the area as quickly as possible, and ensure that you have a basic understanding of that area before conducting further, more detailed research.
- Consult any recommended reading given by the lecturer, and carefully read and digest any advice given by the lecturer on the coursework instructions.
- In most cases (apart from specialist areas not covered in general texts, or where the assessment is in the form of a case study), you should begin by locating the relevant chapters in your textbook (and cases and materials book). This provides a foundation on which to research further material.
- Textbooks provide some additional reading in a specific area (either in footnotes or in reading lists and bibliographies), and this is a useful starting point for locating further secondary sources. Cases and materials texts provide you with an excellent range of secondary (and primary) sources in the legal area, although you still may have to locate and read the full text of some of those materials.

- You should undertake searches on law websites and library catalogues to locate further sources and any new sources since the publication of the texts.
- The textbook normally refers you to the primary sources necessary to answer the question. Identify which ones are particularly relevant, and whether you will need to access the source itself. If so, print off or photocopy those materials.
- Use websites to locate any new cases or statutory developments, and check whether they conflict with your texts and initial research.
- Keep on the lookout for any developments during the period of research and writing up - you will impress the lecturer if you can incorporate new cases, developments, or debates into your answer.
- Ensure that all your research relates to the question and is relevant to answering that question - do not just collect everything on constitutional law/contract/tort. You will locate a prestigious amount of sources, and you need to check them for relevance before printing them off or photocopying them. Websites often provide useful abstracts of articles and books to assist you in this respect. It helps if you are conversant with the legal area, which allows you to identify whether a book, article, or case is relevant.
- You should now be ready to begin writing out your work and including all your research in it. Sometimes you will need to discard material (either because you discover it is irrelevant or because of lack of space), and on other occasions you will need to undertake further research.

## ● Presentation of Law Assessments

It is crucial that students present their work in a professional and suitable manner. Students on undergraduate programmes are expected to display competent writing and presentational skills, and their marks will suffer if they do not follow the basic rules outlined here. Students often complain that they are being marked on their grammatical ability instead of their legal knowledge, but both skills go hand in hand.

- As potential legal advisers, or as graduate employees in general, you are expected to take pride in the presentation of your work and advice and to display competent skills in grammar and spelling.
- Poor grammar and structure make that advice difficult to follow.
- The complexity of the law calls for a clear writing style and a structured approach to addressing questions and problems.
- Undergraduate students are expected to display sound research skills and an ability to cite and use relevant legal and other materials.
- In general, students who gain good honours degrees in law can write competently and display sound essay-writing and problem-solving techniques.

### Word-Processed Work

You will be expected to word-process all your coursework assessments and must display at least reasonable word-processing skills. If you are not 'computer literate' and cannot word-process, then you must learn those skills as soon as possible. If those skills are completely beyond you, you may have to employ someone to do the job for you, but that would be expensive, and eventually you will have to acquire some modest skills. Untidy and careless work does not create a good impression and is penalised, particularly when submitting undergraduate and postgraduate projects (see Chapter 6).

## Concentrate on Content, Not 'Fancy' Presentation

Some students think it is vital to provide elaborate pictures of judges or scales of justice on the front of their work, and spend an inordinate amount of time on this aspect. Such embellishments are not to be discouraged, but ensure that the presentation is not better than the content. Concentrate on a clear and structured layout, eliminating mistakes and untidy presentation. Ensure that pages are in order, and that the bibliography is at the back.

## Spelling and Typographical Errors

Many students submit work with countless spelling and typographical errors. This is unprofessional, creates a poor impression and irritates the marker. It should be avoided wherever possible. Some minor mistakes are inevitable, however much editing you do, and you should leave adequate time to check for these errors.

- Leave plenty of time to check through the work for errors.
- Use the grammar and spell check on your word processor.
- Do not submit the work until all errors have been identified and corrected.

These matters **are** relevant to the quality of your work and to the mark that will be awarded. In particular, for project work it is an essential criterion for awarding marks and determining classification.

## Clear and Coherent Writing Style

Some students have their work returned with comments such as 'You deal with most of the legal issues, but your writing style and structure is poor, and your answer unclear.' This is very frustrating for students who feel that they should be marked on their legal knowledge and not their proficiency in English and their essay skills. However, a good writing style is essential to success in your law assessments.

Law is complicated enough without it being explained in a muddled and clumsy way. Always ensure that you write in a clear and appropriate manner, and that the reader understands what you are saying. Adopt a clear and simple writing style, using correct grammar, as shown in the following example:

> **Example**
>
> 'A legally binding contract requires agreement, consideration and an intention to create legal relations.'
>
> **Not** 'For a contract what you need is an agreement and as well as that consideration as well as intention.'

Learn and employ the basis rules of grammar and punctuation. If you do not know them when you start your course, learn them as quickly as possible. The best way to acquire

HOW TO WRITE BETTER LAW ESSAYS

this knowledge is to read law texts and articles and other good, simple prose. Do not adopt the informal style used on websites or the style used when talking to friends and fellow students. Let us give some examples.

## Casual Language

Many students write in a completely inappropriate way, using casual phrases and presenting work in an informal manner. These lapses 'jump out' at the marker and create a poor impression – that the student does not read legal materials and has not yet learnt how to express him or herself as a law student.

---

**Example**

**Do not say**: 'I don't think Billy has got a chance of winning this case as he was drunk.'

The style is unprofessional and not what is expected of an undergraduate who is aspiring to become a professional lawyer. Can you imagine paying a solicitor for advice and getting that reply? In addition, it is subjective and not based on any authority.

**Instead say**: 'Given that James was drunk and failed to see the sign placed by the hole, it is unlikely that he will prove that the council breached any duty of care owed towards him, as required by the relevant case law [give case name and reference].'

---

The former style is too casual; the latter uses the style adopted by lawyers, textbooks and other legal literature. It *does* matter which style you adopt, and you can learn that style by reading your texts. Assessments are presented in a formal setting and will be marked by someone who uses appropriate language.

So do **not** use phrases such as 'As I said before' ('As mentioned above'), or 'Everyone these days is unhappy about law and order' ('Given the increasing number of serious public order offences committed in England and Wales [provide figures and source], there is increasing public concern with respect to law and order').

You can soon learn how to express yourself by reading legal books, articles, and cases. You will learn how to 'talk the talk,' and expressing yourself in that way will become second nature.

---

**Example**

The layperson might say:

'He went to court and won his case by getting £10,000.'

As a law student you must not express yourself in that way. Instead, the lawyer and the law student would say:

'The claimant brought an action for breach of contract and the High Court awarded him compensation of £10,000, representing his loss of profit.'

---

**Uninformed and Unsupported Opinion**

> **Example**
>
> **Do not say**: 'Everybody knows that judges are snobby and out of touch.'
>
> The comment is too casual and is unsupported by any evidence. It is a throwaway remark likely to be made by an uninformed layperson. You will be expected to be more objective and to provide authority for your opinions.
>
> **Instead say**: 'A common view of the public is that judges are middle-classed and out of touch with the common person. This view is also held by Professor Foster [quote text or article] and indeed figures show that most senior judges received a public school education [provide source and relevant figures].'

**Muddled and Inadequate Explanations of the Law or Cases**

It is essential that you write clearly and that you provide clear and simple explanations of the legal principles and any relevant cases. A muddled style confuses the reader and indicates that you are uncertain on the law.

> **Example**
>
> **Do not say:** 'After the Human Rights Act the judges can now use the European Convention to assist the individual in securing his human rights. Before the Act the judges couldn't do that, but they could take the Convention into account sometimes.'
>
> This statement is confused and vague and does not inform the reader of the position of the Convention in domestic law, both before and after the Act. It also does not give any authority for the proposition.
>
> **Instead say:** 'Before the Human Rights Act 1998 came into force the courts could use the European Convention only in cases where there was an uncertainty in a statute or the common law (authority). However, since the Act came into force, judges must take into account the case law of the Convention (s. 2) and must interpret statutes in line with the Convention wherever possible (s. 3). Consequently, the Convention can be used directly in the domestic courts when adjudicating on human rights disputes.'

The reader now understands what the student is saying, and it is apparent that the student understands the legal position and has consulted the relevant sources. There is little value in mentioning a case or a legal principle if you cannot show that you know its meaning or impact and can articulate that.

In particular, you need to learn how to explain a case in simple and clear terms, often using very few words. Examples of this are given in Chapter 2.

## Clear and Structured Paragraphs

Students should write in paragraphs and not in unconnected sentences or lists. Every paragraph should contain a number of related sentences, dealing with one or more specific legal issues in turn. Let us give an example of how **not** to do it.

Assume that the student is answering the question, 'What are the essential features of the British Constitution?' An unstructured answer might look something like this:

The British Constitution is unwritten, but most other constitutions are written in a formal document.

Some constitutions are rigid and cannot be changed except without a special procedure. This is not true of the British constitution, which is flexible. The sources of the British Constitution are both legal and nonlegal and consist of statutes, case law and constitutional conventions. Parliament is regarded as sovereign and can pass whatever law it wants.

The British Constitution has no formal bill of rights, and Parliament can pass whatever law it chooses. A central feature of the British Constitution is democracy and the House of Commons is elected. Other features are the rule of law and the separation of powers.

The student has made several relevant observations about the British Constitution, but the piece is not written in clear and structured paragraphs. As a result the answer jumps from one point to the next and confuses the reader. The answer requires three or four separate and clear paragraphs identifying the central features of the British Constitution.

**Paragraph 1** - The unwritten nature of the British Constitution. Contrast with other constitutions such as USA and explain why the constitution is unwritten and where the British Constitution can be found.

**Paragraph 2** - The informality and flexibility of the British Constitution. Absence of any formal and rigid constitutional law, reliance on general sources of law, and lack of any higher or supreme law.

**Paragraph 3** - Absence of a formal bill of rights. Explanation of common law system of protecting rights, parliamentary sovereignty and human rights, and the effect of the Human Rights Act 1998 on human rights protection.

**Paragraph 4** - Importance of constitutionalism and the control of government power in the British Constitution: the place of the rule of law and the separation of powers in the British Constitution.

Use the style adopted in textbooks. Undergraduate texts adopt a sound prose style, presenting the work in structured paragraphs under clear headings and sub-headings. You should adopt this style.

- Do not use sub-degree texts that adopt a bullet point style.
- Use headings and sub-headings sparingly and only when necessary to indicate that you are dealing with separate issues.

- Lists should be avoided unless it is appropriate to employ them. For example, during a judgment a judge may have made a list of relevant issues to be considered when deciding whether a claim should be successful.

### Why Don't Students Write in Paragraphs?

- Many students do not write in paragraphs because they have not planned their answers before they start writing and have not thought out what they are going to set down.
- Some students simply copy out points from the book because they are reading them for the first time or they do not realise that certain points are, or are not, connected.
- Some students do not know how to write in paragraphs and have not written in this style before – accordingly they make lists or write in one-sentence paragraphs.

When you are planning your essay, think about what information is going to go into particular paragraphs.

## ● Avoiding Plagiarism

## What Is Plagiarism?

Plagiarism involves the use of others' ideas or words and presenting them as your own. It is a form of cheating, no less serious than cheating in examinations. Plagiarism can take two basic forms.

### Using Someone's Words or Ideas Without Crediting Them

If you copy from a book or an article and do not indicate where you got that information, you are passing that information or idea off as if it were your own. That is cheating because you hope to be credited for that information as if it is your own, when it is not.

For example, you might write '. . . all the cases under s. 3 of the Human Rights Act 1998 indicate that the courts are not yet prepared to take on a legislative role, and are content simply to apply a purposeful approach to the interpretation of statutory provisions in order to ensure compliance with Convention rights.' Without crediting an author, this sentence indicates that the student has done the necessary research of the cases and has formed his or her own opinion on that matter. If they **are** your own words and opinions (congratulations, by the way!), simply refer to those cases in support of your argument. If you have copied the words, or more generally copied that idea from an academic source and you do not credit it, you are guilty of plagiarism.

- This form of plagiarism relates to the use of ideas and phrases from secondary sources such as authors. These individuals have collected legal material and have tried to explain, criticise or analyse the law, and you cannot steal these views and pass them off as your own. In the previous example, the author has examined the relevant cases and has formed an opinion on those cases. That is the author's view on the cases, and it belongs to him or her. If you use that view, you must credit the author with that view and provide the citation and reference (see later).
- The rules do not generally apply to primary sources although – obviously, you cannot quote a judge without crediting that source. If an author copies out a statutory provision or the facts and decision of a case that are not the ownership of the author, you do

not need to cite that author. You should refer to the primary source and not the author (see Chapter 2 for full details). It is only when the author presents his or her view on the primary law that it should be credited. For example, 'The decision in that case can be explained on policy grounds . . . .'

- You do not always have to credit authors for general statements about the law – what is known as trite (accepted) law. If an author says, 'The British Constitution is not contained in one formal document known as a constitution,' you can repeat that statement or idea without crediting it because the author is merely stating a bald fact that every other author in that subject would make in similar terms. However, if the author says, 'Although the British Constitution is not contained in one formal document, the plethora of written legal sources mean that our Constitution cannot be described as wholly, or mainly, unwritten,' this is presented as an analysis and must be credited as such.

### Copying from Other Students

Copying from other students is also plagiarism and is a form of cheating. It involves copying another student's work and passing it off as your own. Although you may be encouraged to discuss an assessment with another student and to share some research material, the written work must be your own. **Never** show a fellow student your written work – either in draft or final form – before submission of the work.

**Remember**, both parties can be penalised if one student knowingly allows another student to copy his or her own work.

## Why Is It Wrong and Why Should You Avoid It?

Plagiarism is a form of cheating, and you will be penalised for such. This penalty may take various forms, from the deduction of marks, to the award of a mark of zero for that piece (or the whole module), to expulsion from the course. In addition, professional bodies such as the Law Society may be informed of such events, jeopardizing your career.

Make sure you read the university's policy on plagiarism and abide by it. If you are in any doubt, consult your tutor, lecturer or course leader.

## Why Do Students Plagiarise?

Most students who plagiarise do not do so intentionally or with a view to gaining an unfair advantage. These students plagiarise because they do not know the rules on plagiarism and do not appreciate that they are plagiarising.

- Some students think it is acceptable to copy from texts without crediting the source. They assume that the lecturer will know that they are using a particular book or article and that it is not their own work.
- Some students do not bother to credit a source in the main body of the work because they have mentioned the source in their bibliography. You must credit the source even though the source is listed in your bibliography.
- Some students do intend to plagiarise to gain an advantage in the assessment. They think that the lecturer will accept the view as the student's own and will be impressed by the student's research or grasp of the law.

- Many students plagiarise because they feel they need to. They have no real grasp of the legal principles or the question and use authors for this purpose. However, instead of plagiarising, the student can credit the author (getting credit for the research) (see later).
- Because many students do not understand the basic principles, they find it difficult to know whether these views are relevant to the question and to providing an appropriate answer. Thus, much of the plagiariser's work is irrelevant to the task in hand, in addition to being plagiarism.
- Most plagiarism is immediately identifiable. Unless the student has a very good writing style and academic approach, the style of the answer shifts dramatically (see the bad answer to the contract essay in Chapter 3). In addition, the lecturer normally is able to identify the source from his or her previous research and knowledge.

## How Do I Avoid Plagiarism?

You can avoid charges of plagiarism by clearly crediting your sources. (Chapter 2 provides fuller information on how to cite and reference legal sources.) If you have read and relied on a source, put it in your bibliography **and** supply the reference in the main body of the essay. Make it clear that the view you are putting forward is not your own, but someone else's.

For example, 'It has been suggested that the case law under the Human Rights Act 1998 has provided very few examples of a "hands-on" approach to the protection of human rights in England and Wales (create a footnote and put "See Foster, Human Rights and the 1998 Act (2005) EHRLR 66, at page 71").' You will be rewarded by the lecturer because the footnote provides evidence that you have researched and read a relevant article, and that you are capable of including a relevant source at an appropriate stage of your work. You can gain extra marks by showing your appreciation of that view, perhaps by pointing to cases that back up or contradict that view, and by putting forward your views on this matter.

## ● Providing Authority

As a law student you are expected to provide legal and other authority for your work, whether it is primary authority – the relevant Act of Parliament or case authority – or secondary authority – textbooks or journal articles. You cannot write law assessments without providing authority and you will fail unless you do so, even if your answer is well written and generally logical. In addition, providing and citing authority avoids a charge of plagiarism (see earlier). There is nothing wrong with the following statement:

### Example

'The Human Rights Act has been described as of great constitutional significance and indeed it provides judges with enhanced powers with respect to the protection of human rights.'

However, a law student must provide authority. The Act's year should be added (1998), the author who described it as significant should be identified, and the provisions which give the judges enhanced powers should be cited.

The rules on providing authority are detailed in Chapter 2, but note the following points:

- Never simply make a statement without providing authority – 'an agreement is not a contract unless the parties have provided consideration and consideration must be sufficient.' (Provide the case name and reference.)
- You do not need to provide authority for obvious statements and accepted principles – for example, England and Wales have a common law, as opposed to a civil law, system. (Even then the student can refer the reader to a textbook for further information.)
- Always provide specific case or statutory authority, rather than saying 'this is covered by statute or a case.'
- Do not just provide your opinion on the law – 'I think the law needs amending as it is unjust.'
- If you are going to provide an opinion, make sure you are aware of academic views on the matter and base that opinion on an appreciation of those views and of the law in general, even if you subsequently wish to disagree with that view.
- If your view is the same as an author's, make sure you credit it.
- If asked to give legal advice (problem questions; see Chapter 4), make sure your advice/opinion is based on a knowledge and appreciation of the legal principles.

## Proper Citation and Referencing of Sources

Proper citation and referencing of sources is discussed in detail in Chapter 2, but you will be expected to adopt the rules on citation and referencing used in undergraduate (as opposed to sub-degree) texts. Citing a case means labelling the case in the appropriate way, giving the case its proper title. Referencing the case means identifying its correct source – for example the law report.

- Always **cite** the case or other legal source properly.

---

**Example**

**Do not say**: 'This was decided in the case of Mrs Donogue.'

**Instead say**: 'This was decided in *Donogue v Stevenson* [reference via footnote].'

Alternatively, if you have already mentioned the case, you can say *'this was decided in Donogue,'* and put either *Donogue v Stevenson* with the reference in a footnote or 'see above' in a footnote.

---

- Always provide the correct **reference** for that source.

---

**Example**

'The "neighbour" principle was established in *Donogue v Stevenson* [1932] AC 562' [Appeal Cases for the year 1932, at page 562].

This is (one of) the official law reports where the case can be located and should be used in course works. In an exam, it is sufficient to put (1932). Do **not** put page 33 of Smith, *Contract Law*, even if you did find the case there.

---

## Using Footnotes

Consult the lecturer as to whether you should use footnotes, but generally footnotes are expected in coursework assessments in law. They give your coursework an air of professionalism and indicate that you are reading the right sort of legal materials and are developing relevant legal and writing skills. Footnotes also allow you to provide legal authority for your answer and to credit relevant sources, avoiding any charge of plagiarism.

Footnotes can be created easily on your word processor.

- Put the cursor at the place where you want to create the footnote mark. For example, 'This can be illustrated by the case of *Donogue v Stevenson*\* (you want your footnote number to appear here and you are going to create a footnote at the bottom of the page).
- Go to Insert at the top of your screen and press on footnotes (or reference, then footnotes).
- Press on footnote and you will given a choice of 'automatic' (in number order) or 'custom' (symbols such as \*).
- Press automatic and then the footnote number will appear and you will be taken to the bottom of the page where you can fill in the appropriate text.
- Click back on the main screen to return to your essay.

## What to Put in Footnotes

Footnotes can be used to give a relevant legal reference – a book, Act of Parliament or case.

> ### Example
>
> 'The leading case in this area is *Smith v Foster*.[1] . . . 'This rule is now covered in the Public Order Act 1986'[2] . . . 'it has been suggested that this case is wrongly decided as paying too little attention to procedural justice.'[3]
>
> ---
> [1][1996] 2 All ER 333
> [2]Section 13(1)
> [3]Foster, S 'Procedural Fairness and the Human Rights Act 1998' (2005) MLR 660, at 668

Footnotes also can be used to provide further, ancillary, information that may not deserve a mention in the main body of your essay.

> ### Example
>
> 'In that case the House of Lords held that the position would be different had the contract been in writing.'[4]
>
> In particular, they can be used in extended essays and projects to refer to a variety of academic sources:
>
> 'This view has subsequently received constant criticism.'[5]
>
> ---
> [4]Per Lord Bridge at page 77. His Lordship also opined that the normal rule would not apply if there was an independent witness to the agreement (at page 81). For a critical account of that obiter, see Foster, S 'A Bridge Too Far' (2005) OJLS 33, at 45
> [5]See Foster [1997] PL 223; Foster, [1998] EHRLR 246; and Foster (1998) MLR 330. For a general discussion on this area, see Foster, *Criminal Law and Human Rights* (OUP 2003)

Be careful when using extensive footnotes; they are common in legal journals and text-books, but may be discouraged in student assessments. Check with the lecturer whether they count towards your word limit. Some lecturers may not read any text in footnotes.

## Appropriate, True and Properly Cited Bibliography

You should provide a list of sources that you have used for the research and preparation of the assessment at the end of the work, on a separate page. The rules on bibliographies are discussed in greater detail in Chapter 2, but note:

- It should contain an appropriate range of materials (depending on the level of your study and the nature of the task) from textbooks, journal articles and primary sources.
- It should contain all the material that you researched and read for the work.
- It should not contain anything that you have not read (at least in part).
- It can contain material not specifically referred to in the main text of the work, but generally you should try to refer to as many references as possible during the work. If you don't, the lecturer may draw the conclusion that much of your bibliography is purely for show.
- Ensure that the bibliography is properly cited and referenced (see Chapter 2 for details).
- You may wish to separate primary and secondary sources. You also may wish to separate specific primary sources (Acts of Parliament, cases, treaties) and secondary sources (books, articles). Consult your lecturer on these details.

## ● Reading Over Your Answer

The basic advice of reading over your answer is ignored by many students, not because they don't care whether they submit clear and structured work, but because they leave insufficient time to check over their work before submission. Presenting sloppy work with countless errors and which ignores basic legal and English skills gives a poor impression (see earlier under *respect for the module and the module leader*) and leads to marks being deducted; in extreme cases the student may fail. Lecturers are impressed by well-written, structured and logical answers; it allows them to concentrate on the legal content and gives them the impression that the student knows what he or she is talking about.

- You should spend almost as much time checking your original work as you do writing the assessment.
- Check work for basic spelling and typographical mistakes and for poor grammar, unclear structure and inadequate explanation.
- Do not submit your first draft – work on the piece until it is acceptable.
- Give yourself at least a whole day to check your final draft.
- If you get a friend to read the work, ensure you choose someone who is very competent in English (do not use a fellow law student on the course because of the possibility of plagiarism).
- Use the grammar and spell check functions on your computer, but be aware of legal phrases that the computer may not be aware of (e.g., Latin phrases). A common error is students describing a tortious action (an action in tort) as 'tortuous' on the instruction of the computer.

## Why Don't Students Follow These Rules?

Students don't follow these rules either because they do not care how the work is presented (this is uncommon, but some students feel that presentation is irrelevant), or because they do not have the time or inclination to check the work before submission. The problem starts earlier, with late preparation, poor research and hurried writing. The student is left with little or no time to check the work for even basic errors.

## ● Answering the Question

Many students fail their assessment because they do not answer the question. Even if the content of the answer is sound, many students fail, or fail to get good marks, because they have not understood, or have deliberately ignored, the question.

- Lecturers set questions that they know the answer to (or at least have a sound idea of what should be included in the answer).
- Lecturers deliberately set testing questions and in the main avoid wholly descriptive questions, such as 'What are the essential requirements of a legally binding contract?'
- Lecturers tend to set questions which require research beyond the basic text or which require analysis or (in the case of problem questions) application to the facts of a scenario.

### Answer the Question That Is Set

#### Do Not Select Your Own Question

Many students choose to ignore the question set by the module leader and instead select their own question. For example, a student when asked the question 'What is a constitution?' or 'What is the purpose of a legal system?' may turn the question round and instead address the question 'What are the sources of the British Constitution?' or 'What are the features of the English legal system?'

In doing so the student has ignored the question (carefully) selected by the module leader and has given an answer to another question. Even if the student touches on the specific question, the answer, logically, does not follow the pattern expected by the module leader, and in the worst-case scenario the answer is totally irrelevant. Equally important, the answer does not address the specific nuances of the question. In the above-cited example, the question asks the student to look at constitutions or legal systems in the abstract – it asks the student to identify the characteristics and content of a constitution/legal system – and the answer instead gives information about one particular constitution or legal system. The student does not display the knowledge and understanding required from the question and has not answered the question.

Although this may be tolerated to a great extent on sub-degree courses, it is not tolerated at undergraduate and postgraduate levels. A specific skill required of law students is that they can give legal advice in response to specific inquiries or facts. The module leader expects you to identify the specific legal problems raised by the question, and to address those aspects in your answer. Otherwise the module leader would set questions such as 'Write all (or anything) you know about constitutions/legal systems.'

## Do Not Write in the General Area – the 'Scatter-Gun' or 'Dartboard' Approach

In addition to the case where the student turns the question round, some students simply identify the general legal area and write in that general area. Imagine if a client asked a solicitor about a personal contractual problem and was met with a mini lecture on the law relating to the formation of a contract. The client would feel cheated because the solicitor has merely told the client the general legal position and then, in effect, told the client to answer the specific question him or herself.

## Analyse the Question and Its Components and Make a Plan of Your Answer

Look at the question carefully and identify the relevant area of law and the main components of the question.

### Example

*'In terms of procedure and purpose, what is the distinction between civil and criminal law? Is this distinction always sustainable in practice?'*

The question is about the difference between civil and criminal law, but cannot be answered simply by listing the basic distinctions. You can start with basic definitions and distinctions, but your answer must concentrate on the headings of procedure and purpose. You can then address the final part of the question by giving examples of both divisions, and, more importantly, giving examples where the distinction is blurred.

- Define criminal and civil law and explain the basic distinction.
- Explain the difference in respect of legal procedure – how a case is brought, parties to an action.
- Explain the difference with respect to the purpose of both – regulating private relationships and activities, providing compensation, as opposed to protecting society, punishing.
- Give examples where the distinction is uncertain or blurred, for example, where some conduct might attract criminal and civil liability, private criminal prosecutions, juries in civil cases, exemplary damages.

Before you begin to type your answer and before you finalise your research, you must make a plan of your answer. You should know what you are going to say, and in what order, before you begin writing. You can refer to that plan in structuring your answer and check your work at the end to see whether you have followed that plan and answered the question.

### Example

*'The British Constitution is unwritten, informal and flexible. Indeed, it could be argued that there is no British Constitution. Discuss.'*

- You could start with a brief definition of a constitution and what a constitution is and what it should contain.
- You could then discuss what is meant by the terms 'unwritten, informal and flexible' with respect to the British Constitution, comparing it with written, formal and rigid constitutions.

- You could answer the second part of the question by examining the relevance of those characteristics to the question of whether a constitution exists.
- You could provide evidence of the British Constitution to argue that it does exist – that there is an established system of government and established principles of constitutional conduct, recent constitutional reform.
- You could provide evidence to support the argument that it does not exist – lack of a fundamental, supreme law, sovereignty of Parliament as opposed to sovereignty of the constitution.
- You could then reach a conclusion as to the truth of the statement.

**Introductions, Main Text and Conclusions**

Courseworks should be approached in three stages – the introduction, the main text and the conclusion. In other words, say what you are going to say, say it, and say what you have said.

Your **introduction** should be brief and tell the reader what needs to be covered and how it is to be covered.

---

**Example**

'This question (*"Is law the same as justice?"*) asks whether the formal law is equivalent to the general notion of justice. To answer the question one needs to appreciate the various meanings of both law and justice, and to identify the central characteristics and qualities of each. Thus, by examining various definitions and ideas of both, and by providing a number of examples, one should be able to conclude whether the two concepts are indeed the same.'

'With respect to law, we can note that law has been defined as. . . .'

---

With problem questions, the introduction can identify all the relevant legal issues.

---

**Example**

'This question relates to the formation of a contract and whether X and Y have entered into such a contract. In particular, it must be determined whether X made an offer, whether Y accepted that offer, and whether both parties have provided sufficient consideration for each other's promises.'

---

Alternatively, you may dispense with a general introduction and include a specific introduction as you deal with each point.

---

**Example**

'The first point to consider is whether X made a firm offer to Y, or whether his or her statement was a mere invitation to treat.'

---

HOW TO WRITE BETTER LAW ESSAYS

The **main text** should deal with each point in turn, addressing all aspects of the question and providing relevant legal authority for each point.

The **conclusion** should contain a summary of the issues dealt with in the main text, along with the student's own concluding remarks.

### Example

'In conclusion, therefore, it can be submitted that the notions of law and justice do not necessarily coincide, and that formal law can exist without it meeting the requirements of basic notions of justice. [You can expand by referring to some specific points in that respect and by referring to authority already referred to in the main text.] However, provided the substantive law contains those requirements and reflects such notions, it can be seen that law is, or perhaps should be, the same as justice.'

### Note

Do not include new information or ideas in your conclusion. Many students do this because they remember a point that that they have left out in the main text. This causes confusion to the reader and suggests that the student is either muddled or poorly organised.

### Make Sure the Content of Your Answer Is Relevant

You should check continually whether what you are writing is relevant to the question. It should be easy to do this provided you have the necessary knowledge to identify the main points raised by the question and have made a clear plan of the answer.

If it is a problem question, place yourself in the position of the person to be advised: Would he or she need to know that information? Is the point relevant to his or her situation? In an essay question, check that you are addressing all the issues, and that you are not including information simply because it is covered in the textbook and relates to the relevant legal area.

### Address the Problems in Problem Questions

Chapter 4 addresses the techniques necessary to answer problem questions. Remember, you are asked to give advice to the affected parties, not to write generally in the legal area. The scenario raises legal and factual problems.

- Was a contract concluded at that stage?
- Did the parties follow the legal formalities of a contract?
- Did their behaviour indicate agreement?

The parties want these problems addressed and answered, and you will not be able to avoid them by simply writing in the general legal area.

### Why Don't Students Answer the Question?

There are many reasons why students do not answer the set question:

- They simply do not understand the question or what the question is getting at.
  This can be particularly so with problem questions (addressed in Chapter 4), where students cannot identify which aspects of (contract) law are raised in the scenario. In such

a case students either (wrongly) guess at what areas are alluded to, or write everything about the law of contract just to be on the safe side.

In addition, the wording of, or the words used in, the question can confuse students: 'The British Constitution is mythical and principally unconstitutional. Discuss.' Here students do not appreciate the use of the words 'mythical' and 'unconstitutional,' but having seen the words 'British Constitution' feel that it is safe simply to explain the sources and features of the British Constitution.

● They understand what the question is getting at, but do not have the knowledge or research time to provide the answer.

For example, in exams students identify what a problem question is getting at, but do not know anything about (consideration/misrepresentation). Instead of writing nothing, they talk about what they do know (offer and acceptance/intention to create legal relations). So too with coursework assessments, a question asking for personal or academic analysis (or for them to get to grips with a concept such as 'constitutionalism') is ignored by students because that would require further research or asks students to articulate on a topic they have little or no views on.

● They know the answer to another, simpler question – generally one that can be answered by reading and copying out the general textbook.

Students ignore the question and substitute another question which they do know the answer to, and which can be answered by looking at the general textbook. 'What is the purpose of law?' may become 'How is the law classified?' Students do this because the text provides lots of information on the classification of law, but little on what law is and its purpose.

Below are some examples of some testing questions that are likely to be misread or misunderstood by students.

---

**Example**

*What is a legal system and what is its purpose?*

This question is **not** asking you to outline the nature and sources of the **English** Legal System. Many students simply describe the English Legal System because that is what they find in their textbooks. But the question is asking you to define **a** legal system and to explain its purpose.

You need to appreciate the nature and purpose of a legal system – what it does, what it consists of, how it interacts with the law and the constitution. You can then describe its purpose (which should become evident once you have defined a legal system) – that it consists of the machinery for passing, executing and adjudicating upon the law, that it provides a system for resolving disputes and obtaining justice, that it relates to the relevant institutions, its personnel and the procedure of the law's enforcement.

You can use features of the English system to illustrate the answer. For example, it would be proper to say that 'a legal system will contain a hierarchy of courts, and in the English legal system the highest court is the House of Lords.' Here, you are simply using the information as an example of a wider and more general principle (that all legal systems contain

---

a court hierarchy). Similarly, you may mention that there are different legal systems, and use the English (common law) system as an example. However, you must not explain every rule on the English system without explaining what a legal system is. You should not be drawn into explaining the rules and characteristics of the English system.

## Example

*What is a constitution? What is meant by acting 'constitutionally'?*

This question is **not** asking you to outline the nature and sources of the **British** Constitution. Most students go down that path because most textbooks give that information. As with the question on the legal system, examples of the (British) Constitution can be used once a constitution has been defined, but only to illustrate a particular characteristic of a constitution. For example, 'a constitution will identify the supreme power within the state, which in the British Constitution is Parliament.'

**Neither** is the question simply asking you to list **the different categories** of constitutions – formal and informal, flexible and rigid, written and unwritten. Instead, you should provide a number of definitions of a constitution – a document (or various laws and practices) containing the rules of government, the fundamental and supreme law of the state, a defender of liberties, a controller of government. By doing this, you can identify the central features of a constitution and are in a good position to address the second part of the question.

The second part of the question confuses many students, particularly if they have simply explained the rules relating to the British Constitution in the first part. You need to define constitutionalism and appreciate its various meanings: It either means following the formal rules of the constitution or acting in conformity with accepted ideas of constitutional fairness (following the rules of natural justice, upholding fundamental rights)

## Example

*What is a contract? Why do people enter into contracts?*

The question is **not** asking you to explain all the rules about the formation of a contract. Many students go down that path because that follows the format of the first chapter in the text and the first few contract lectures. Rather the question asks you to identify the central characteristics of a contract – that it is based on **agreement**, that it is a **bargain** that it may be made in writing or orally. You must start with a definition of a contract and then must identify those central characteristics.

You can use some of the basic rules on contract formation to illustrate the answer, **once** you have identified the relevant characteristics. It would be inappropriate simply to say that every contract requires an offer and explain the relevant rules and case law. By doing this you are explaining the rules of contract without telling the lecturer **what** a contract is. It is acceptable to say that 'a central characteristic of any contract is that the parties are in agreement and that there is a meeting of minds with respect to the essential terms. To achieve this, every contract must contain both an offer and acceptance (relevant case law), and the terms of their agreement must be stated in sufficiently clear terms (relevant case law).'

The second part of the question requires a basic understanding of modern commerce and some commonsense observations about why contracts are concluded. It does **not** require you to explain the rules of contract. It requires you to think about why people arrange their affairs via contracts and to appreciate what qualities a contract has and what purposes it achieves. A knowledge of the rules of contract may help you appreciate the reasons why people enter into them – they formalise the parties' agreement, provide evidence of their agreement, finalise the terms and the rights and duties of the party, allow individuals and companies to arrange their business affairs and to provide redress if the agreement is breached. Simply stating the law does not address the question why people enter into them.

In all of the examples provided, you have been asked a searching question that cannot be answered simply by looking at the textbook. It requires you to appreciate particular concepts and to think why the law (or a legal system or a constitution) exists. The lecturer is asking you to reflect on what you are studying and what you have been taught. In most cases the lecturer has addressed these issues in lectures and seminars, and if you have not attended lectures and engaged with the subject (or you are not prepared to research beyond the main text) you will be left floundering. As a result you will provide the wrong answer or, more commonly, an answer to another question.

### How Can I Avoid Not Answering the Question?

Misreading or misunderstanding the question can happen to anyone, particularly during the tension of an examination. However, you can avoid this problem by taking into account the following:

- Read the question carefully, and in the case of coursework assessment read and follow any guidance given by the lecturer and discuss the title with (reliable and knowledgeable) fellow students.
- Ensure that you are conversant in that legal area before you begin writing the answer. Many students answer the wrong question because they have a limited knowledge of the area and are unable to identify the central issues.
- Attend all relevant classes where the question or at least the subject area will be discussed.
- If the question uses unfamiliar terms, find out what they mean and do the necessary research beyond the text to allow you to tackle the question.
- Expect the question to be demanding and for it to require you to think about the answer and to do further research.

## A Choice of Questions

If you are given a choice of questions, choose one that suits your knowledge and your specific skills.

- If one area has been covered in lectures and seminars and the other needs individual research, you may be better advised to choose the former, unless you have good research skills and you are particularly interested in that legal area.

- Some students prefer to tackle problem questions rather than essays (see Chapter 4).
- Some students are more confident with analytical questions ('Critically examine the central features of the British Constitution.'), rather than more descriptive questions ('Using case law, explain how section 1 of the Theft Act 1968 has been interpreted by the courts.').
- Some students prefer interdisciplinary questions, requiring a (political) perspective ('To what extent is the British Constitution consistent with basic notions of democracy?').

## Different Types of Questions

You should identify early on what type of question has been set. This dictates your research, your writing style and your overall approach to answering the question.

### Questions on Legal Theory, Concepts and Institutions or Substantive Law

Some questions relate to substantive legal topics (contract, tort, criminal law) and require the student to be conversant with specific legal principles.

> **Example**
>
> *What is a contract? What are the essential requirements of a legally binding contract?*
>
> *The courts will only impose a duty of care on the defendant if they feel it is just to do so. Discuss.*
>
> *In what circumstances does and should the criminal law impose strict liability?*
>
> These questions require a knowledge and discussion of the relevant substantive law. They can be answered adopting a critical approach, and some require an appreciation of specific concepts (such as justice), but essentially they require you to be conversant with the relevant legal principles and sources.

Others questions refer instead to legal concepts (e.g., the law, the rule of law, justice), or institutions (e.g., constitutions, legal systems, courts).

> **Example**
>
> *What is law? Is law the same as justice?*
>
> *Explain what is meant by the rule of law. Why do we prefer to live by the rule of law rather than by the rule of men?*
>
> *What is a constitution and what purpose does it achieve?*
>
> *What is the function of a legal system?*
>
> These questions cannot be answered by simply explaining specific legal rules. They are asking you to appreciate and explain certain concepts or ideas. You need to employ accepted definitions and views on, for example, what law is, and to discuss those concepts and views in the context of the question.

For example, you cannot answer the question 'What is law?' by saying that *the law of contract is an example of law and the rules of contract are as follows . . .'* However, once you have identified what law is, you may be able to use specific laws in illustration: *'. . . law can govern and regulate private relationships and activities, such as family law, contract law or property law.'*

When you have defined justice you can use a law to illustrate a specific aspect of justice: '. . . a fundamental principle of justice is that every citizen should have access to the courts and, where necessary, access to free legal advice and representation. In this respect, the Access to Justice Act 1999 provides that . . . .'

### Essay and Problem Questions

The skills required to tackle problem-type questions are addressed in Chapter 4. For present purposes, essay questions test the following skills:

- your ability to research a specific legal topic;
- your legal knowledge of that legal area;
- your ability to offer a critical and analytical account of the law;
- your ability to address the question and to structure a logical and academically sound answer;
- your ability to use relevant legal sources in support of the answer and to employ relevant citation and referencing skills.

Problem questions require you to employ most of the above-listed skills, but in particular you must concentrate on the following:

- identifying the relevant legal areas and the specific legal problems faced by the parties;
- applying relevant legal principles and cases to the facts of the scenario;
- providing the parties with clear, correct and constructive legal advice.

In problem questions, the style of the answer will be different in many respects – your account of the law will be less academic and critical and your advice will be more practical. However, you will still be expected to employ other academic and writing skills, such as sound grammar and spelling, clear use of case law and other authority and proper citations and references.

### Descriptive and Analytical Questions

Some questions require a reasonably descriptive account of the relevant legal principles and sources. They are principally testing your legal knowledge and your ability to give a clear and correct account of the law.

> **Example**
>
> *'What is the difference between a contractual offer and an invitation to treat?'*
>
> This question can be answered by examining the legal principles as established in the relevant case law, and by giving examples of offers and invitations. It does not call for any critical account of the law or the cases, although a good answer would highlight and comment on any illogical or inconsistent case law and would include some academic opinion.

Other questions call for a much more critical and analytical approach of the law. Here you need to appreciate the law and its rationale and to be able to critically assess its effectiveness.

Example

*'The existing case law with respect to the adequacy of consideration shows that the courts have failed to settle on any definite legal principles. Discuss.'*

This question cannot be answered by simply outlining the principles and case law on consideration. It is asking you to address the quote, which implies that the law is in a state of confusion and lacks principle, relying instead perhaps on flexibility, which is causing confusion. You must identify the relevant legal areas (performance of existing duties, part performance of contractual obligations) and analyse those decisions to see whether the statement is indeed true. You should be conversant with academic opinion in this area and should use textbooks and journal articles to support your answer.

In addition, some questions ask for the student's own opinion or assessment of the law.

Example

*'Critically examine the provisions of the Human Rights Act 1998. In your opinion, do you believe that the Act is democratically and constitutionally sound?'*

Part one of the question asks for a critical assessment. You need to highlight the controversial provisions of the Act – not simply list each and every provision – and highlight the legal and constitutional problems. You need to be aware of, and to use, academic opinion in this respect.

Then you are asked for your own opinion. This often throws students, who either feel that they can say anything at this point or are uncomfortable with offering their own view. For the former group, the question is not giving you *cart blanche* to comment on the Act. Your opinion must be based on an appreciation of the Act's provisions and of the arguments for and against the passing of the Act and of its provisions. For the latter, you are not expected to provide an entirely individual view on the matter and can base your views on accepted academic commentary.

It is perfectly acceptable to say, '. . . although the Act appears to allow a shift of power between Parliament and the courts, it should be stressed that the court's new powers have been granted by Parliament itself. This view is supported by Foster [provide citation and reference] who feels that the Act is neither undemocratically nor unconstitutionally unsound. Thus, in my opinion, the Act is neither undemocratic nor unconstitutional simply because the courts are vested with greater powers.'

It is not acceptable to give entirely subjective and unsupported opinion: '. . . In my view it is unacceptable for the judges to question the law and to decide whether the law is in breach of human rights. That is not the court's job – they are not elected like Parliament, and they should just declare what the law is.' This opinion exposes a lack of understanding of the role of the courts in protecting human rights and is unsupported by established legal opinion.

## What Is the Lecturer After? What Does the Lecturer Expect From the Student?

The lecturer's expectations depend on the nature of the question (see earlier).

- If the question is largely descriptive, the lecturer will expect you to show a sound understanding of the legal area and the cases based on sound research.
- If the question relates to a legal concept or idea, the lecturer wants you to show that you have grasped that concept, and that you can articulate your understanding of it by using relevant sources and examples.
- If the question is analytical, the lecturer wants you to show an appreciation of the law – why it exists, what problems it causes, whether it has been applied correctly or justly. The lecturer wants the student to appreciate specific notions of fairness or justice or to comment on the consistency of the law with those notions.
- If the question specifically asks for your opinion, the lecturer is looking for an appreciation of the relevant contentious issues and arguments and counterarguments and a willingness on your part to commit (not necessarily unconditionally) yourself to a particular view.
- In general, the lecturer is testing to see whether you have grasped what you have studied on the module or what you have researched and read.
- Whatever the nature of the question, the lecturer wants you to employ sound writing and legal skills, consistent with you being on an undergraduate law programme.
- The lecturer does not expect you to be a legal expert or to reject established expert legal opinion.

## Is There Anything Particularly Difficult About the Question?

Once you have got the question you should immediately identify whether there is anything particularly difficult about the question, or whether it going to be difficult to research or answer. Some questions relate to **complicated (or vague) concepts**, such as justice, the rule of law, constitutionalism. Before you can answer the question, you have to understand and be comfortable with those concepts. The general text might not provide a definition or a suitable explanation, and you may need to conduct some further research to obtain the necessary knowledge. Leave yourself plenty of time to research this information and to acquire this knowledge. If you get the basics early on, this will give you adequate time to address the issues in the question.

Other questions can be difficult because they deal with **very wide and general areas**, requiring you to trawl through a great amount of information and select specific information for inclusion in the question. For example a question such as 'What is law and what is its purpose?' seems to cover an enormous area and poses a number of problems for the student:

- What am I going to include in the answer?
- How am I going to research this huge topic?
- How am I expected to provide an answer to such a general and fundamental question?

The question requires you to cover the basics and to show a general understanding of the concept of law, various views on its nature and scope, and what its purpose is. Find textbooks which provide a number of definitions of the law and which explore a number of theories of the law and its purpose; those texts also may refer you to other texts and articles. Use those established theories as a basis of your own views and to question those views.

Definitions are of particular assistance in this type of question. Use a number of them and do not simply quote them and move on to the next point. Show that you understand the quotation and elaborate on it.

## Example

'Law has been defined as a **set of rules, enforceable in a formal setting**, and which **govern** society and its citizens.'

From this definition, one can explore numerous characteristics of the law and its purpose – that it exists in the form of rules, that these rules are formal and binding and can be enforced formally in courts of law or by other formal mechanism and that these rules govern and regulate the conduct of society and its citizens. If you then use another definition or theory, you will be able to identify new characteristics of the law, for example:

'Law is a mechanism for **controlling the masses and retaining the power of the ruling classes** . . . ' or law is the means by which **justice** can be achieved.'

Once you have identified and explained a number of theories, answering the second part of the question becomes much easier; in other words the two parts of the question are related.

Other questions are difficult for the following reasons:

- They require you to **cover a number of legal areas** (for example, a problem question which covers offer and acceptance, consideration, breach and damages). You need a broad knowledge of the course to tackle these questions (attending lectures and seminars on a regular basis helps enormously), and you need to dedicate an appropriate amount of time to each area.

- They require you to **display a thorough knowledge of a specific legal area**, or a case or number of cases. For these questions you need to research beyond your basic textbook and may need to access full law reports and case notes on relevant cases.

- They require you to **employ skills such as statutory or case interpretation**. The answers to these questions do not appear in any textbook and you need to look carefully at the wording of the statute or the decision of a previous case to allow you to answer the question. Never underestimate the acquisition of general and basic skills in tackling questions in substantive legal areas.

- They require you to have **some knowledge of recent events or political and social affairs**. A lot of students struggle with questions which require some knowledge of politics or recent affairs. If you are not naturally a 'political animal,' acquire a textbook that adopts a more political approach to the subject and try to get to terms with at least the basic political or other arguments. As a law student you should buy and read a good broadsheet newspaper, particularly if you are studying subjects such as Public Law or Law in Society.

## What Sort of Skills Do I Have to Employ?

You should examine the question closely at an early stage and consider the sort of skills you are going to need to tackle that question. This allows you to acquire the skills before you write the assessment. In general, to tackle law assessments you need to employ the following skills:

- Careful and selective research
- An ability to grasp concepts and legal principles
- A sound knowledge of the relevant legal area
- An understanding of cases and other legal sources and their relevance to the question
- An ability to explain concepts and legal sources in a simple and clear fashion
- Clear writing and English skills

In addition, the question might expect you to show other skills, such as critical analysis or contextual awareness. In such a case you need to acquire and practice those skills in preparation of the presentation of the work.

## How Much Knowledge Do I Need? What Depth of Knowledge Is Required?

At level 1 of your law studies you will be given assessment that tests your basic knowledge and understanding of the law, the institutional framework and basic legal concepts. In addition, the assessment will test your ability to write in a way that is consistent with you being an undergraduate, including showing skills expected of a law student – handling of legal materials, proper citation and referencing skills. At this level you will not be expected to display enhanced academic skills or an advanced knowledge or appreciation of the law. Also, you will not be expected to conduct extensive research at this level.

- Ensure that you display a knowledge of the basics.
- Try to give the impression that you have understood what you have learnt in lectures and seminars.
- Be sure to employ basic writing and legal skills.
- Ensure that you make good use of legal sources such as cases, statutory provisions and secondary sources.
- Be prepared to conduct some research beyond the main textbook – other texts, articles and primary sources.
- Avoid esoteric or advanced arguments and articles unless you fully understand them and can comment on them in a constructive manner. It is better to answer the question soundly, rather than risking failure by including material and arguments that you do not understand.

You will be expected to display greater skills at levels 2 and 3 of your studies (see Chapters 2 and 6), but for the time being you are learning the fundamentals so concentrate on the simple things, especially in your first assessments of the year.

HOW TO WRITE BETTER LAW ESSAYS

# Showing Individual Understanding

The ability to display individual understanding and to show the lecturer that *you* understand the legal area and what you are saying is related to the problem of plagiarism. As noted previously, many students plagiarise because they have no knowledge and views of their own and feel the need to hide behind other's views and ideas. Similarly, some students in that position rely (and often credit) those views so heavily that they fail to show any understanding of the issues or of the question. In addition to using and crediting sources, you must show that you are comfortable with the legal principles and all relevant sources.

## Using Relevant Sources

By using relevant cases, statutes and academic opinion you are showing that you understand the question and have identified the relevance of that source in addressing and answering the question. If you use irrelevant (cases), or simply include all cases in the general legal area, you expose your lack of appreciation of the question and its scope.

## Giving Relevant Examples in Illustration

You can illustrate general or complicated concepts and principles by giving clear and simple examples, either real or hypothetical. This shows that you have truly understood what you have read and included in your answer.

For example, 'A fundamental principle of the rule of law is that all law should be prospective as opposed to retrospective.' Anyone can write that down from a book, but to show your understanding of that idea you can give an example. 'For example, if an Act was passed in June 2005 which made it unlawful to smoke on the streets, and that law applied to such conduct whether it took place before or after the coming into effect of that Act, the Act has retrospective effect. This will undermine the rule of law, for people will be subject to criminal liability even if their conduct was not unlawful at the time of committing the relevant act.' If you have found this example in a secondary source, you must credit and cite that source: 'As Foster has indicated, if an Act was passed . . . .' However, you may wish to use a similar example that you have thought of, in which case you will be rewarded for your individual understanding. Alternatively, you could use a real case example (*Burmah Oil*) to illustrate the principle and unfairness of retrospectivity – examples could be found in the textbook and you can then use it in the context of the question that you are answering.

## Explaining Cases and Other Primary Sources

Anyone can copy out a case or statutory provision. Try to show that you have understood the source and its relevance to the question:

> **Example**
>
> *'There is a clear difference between an offer and an invitation to treat. Discuss.'*
>
> 'In *Carlill* it was held that the advertisement was indeed a contractual offer. **This is because the advert was in sufficiently clear terms and the company had expressed their contractual intention by depositing £1000 in the bank. Hence, an advert Is not necessarily an invitation to treat and it is not always clear whether those who place an advertisement in a newspaper intend to be bound if someone attempts to accept it.'**

*'To what extent does the Human Rights Act 1998 change the role of the judge with respect to the protection of human rights in domestic law?'*

'Section 3 of the Human Rights Act states that the courts must so far as is possible – interpret legislation in a manner that is compatible with Convention rights. **Thus, although the section does not give the courts the power to ignore clearly incompatible legislation, it does provide them with an increased duty, and power, to ensure that legislation is interpreted consistently with human rights.**'

### Explaining and Criticising Authors' Views or the State of the Law

You will not be expected to compete with recognised academic opinion. However, you should not simply quote an author and his or her views without offering some analysis or explanation. Try to sum up in simple terms what the author is saying and perhaps offer an example in illustration.

'Foster claims that the courts have continued to show a deferential approach towards the executive, and have thus refused to take a dynamic or robust approach in cases concerning a conflict between human rights and official policy [reference to article/book and page number]. **What Foster means by this is that in certain cases, most notably those cases relating to national security [provide reference to a case], the courts will be reluctant to interfere with the decision of a public authority. Here the courts might feel that to interfere would impinge on the authority and autonomy of that body and thus breach the separation of powers.**

You also may want to criticise the academic opinion. You can do this provided you have the authority to endorse that criticism; you cannot simply say that *'I do not agree with Foster.'* You can say, *'However, that view ignores the fact that several decisions relating to national security have been challenged successfully.'*

If you are disagreeing with a more abstract or subjective opinion, such as 'the law should not criminalise speech purely because it clashes with public morals,' then you should only give your subjective opinion once you indicate that you have understood the first opinion. You can't just say, *'I don't think people should be able to express themselves in an immoral way.'* However, you can say, *'Whilst agreeing that speech should not be restricted simply because it is controversial or causes offence, I do believe (or it could be argued) that there exists in society a common belief in morality which is worthy of protection from attack.'*

## Receiving and Digesting Feedback

When marking your work the lecturer should put a number of comments on the script and provide you with reasonably detailed feedback, including guidance on how the work could have been improved. Some lecturers hold extra sessions to go over the work in class, pointing out common mistakes. In addition, you may be able to make an appointment with the lecturer to discuss specific points about your work and its shortcomings. Take advantage of these facilities and ensure that further work is improved in accordance with any guidance or comments.

- Ensure that you collect your work as soon as it is available. If you miss the handing-back session, make an appointment to collect your work as soon as possible.
- Do not just find out the mark and leave the work uncollected – you need to look at the comments whatever mark you received.
- Read and digest the comments carefully and ensure you do not make similar mistakes in further work.
- If there are legal errors or omissions in your work, ensure that you correct and update them in your notes.
- If the lecturer complains about writing style, grammar, poor referencing skills, or inappropriate use of legal materials, work on those skills in time for the next submission.

## Summary of Points on Writing and Presenting Law Assignments

At the end of this chapter you should have learnt or enhanced a wide range of basic academic and writing skills to assist you with your general law study, but most specifically with the writing of your law assessments.

- Engage with the course and the relevant module and get the most out of the lecturer and the teaching sessions.
- Research your assessments as early as possible and get to know the legal area thoroughly.
- There is no substitute for knowing your law, although your work will be enhanced by good writing skills.
- Learn how to cite and reference legal sources.
- Ensure that you have understood the question and that you know what the lecturer is after.
- At the very least, show that you have understood the basics.
- Avoid any possible claim of plagiarism.
- Avoid complicated legal jargon and esoteric and too advanced sources.
- Check your work thoroughly before you submit it.
- Take note of any comments made on your work and address any shortcomings before submitting further work.

You can test your skills by carrying out the relevant excercises on the Companion Website (www.pearsoned.co.uk/foster)

# Writing Legal Essays: Specific Legal Skills

**2**

## ● Introduction

Although the basic rules relating to good essay technique apply equally to law assessments, because of the complexity of the law and legal concepts, and because the law is often vague and/or open-ended, students will be required to display even greater and clearer writing skills. Some of these rules are outlined in Chapter 1, but this chapter provides more detailed information and guidance. In addition, students must develop specific skills in the research and writing of their assessments. This chapter explains those skills and teaches the reader how to employ them. In particular, this chapter examines:

- The use of legal materials, both primary and secondary, in the presentation of law assessments, including specific guidance on the use of cases and statutory provisions and the use of books, journals and other secondary sources.
- The rules relating to legal referencing and citation of authority, including how to cite cases, statutes, books, journals and other sources. **(Please note that if the name Foster is used, the case, article or book is fictitious and is being used to illustrate general citation and referencing skills.)**
- Advice on researching law assignments, including where to locate necessary materials and which materials to use for specific questions, depending on the nature of the question and the level of study.
- A general overview of the sorts of skills needed to tackle law assessments.

## ● Using Legal Materials

As with the study of any academic subject, law students must give authority for their views and in their assessments. In particular, students must use a variety of legal sources, both **primary** and **secondary,** in presenting their work and any argument. The use of these sources is governed by a number of rules, some of them specifically applicable to legal materials, and you must learn and apply these rules when submitting your assessments.

### Providing Authority

As with all academic subjects, a student must provide authority for the things they say in their assignments. You cannot simply make a statement relating to the subject without providing the source of that statement and providing evidence that what you are saying is correct and established:

'Serious crime is on the increase these days.'

Where is the evidence for that? Are the figures contained in an official document? Has someone undertaken research?

'It is unlawful for a person to commit an act of theft.'

Is this the law? If so, which law, in which particular provision is this law located, and what does that provision actually say?

'There are a number of cases that show that the courts are prepared to uphold the sovereignty of Parliament.'

Which cases support that proposition? Has an author assimilated those cases and analysed or criticised them?

In all these cases, some evidence exists to back up what you are saying. This will provide evidence that you have read the primary or secondary sources (see the following Note) and are relying on those sources. It will also provide you with the opportunity to display your academic and legal skills in citing and referring to those sources (see the following Note).

---

**Note**

**You should not use lecture notes, or statements made by lecturers, as legal authority.**

---

- Lecture notes are *not* authority for the law and they should not be referred to either in the main body of your work or in the bibliography. In other words, avoid 'See Lecture notes on Offer and Acceptance' or, in your bibliography 'Foster, Lecture Notes.' This might be acceptable on sub-degree courses but is not so on undergraduate courses.

- So too, lecturers are not authority unless they have published (a book or an article in an official journal or newspaper). In that case, by all means refer to their views (if relevant) and provide the reference.

- If secondary sources have been distributed in class, give the proper reference for that source; do not put 'article distributed in class.' If the source of the article is not clear, find it out.

- You can, and should, however, listen to what the lecturer has to say on the law and keep those views in mind when researching your work and structuring your argu- ments. The lecturer will expect you to have picked up these points and to show that you have understood them. Always back those points up with proper authority.

- Do not simply follow the pattern of, or copy out, lecture notes. This suggests you have not looked at proper secondary sources. You can, however, use the lecture notes for general guidance on how to order specific points.

## Do I Always Have to Give Authority?

As indicated in the following examples, you are not obliged to give authority for obvious statements, such as 'The United Kingdom consists of Great Britain and Northern Ireland, but not the Republic of Ireland.'

Also, if you have been asked for, and are giving, your opinion, then you do not use authority, because it is *your* opinion. For example, 'In my opinion, it should not be an offence to blaspheme against established religious views because free speech should be more important than protecting even religious sensibilities.'

However, if your opinion is based on another source, you must credit that source.

### Example

'With respect to the protection of human rights, I am more convinced by the natural lawyers rather than utilitarian arguments, because the utilitarian view might lead to the suppression of minority rights.'

In this case, you need to show an awareness of those arguments and to refer to specific authors (secondary sources). If your opinion is one that is shared by an author, then you should indicate that.

You must also ensure that your opinion is consistent with the legal facts.

### Example

'In my opinion, judges should not be so reluctant to interfere with decisions made by the Home Secretary and should strike down such decisions if they are inconsistent with human rights.'

This would be a valid point to make, provided the case law supports the statement. In this case, there are a number of cases in which the courts *have* interfered.

## The Difference Between Primary and Secondary Sources

Many students get confused between primary and secondary sources, and this leads to further confusion with respect to the crediting and referencing of such sources.

A **primary source** is the original source of that law, where that law originates; without that source, the law would not exist. For example an Act of Parliament, an EC Directive, a piece of delegated legislation, an international treaty and a case are all primary sources and must be treated and sourced as such.

### Example

If you say, '. . . it is offence to commit an act of theft,' you are referring to the law on theft, and there is a primary source for that law (Section 1 of the Theft Act 1968 (as amended)). Without that primary source, that law would not exist in England and Wales, and thus you must refer to that source. This is the case even if you read about that law in a textbook, a website or an article. Consequently, you cannot say '. . . it is an offence to commit an act of theft' and then credit that statement by putting (Foster, *Criminal Law*, at page 67.) You have referred to a secondary source (see the following example) and have indicated that this author is the primary source, which of course he is not, because the law of theft would exist even if that book had not been written. So too, you are not guilty of plagiarism by failing to mention the book in such a case. The law does not belong to that author, and you simply must refer to the primary source.

With cases, you must refer to the case itself, and not the book that you read the case in. You can then give the appropriate reference to that case - usually the official law report. Thus, do not do this:

## Example

'An advertisement can be construed as a contractual offer (See Foster, *Contract Law*, at page 16)'.

In such a case you must refer to the case itself and provide the reference (*Carlill v Carbolic Smoke Ball Company* [1893] 1 QB 256).

A **secondary source** is where an account of or a commentary of the law can be found. For example, a textbook, a journal article, a website and a conference paper are all secondary sources. They are not the original source of the legal rule, and if they did not exist the law would still be there (in its original source). Thus, do not refer to them as primary sources.

This rule also applies to information found on websites.

- If you access primary sources on websites (e.g., treaties, Acts of Parliament, cases), refer to the primary source (and its proper reference) and not the website. Do not put *Smith v Hughes* (see www.casefind.com).
- You can, however, put a website in your bibliography to indicate that you have researched and accessed that source.
- It is permissible to refer the reader to a website to gain primary sources: 'The Human Rights Act 1998 can be downloaded by accessing www.statuteuk.co.uk.
- If you are using the website as a secondary source (for views or explanations of the law), refer to that website as your source.
- Try not to use websites as a substitute for textbooks and articles. If you access such materials on the website, obviously refer to the book or the article, not the website.

## Using Secondary Sources

You can use secondary sources to explain, criticise or summarise the law. An author will have read the primary source and is now explaining to the reader how that law originated, how it has been interpreted and applied, whether it is correct or just, whether it should be amended and so on. If you are making use of other people's academic efforts and views, you must credit them. This is the case even if you are not copying those views word for word.

- If you are copying word for word, use inverted commas and provide the reference.
- If you are taking the thrust of the author's work or view, make it clear that you are using another's views and credit that author.

By using the words 'it has been suggested,' the student is obviously referring to an established view on this aspect of the law. He or she must, therefore, credit that source (Foster, 'The Human Rights Act and its application' (2004) 66 MLR 333, at page 346). The student should also refer somewhere – either before or after the statement is made, or in a footnote – to the primary sources (the case law that is allegedly uncertain).

If this view is taken from an author, it should be credited as such, like this: 'Foster has noted that . . . '; then provide the reference or put the opinion in quotes and then provide the reference. Again, there should be some reference to the primary sources that are alluded to in the statement.

If this is an author's subjective view, it must be credited as such; you cannot pass it off as your own. Thus, you must either put the words in inverted commas and then give the reference, or precede the statement by saying that 'Foster argues that . . .' and then providing the reference.

You can then indicate whether you agree with that view (and submit your own opinion), or whether it is supported by primary or academic authority (providing that authority either in support or in opposition of the view).

Unless the student is conducting extensive research, the student here has copied this footnote from a text or article. He is thus relying on the author's own research and hard work; unless he credits it, he is passing this work off as his own – giving the impression that he has looked up and assimilated all these sources – and is guilty of plagiarism. In such a case, make it clear that this compilation is the work of another: Foster provides a number of cases from other jurisdictions which support this view (reference to the article or book).

## Secondary Sources Within Secondary Sources

Some textbooks, articles, websites and so on refer to other secondary sources, either to support their arguments or to assist in the explanation of the law. This is particularly true of cases and materials books, where a book will provide a number of (secondary) sources.

- You must refer to the original secondary source and not the text or article that referred to such a source.

> **Example**
>
> 'Dicey always maintained that there should be no separate public law and that the government should be bound by the ordinary private law (Foster, *Constitutional Law*, page 23).'
>
> This reference is wrong; you should refer to the original source of Dicey's views (AV Dicey, *Introduction to the Study of the Law of the Constitution* (1885), at page 22).

- You should read the original source if possible or practicable. If the original secondary source is not available, then it is permissible to rely on the later source. In such a case indicate that you have not accessed the original source.

> **Example**
>
> Locke J, The Second Treatise of Government (1689), as cited in Foster, *Constitutional Law*, at page 32.

## Do I Always Have to Credit Secondary Sources?

To be on the safe side, or because they are not sure about the rules on crediting, some students credit the author with everything they put in the assessment. This is not always necessary and gives the impression that you have no understanding of the subject beyond what you are taking from the textbook.

- As mentioned previously, do not credit the author for primary sources, even if you learnt about that source from the textbook or other secondary source.
- You do not have to credit the author with the facts and decisions of cases (as opposed to the author's analysis of that case or her views on it). They do not belong to the author, and you can copy the facts and decision from the textbook (or casebook, or,

where appropriate, the law report). Very often, students get into difficulties by trying to give their own version of the facts and the decision – if you find a simple and appropriate account of the facts and the decision, you can use it.

- Avoid using one author for all the statements you make – this will indicate that you have only read that source.

- You do not have to credit the author for trite law (obvious and accepted legal statements) such as 'the British Constitution is unwritten' and 'England and Wales have a common law system.'

- You do not need to credit an author if you make a general legal comment and use different words than those employed by the author. For example, if an author says 'In all but exceptional cases, a contract is based on the agreement of the offeror and the offeree,' you can say 'In most cases a contract will be based on agreement between the parties.'

## Can I Use the Author's Style of Writing and Format?

Generally, it is acceptable to employ the same sort of style and format adopted by an author; indeed, students will be encouraged to employ a similar style.

- Adopt the legal style used by authors and employ appropriate phrases such as these: 'The claimant brought an action for breach of contract' (not 'The innocent party sued the other in court'); 'His Lordship referred to a number of authorities' (not 'The judge looked at a lot of cases before making his decision').

- Adopt authors' methods of explaining legal principles, cases, statutory provisions and so on, including the order in which points are made and the structure of the explanation. Thus, if a number of authors deal with a legal issue (e.g., contract formation) in a particular manner (e.g., offer and acceptance, consideration, intention, capacity), it is acceptable for you to follow that order. If one author adopts an unusual approach, then you may credit that author for such: 'On the other hand, Foster believes that the following approach should be used in determining whether a contract exists.' (Foster, *Contract Law*, page 6).

- In particular, follow an author's *style* (not the exact words) in how he or she uses legal materials to explain and illustrate the law – how to cite and refer to a case or Act of Parliament, how to explain the significance of a case, how to introduce a case into the discussion and so on.

- Do not use the style adopted in sub-degree texts – lists, bullet points, questions and so on. That style is inappropriate for undergraduate work.

## ● Using Cases

Case law is central to answering many (though not all) legal questions – essays or problem-based – and it is essential that you are comfortable with using this source.

A large number of students struggle when using cases in their written work. They are not sure why the case must be used, how to use it, what the case is saying and so on. Because of this confusion, the student's answer is often made worse by the inclusion of case law.

- Learn how to use cases and become familiar with how they are written and structured.
- Read as many cases as possible and become familiar with law reports.
- See how textbooks and articles use cases and acquire that style and those skills.
- Do not rely on lecture notes when providing an account of the case; read the law report, a casebook or, at the very least, a good account of a case in a textbook.

## Why Use Cases and When Do I Use Them?

Cases can be used to provide legal authority or to explain and illustrate a legal principle or argument. Students should use cases to enhance their work, by displaying legal skills in respect to citation and referencing or by using cases to better explain particular rules or views. They are not to be used simply to show that you know a case; they should be relevant and fulfil some purpose in the presentation of your work.

### Cases as Simple Authority

Cases can be used as simple authority for a legal proposition and can be cited as such.

---

**Example**

'Generally, for an acceptance to be valid, it must be communicated to the offeror.'

There is case authority for that proposition (*Entores v Far Eastern Miles Corporation*) and you can use that case, along with its reference, to provide such authority. This follows the principle that you always provide authority for any statement made in assessments. In addition, you can also display your skills in citing and referring to cases properly.

---

### To Illustrate a Legal Principle

A case can be used to explain the law and to provide an illustration of how a legal principle is applied in practice. In this way, you are not merely providing authority but using the case to enhance your work and your explanation or analysis of the law.

---

**Example**

'Case law is a major source of the British Constitution, and some cases have established fundamental constitutional principles, such as the rule of law and the accountability of government. Thus, In *Entick v Carrington* (reference), it was held that government officials had to show legal authority in order to enter an individual's land, and could not rely on the arbitrary principle of state necessity.'

Here, the case is being used to explain what would otherwise be a rather dry and abstract principle. It shows that you understand that principle and you have brought the law to life by providing a real case example.

---

### To Support an Analysis or Criticism of the Law

You can use a case to support an academic argument.

'Foster argues that there is no need for a written constitution, because the courts will protect individuals from arbitrary and unreasonable interference with their liberty via the common law. This can be illustrated by cases such as *Entick v Carrington* (reference), where the individual's rights were upheld within the traditional common law principles of trespass.'

Alternatively, it can show your analytical or critical skills.

'Although the quote in the question (that 'human rights are best protected by the general law') can be supported by cases such as *Entick v Carrington* (reference), it should not be forgotten that the courts have on occasions failed to recognise certain fundamental rights. Thus, in *Malone v MPC* (reference), the domestic courts failed to recognise a general right of privacy.'

### To Assist You in Answering Problem Questions

Specifically, cases can be used to help you answer problem questions and to give advice on the likely outcome of a dispute.

'It is to be noted that in this case Jack, by offering to pay only half of the original debt, appears not to have provided any fresh consideration for Bill's acceptance of that offer. In this respect, one could refer to the principle in *Pinel's Case* (reference) and conclude that in the absence of any fresh promise, Bill will not be bound by that acceptance.'

So, too, you can use the facts and decision of a previous case and apply it to (or distinguish it from) the present facts.

'In our case the advertisement states quite clearly that the customer merely needs to "take the voucher to the store to receive a discount on those goods." This is similar to the situation in *Carlill v Carbolic Smoke Ball Company* (reference), where it was held that a contract was concluded when Mrs Carlill followed the company's instructions and used the smoke ball without success and claimed a reward that had been promised in a newspaper advertisement.'

## Do I Have to Give (All) the Facts and Details of the Decision?

This will depend on whether an account of the facts and the decision will assist you in answering the question. As indicated previously, you can use cases for a number of purposes, and sometimes the facts of and decision in the case are not relevant to the point that you are trying to make.

- It will be rare for the lecturer to expect you to give the full facts of a case and/or a full account of the decision in that case. However, you may need this information if the question is principally concerned with one or a limited number of cases, or where you are asked to write a case note on a specific case.
- Giving the facts of the case might help readers (and students) understand a legal issue (and why it was in dispute), and help them explain the decision and its rationale. If you are explaining something theoretical or legally complex, the facts of a case might help readers engage with the area and the specific issues.

### Example

'The rule of law demands that government is equal before the law and should not rule via arbitrary discretion.'

Giving the facts of (and decision) in *Entick v Carrington* might help the reader understand the significance of that case and the principles it upholds.

- In problem questions, only give the facts of a case if they are similar to the ones in the scenario, or if they allow you to draw a distinction between the case and your facts.
- Generally, it is more important to explain the principle behind the case (or its rationale or significance) than to tell the lecturer what happened and what was decided in that case.
- Often it is better to give an extract from the judgment rather than the facts and the decision.

### Example

'Recent case law suggests that the courts are prepared to interfere with executive discretion where fundamental human rights are under threat. Thus in *A v Home Secretary* (reference) Lord Bingham stated that 'Even in a terrorist situation, the courts were not precluded by any doctrine of deference from scrutinising the issues raised.' (Provide reference to page or paragraph number in the law report.)

- If the facts and decision are relevant to answering the question, and if you have time and space to give the facts and decision of the case, ensure that you do so as briefly as possible. Learn how to digest the facts and decision of the case in one or two sentences.

### Example

'In Carlill it was held that an advertisement which clearly stated that any person who used the company's product and still caught influenza could claim a reward of £100 constituted a contractual offer, which was accepted by the claimant when she followed the relevant instructions.'

▼

That would be sufficient to inform the reader of the basic facts and decision and to make some accompanying comment such as 'Thus, an advert can be an offer if it is couched in sufficiently clear terms,' or 'Thus, in such cases the acceptance is valid on performance of the act.' If the case is being used in a problem question as an analogy (or otherwise), then you could give more detailed facts (perhaps mentioning that the company deposited £1,000 as a mark its sincerity).

## Is It Sufficient to Give the Case Name?

If you are using the case simply to provide authority for a general legal principle, then it is sufficient to give the name of the case (either in the main body of the work or by creating a footnote).

**Example**

If you are answering a problem question on judicial review, and the scenario raises a specific ground of review such as natural justice, you might want to make a general point about the general grounds of review:

'Lord Diplock has identified the general grounds of judicial review as illegality, irrationality and procedural impropriety.'

You can then refer to the case (*Council of Civil Service Unions v Minister of State for the Civil Service*) and then give the reference ([1985] AC 374), either in a footnote, or by putting 'In *Council of Civil Service Unions v Minister of State for the Civil Service* (create footnote for the case reference), Lord Diplock identified . . .'

There is no need to give the facts or the decision in that case, or even to analyse the significance of the case. You are using the case simply to provide authority for a general point, and it is acceptable to give just the case name and reference.

## Do I Need to Read the (Whole) Law Report?

You will be encouraged by your lecturers to get into the habit of accessing law reports and reading a case in its entirety. Most lecture notes and reading lists for seminars and coursework will refer you to the official law report.

- By reading the law report, you will get a fuller picture of what the case was about, what legal and factual issues were raised and how the case was decided. You will also become familiar with the style of language used by judges, which will help you in explaining, distinguishing and analysing cases.
- If you are going to use the law report, you might not have to read the whole judgment(s). If you read the head note to the case, you will be referred to relevant and the most important parts of the judgment. Practise locating the most important sections and getting the essential gist of what the judge is saying.
- If you have read the law report, make sure you get the benefit of that research. Indicate to the lecturer that you have taken the trouble of accessing the law report, by, for example, quoting from the judgment(s).

- Remember, many law reports (and other sources) can be accessed via websites; you do not always need to go the library to read a case. Make sure the site provides proper references to pages or paragraph numbers.

However, it is not practicable for you to access the law reports for every case that you are referred to.

- Use the law reports if it is necessary to access the full case and to get a complete picture of the case.
- In many cases you can rely on a good casebook to give you an account of the case and its decision. The advantages are that the casebook will digest the facts and the judgment and provide you with a relevant analysis of the case and its impact on the general law (in which case, if you use that information you should credit it – beware of plagiarism).
- Do not use casebooks that provide the barest detail – one or two lines on the facts and then the same on the decision. They will not provide sufficient depth or analysis for coursework purposes.
- Sometimes your textbook might provide a sufficient account of the case, and you can use it in your work. This can be done if you are using the case as simple authority or giving a very basic account of the case.
- You can often find suitable accounts of cases in journal articles. Sometimes the author will examine a case in detail, and you can get the facts and decision from this source. Ensure that you distinguish the account of the facts and the decision from the academic commentary provided by the author. You will need to credit the latter; otherwise you will be guilty of plagiarism.
- Beware that some authors will not refer to the facts (or decision) of the case, but will simply analyse or criticise the decision. In that case, find out the facts and decision (if they are relevant) and do not make vague statements such as '. . . the case of *Foster v Foster* shows the courts' reluctance to interfere with domestic arrangements.'
- When you get the facts and decision of a case from a textbook, casebook or article, do not refer to that secondary source, but use the primary source. In other words do not say, 'This was decided in *Foster v Jones* (See Foster, *Contract Law,* page 6, or Foster, Analysing offers (2004) OJLS 213, at 216).'

## Newspaper and Journal Reports

Students will be encouraged to scan the respectable newspapers (*The Times, The Daily Telegraph, The Guardian* and *The Independent*) and to read their daily law reports. Cases are normally reported within days of the judgment, and reading these reports is a useful way of keeping up to date with new cases.

- Most of these reports will be fairly brief and thus provide only a superficial account of the case; you will normally need to research to find a fuller report of the case.
- Some such reports are more comprehensive and provide a useful account of the case; unless the case is particularly important for your studies, this report may suffice.
- Always check to see whether the case has been subsequently reported in the official law reports, and cite that reference if possible.

In addition, journals such as the *New Law Journal, Legal Action, Criminal Law Review, Solicitors Journal, European Human Rights Law Review* and so on have their own law reports; in the absence of something more official, you can use that reference: *Foster v United Kingdom* [2005] EHRLR 236.

Many journals have case commentaries by academics, in which the case is analysed and criticised. These are not reports of the case and should not used as such. You can, however, refer to them as a secondary source after referring to the official report:

---

**Example**

This was confirmed in the recent House of Lords' decision in *Foster v Smith* [2005] 2 AC 333. For an analysis of the case see Foster, 'What was wrong with the decision in *Foster v Smith*?' (2005) 68 MLR 298.'

---

## Unreported Cases

Some cases are not reported in the official law reports or elsewhere. In such a case follow these rules:

● If it is not reported in the official law reports, or subject specific reports, but has been reported in a reputable newspaper law report (see the preceding section), it is acceptable to use that reference: *Foster v Jones*, *The Times*, 1 April 2005.

● If it has not been reported in official, specific or newspaper law reports, you may use a reference from a legal journal (see the preceding point).

● In the previously mentioned situations, check whether the case has subsequently been reported in the law reports or a newspaper law report. You can do this by accessing websites such as LAWTEL or WESTLAW.

● Cases are now given a neutral citation, separate from any particular law report. Different abbreviations are given, which depends where the case was heard – the House of Lords (UKHL), Court of Appeal (EWCA Civ or EWCA Crim) or the High Court (EWHC). If the case has not yet been reported in a law report, you can use the neutral citation – *Foster v Worthington* [2005] UKHL 2657. Check whether the case has subsequently been reported elsewhere.

● For cases without any reference at all, refer to the name of the court and the date of the decision – *Foster v Home Office*, unreported, decision of Manchester County Court, 14 April 1987

● Unreported decisions of the European Court or Commission of Human Rights can be referred to via the application number – *Foster v United Kingdom* (Application No 23456/04).

## Multiple References

A case may have been reported in a number of law reports and thus have a number of references. For example, an important case may be reported in the Appeal Cases (AC), the Weekly Law Reports (WLR), the All England Law Reports (All ER) and various sections of the Law Reports (Queen's Bench Reports (QB), Chancery Reports (Ch) and Administrative Law

Reports (Admin LR). In addition, it might be reported in specialist law reports such as the Industrial Relations Law Reports (IRLR), Human Rights Law Reports (HRLR) or the Criminal Appeals Cases (Cr. App R).

- If the case has multiple references, generally refer to just one established report; you do not have to use all the references - WLR. All ER, AC and so on. It is, however, quite common for texts to refer to both a newspaper report and an official report.
- Some journals tend to use one particular report (e.g., the WLR), but unless your lecturer specifies which report should be used you can use any of the established ones. Having chosen one, try to use that one consistently (unless the case has not been reported there; in which case, use another).
- If it has been reported in the official reports, ensure that you use that reference and not one from a newspaper or journal.

## Footnotes and Cases

Check whether you are required to use footnotes in your coursework. You can then follow these basic rules:

- You can use footnotes to locate the case reference:

### Example

'This was established in *Jones v Foster*[1] . . .'

---

[1] [1876] AC 23

Note that you do not have to give the case name in the footnote, as you have already supplied it in the text.

- You can also use footnotes to place the whole case reference:

### Example

'The Court of Appeal has established that a Minister's decision in this area can be subject to judicial review.'[2]

---

[2] *Foster v Secretary of State for the Home Department* [2004] WLR 234.

- Some texts cite the year of the case and then create a footnote:

### Example

'This was decided in *Foster v Brown* (1998).'[3]

Check with your lecturer whether this is acceptable.

---

[3] [1998] 2 WLR 67.

- You can also place additional cases in footnotes.

- You can use a footnote to refer to a part of the judgment:

## How Many Cases Should I Use?

Students often ask this question, and the answer can be very frustrating: 'It depends; how long is a piece of string?'

Of course it does depend, and all we can do here is highlight relevant factors to decide how many (and what type of) cases you should use:

- It will depend on the nature of the question. Some questions deal with institutions and procedure rather than substantive law, so you will not be expected to use cases to illustrate your answer. For example, 'Outline the court structure in the English Legal System and suggest proposals for reform.' If the question is on theory – 'What is justice?' – the answer should concentrate on conceptual and theoretical and arguments, and does not require much case law in illustration. What case law you use in such questions must illustrate the theoretical principle (e.g., the fairness and justice of the case), rather than the substantive legal issues (e.g., whether a duty of care existed and was broken on the facts).

- Questions that deal with substantive legal areas (the substantive areas of contract, tort, employment or property law and so on) will require you to be familiar with the leading case law in that area. You should include, or refer to, the leading case authorities, either to illustrate your answer or to provide authority.

- Your textbook will give you a fairly good indication of the leading cases in that area, but make sure they are relevant to the question you have been set, and always ensure that you include recent cases not included in your text.

- For more advanced work, you will be expected to be conversant with all significant decisions in that area. Even if you cannot comment on them all, ensure that you indicate your awareness of them in footnotes and so on.

- Some substantive legal areas are governed primarily by statutory provisions and, thus, there may be little case law. In this situation concentrate on the wording and interpretation of the statutory provisions to make up for the lack of case law.

- Use case law whenever it helps you answer the question. Do not cite cases just to show that you know that case or to show off your knowledge of a range of cases.

- If you use a case as authority or to illustrate a point, do not use other cases unless that enhances your answer – if it shows how the case was distinguished, applied to different circumstances and so on.

- You can refer to similar cases in footnotes: 'This principle was also applied in the subsequent House of Lords' decision in *Foster v Harrison* (reference).

- For problem questions, only use cases that are relevant to addressing and answering the specific issues raised by the scenario (see Chapter 4, 'Answering Problem Questions'). If you do refer to a case as authority for a basic point, merely give the case name and reference.

- Hence, there is no strict rule on how many cases you should use. If you look at the 'good' answers in Chapters 3 and 4 of this text, you will see that the student uses between ten and fifteen cases to answer the question. However, it is more important to bear in mind the rules set out here, rather than saying, 'I must use *X* number of cases.'

## Make Cases Work for You

Remember, you use cases to enhance your answer. Ensure that the case has made your answer more authoritative and more convincing.

Do not make your answer less impressive by the use of cases, by a muddled account of the facts and decision or by a confused explanation of its ratio or importance.

### Example

'The courts have always upheld individual liberty and have safeguarded such liberty from arbitrary governmental interference. In *Entick v Carrington* (reference) the court upheld the individual's right to privacy when they held that the police had no right to seize the plaintiff's property, even thought the Secretary of State said they could do it. This case shows that freedom of expression has always been important.'

The initial point is well made, but when the case is introduced, the author has made some mistakes on the facts, the relevant law and the ratio of the case, and the reader is thus confused about what happened in the case and its importance.

## Introduce the Case in the Context of the Question or the Point That You Are Trying to Make

Many students just drop cases into their answer without explaining their relevance or what purpose the case is serving.

### Example

'The grounds of judicial review include substantive as well as procedural wrongdoing. In *Congreve v Home Office* the minister had recalled validly granted television licences and Congreve claimed that this was not allowed. It was held that the minister had no right to revoke the licence.'

This account of the case does not tell the reader why this case, as opposed to others, has been chosen in illustration. Neither does the student use the case to illustrate the previous statement: It does not tell the reader whether there was substantive or procedural wrongdoing, what the difference is between the two or why the court thought it was beyond the minister's powers to do what he did.

Instead, after the initial statement he could say:

---

**Example**

'A public authority might have gone beyond its substantive powers by exercising them for an improper or unlawful purpose. Thus, in *Congreve v Home Office* it was held that a minister could not exercise his statutory right to revoke television licences (refer to the relevant Act of Parliament and its section) in order to raise extra revenue for the government. The minister's substantive powers were restricted to cases where the individual had broken the terms of the licence or had failed to pay the fee.'

---

This account of the case provides a good clear example of the point that the student made originally and explains the court's reasoning.

## Explain the Ratio and the Rationale of the Case

- You can use a case to give an example of how the law operates or to illustrate the law's fairness (or otherwise).

Too many students spend too much time explaining the facts and decision of the case, instead of concentrating on the legal ratio and the general reasoning of the case. For example in the preceding *Congreve* example, although the facts and the decision are quite interesting, and might be useful in helping you to illustrate a point, it is the ratio and rationale of the case that must be stressed. Thus, you should indicate why the court came to this decision, the ratio (that public authorities must not act for an improper purpose) and its rationale and significance (that courts will ensure that public authorities do not abuse their public powers).

## Explain the Significance of the Case, Not Just the Decision

The decision in a case only affects the parties to that dispute. It is the ratio of the case and the principles it upholds that are significant.

- Do not just give the facts and decision of the case, without explaining why this case is significant in answering the question.

---

**Example**

'An offer has to be distinguished from an invitation to treat. In *Fisher v Bell* a flick-knife was placed in a shop window and the shopkeeper was charged with offering for sale an offensive weapon. It was held that the display was an invitation to treat.'

---

HOW TO WRITE BETTER LAW ESSAYS

Here, the student has used the case of *Fisher v Bell* without telling us why the court decided the case as it did – why was the display not an offer? Also, why has he used *Fisher v Bell* to distinguish offers from invitations to treat, or a case on shop window displays?

Let's try again:

The student has left out the facts and has given a brief account of the decision, so that he can concentrate on the important point – that shop window displays are normally invitations – and explain the rationale and effect of such a rule.

## The Two/Three/Four/Five Step Approach

As mentioned previously, you should introduce the case properly into your work and within the context of the question, making it clear why you have used that case.

- If you are going to use the case as simple authority, then ensure that it is relevant and appropriate:

**Example**

**Step One**   Make the legal statement. ('Not all adverts are necessarily invitations to treat.').

**Step Two**   Refer to the relevant authority (*Carlill*).

- If you are going to use the case to explain a point, then ensure that you not only refer to it but explain its significance:

**Example**

**Step One**   As in the previous example.

**Step Two**   As in the previous example.

**Step Three**   Thus, an advert can be construed as an offer if (as in *Carlill*) the terms are certain enough.

- If you are going to explain the facts and decision of the case (because of its importance), ensure that you introduce the case properly, that the facts and decision are explained clearly and that you explain the ratio and significance of the case.

- If you are going to explain the decision of the case but you are not going to give the facts (because of lack of space or because they are not particularly relevant, then follow the five step approach, but leave out Step 3 in the above example.

## Read Cases Properly

It is essential that you read the case as carefully and as fully as possible, and that you understand the case before you include it in your work.

- Do not rely on your notes for the facts, decision and ratio of the case.
- At the very least, take the facts and decision form a suitable textbook or a casebook.
- You may need to read the full report to get appropriate detail or to use quotations from the judgment(s).
- Ensure that your account of the facts and of the decision is correct.
- Do not use a case in illustration unless you understand the facts and decision and the significance of the case.

## Explain the Facts and the Decision Clearly

If you are going to provide the facts and the decision of the case, ensure that you do so clearly and simply. A muddled account of the case will detract from the quality of your answer and confuse the reader:

European Convention allows a state to derogate from article 5 of the Convention and the Home Secretary claimed that this detention was necessary in times of emergency. The House of Lords held that the Act of Parliament was incompatible with article 5 of the Convention and that the courts should not be reluctant to interfere simply because there was a state of emergency. Lord Hoffmann held that there was no state of emergency, but the House of Lords held that the detention of the foreign suspects was disproportionate, even though they were detained to prevent them being tortured. Lord Walker held that the detentions were lawful and that there was a state of emergency.

This account of the case shows that the student is confused on the facts, the background of the case, the relevant statutory provisions and the decision (and which of the Lordships were dissenting). There is no logical sequence to his account of the facts and decision, and he jumps from one point to another. Consequently, the reader is confused as to what was held and the significance of the case.

Let's try again:

### Example

In *A v Secretary of State for the Home Department* the House of Lords held that the detention without trial of foreigners suspected of terrorism, under s. 26 of the Anti-Terrorism, Crime and Security Act 2001, was contrary to Article 5 of the European Convention, which guarantees the right to be brought before a judicial authority. The provision had been introduced in order to detain individuals who could not be deported to another country because of the risk of them facing torture (thus complying with the European Court's decision in *Chahal v United Kingdom*). The government had lodged a derogation order with respect to Article 5, claiming that there was a public emergency threatening the life of the nation and that it was necessary to derogate from Article 5. The majority of the House of Lords accepted that there was such an emergency (Lord Hoffmann dissenting), but held that the provisions were discriminatory and disproportionate and thus incompatible with the government's right (under Article 15 of the Convention and s. 14 of the Human Rights Act 1998) to derogate from its Convention obligations. In reaching that decision, their Lordships (Lord Walker dissenting) stressed that the courts would not show deference to Parliament in cases of national security where fundamental human rights were endangered.

This account clearly sets out the facts of and the background to the case and summarises the main thrust of the decision. It also highlights (albeit briefly) the impact of the case on the constitutional role of the courts. This student has only used fifty more words than the other account, but the difference in quality and clarity is marked, and the lecturer will appreciate this and will reflect this in the marking of the script.

## Using Extracts From the Judgment

You can quote from the judgment in the case to highlight any specific aspect of the decision or the judge's reasoning process. This will also indicate to the lecturer that you have accessed the full law report and have read the case fully.

- Ensure that the extract is relevant and that it supports the point you are trying to make.
- Ensure that the extract is properly cited and referenced and that you highlight the extract appropriately.
- Try not to use too long an extract.
- You should refer to the case name and reference, and provide a separate reference for the relevant extract.
- You might wish to highlight particular words in the judgement to stress a particular point. If the judge did not highlight the words, but you want to stress them, then put 'italics added.'

---

**Example**

In *Smith v Foster*[1] it was held that a contractual acceptance does not have to be recorded in writing and that it could be made orally. Explaining that decision Harrison LJ held that: 'although for evidential purposes it is obviously preferable for the acceptance to be communicated in writing - so that both parties have an official record of such acceptance - *a written acceptance is not a formal requirement of a legally binding contract* (italics added). An oral acceptance is in law just as effective, despite the evidential difficulties such a method might cause.'[2]

---

[1] [1990] 2 AC 236.
[2] [1990] 2 AC 236, at page 240 (or *Ibid*, at page 240).

Here the student has made the general point and has then illustrated it by the extract, highlighting the most pertinent words. The student has also referenced both the case and the extract, can comment on the extract and can refer to subsequent authority in a footnote.

- You can then comment on that extract and add further information.

---

**Example**

Thus, in that case his Lordship drew a distinction between legal and practical difficulties and this approach has been followed in subsequent cases.[3]

---

[3] See *Holmes v Foster* [1998] 1 AC 333, and *Foster v Jones* [2000] 2 AC 444.

## Use Relevant Cases

This may seem an obvious point, but a common complaint of lecturers is that many students use irrelevant cases in their answers.

- Do not use cases just because you know them and they are in the right general legal area. Many students will do this (particularly in examinations) when they do not understand, or cannot answer, the question, in the hope that the lecturer will be impressed by their general knowledge and their ability to remember lots of cases.

- You are more likely to use relevant cases if you have a sound knowledge of the legal area and you have attended classes and contributed in seminars. This is because you will already have engaged in that subject and subject area, and will recognise what the question is about and what cases are needed to address the question.
- Look at the question carefully and compile a list of relevant cases to use in the answer.
- Always ask yourself whether that case is assisting you in answering the question or addressing the issue.

## Cases With More Than One Ratio

Many cases deal with more than one legal issue and have a number of ratios. For example, a case might raise the following issues: Did the defendant make a valid offer; if so, did the claimant accept that offer; if so did both parties provide consideration? In such a case students must ensure that they use the relevant part or ratio of that case, and that the question concerns that part of the case.

For example, *Carlill* deals with a number of issues: Was the advert an offer? Was it accepted? Was there any intention to create legal relations? Did Mrs Carlill provide any consideration? In such a case it is relatively easy to use the wrong ratio to explain the point you are supposed to be making:

### Example

'Not all advertisements are invitations to treat. Thus in *Carlill* it was held that Mrs Carlill had provided consideration for the reward by simply using the product. In addition it was not necessary for her to communicate her acceptance by indicating that she was going to use the smoke ball.'

What the student has written is correct, but it is not relevant to the point he was trying to make. He deals with two legal issues raised in the case, but neither is relevant to the question of whether the advert was an offer. He knows the case is relevant to the question (because it is on the reading list or on the lecture handout), but he fails to recognise that the case raises several points and that he should be talking about the issue of offers and invitations to treat. The student has gone to the case in the book (or his notes) and has not checked whether this is the relevant point to make. You are unlikely to make this mistake if you are conversant with the relevant legal principles and have attended all sessions, because in such a case you will have spotted that the case has come up on several occasions and deals with different issues.

## Use Up-to-Date Cases

As a law student, you will be expected to keep up to date with new cases and to conduct the necessary research in order to locate them.

- Although 'old' cases are still valid, particularly in subjects such as contract and property law, you should ensure that you are aware of new case law in the relevant legal area.

- This is particularly so where the case deals with a traditional legal principle in the context of modern technology (e.g., the application of the postal rules to emails or faxed communications) or if it reflects a modern political or other problem (e.g., a challenge to recent government policy).

- You can access these cases by reading newspaper law reports, journal articles (particularly the weekly journals such as the *New Law Journal*) or by searching for new case law on websites.

- Check your lecture and seminar materials to see if there is any reference to new cases and other legal or political developments.

- Don't just rely on your textbook in this respect; the text will be at least six months out of touch with new cases.

- Always ensure that the case that you use is consistent with recent authority and that it has not been overturned or qualified by more recent cases.

## ● Using Statutory Materials

The rules in the preceding section relating to the use of case law also apply to the use of statutory materials.

Statutory materials are primary law, the law's original source, and include Acts of Parliament and its sections, Parliamentary Bills and its clauses, and delegated legislation such as statutory instruments. It also includes European Union legislative provisions such as treaty articles, regulations and directives.

You may also have to refer to provisions (articles) contained in international treaties such as the European Convention on Human Rights and Fundamental Freedoms (1950) or the Universal Declaration of Human Rights (1948).

### Quote the Relevant Section or Subsection and the Year of the Act or Regulation

- When you are using an Act of Parliament as authority, you should refer to the specific section of the Act as well as its short title (the Human Rights Act) and the year it was passed (1998), rather than the year it came into force.

---

**Example**

'Section 3 of the Human Rights Act 1998 provides that . . .'

**Or:**

'. . . the courts are now empowered, so far as is possible, to read and give effect to primary and subordinate legislation in a way that is compatible with Convention rights.' [15]

---

[15]Section 3 Human Rights Act 1998

---

- If the section has sub-sections, then you should cite that as well: 'Section 4(2) of the Human Rights Act 1998 provides. . . .' **Or** '. . . sub-section (2) of the section 4 provides . . .'

- When you are using the word *section* in the middle of a sentence, you should abbreviate it to *s.*; likewise, the word *sections* should be abbreviated to *ss.*

## Learn to Extract the Relevant Words of the Statute, Rather Than Copying Out the Whole Section

- If the statutory provision is particularly central to the question, then you may quote the whole section as long as it is of manageable size.

For example, if the question is about the courts' new interpretative powers under the Human Rights Act 1998, then it would be appropriate to quote at least sub-section (1) of the section (s. 3) in full early on in the assessment so that you can refer to the wording as you answer each aspect of the question:

- If however, s. 3 is just one of a number of sections that you are referring to, then you can paraphrase the wording, provided you get the gist of the provision:

- If the provision is long, or technical, then try to paraphrase it, rather than copying it out in full.

For example, s. 3(2) of the Human Rights Act provides as follows:

(2) This section –

- **(a)** applies to primary legislation and subordinate legislation whenever enacted;
- **(b)** does not affect the validity, continuing operation or enforcement of any incompatible primary legislation; and
- **(c)** does not affect the validity, continuing operation or enforcement of any incompatible subordinate legislation if (disregarding any possibility of revocation) primary legislation prevents removal of the incompatibility.

It would not really be appropriate to copy out the whole of s. 3(2), particularly in an essay with a word limit. Instead, you should paraphrase the sub-section and contain the gist of that provision in your answer:

---

**Example**

'Sub-section 2 states that this new power can be used in respect of both primary and secondary legislation, whenever enacted. However, s. 3(1) does not affect the validity of incompatible primary legislation, or of secondary legislation where the primary legislation would prevent the removal of the incompatibility.'

---

- Paraphrase the technical words of a statutory provision and allow time and space to explain or analyse the provision.

The use of a statutory provision will not necessarily assist in you in explaining the law. You will need to add comments and analysis to show that you understand the provision and its relevance to the question.

---

**Example**

'Sub-section 2 states that this new power can be used in respect of both primary and secondary legislation, whenever enacted; in other words, either before or after the coming into effect of the Human Rights Act. However, s. 3(1) does not affect the validity of incompatible primary legislation, or of secondary legislation where the primary legislation would prevent the removal of the incompatibility. Thus the sovereignty of Acts of Parliament is preserved and the courts have no power to strike down legislative provisions which have been clearly sanctioned by Parliament.'

---

## If You Are Paraphrasing the Provision, Ensure That You Convey the Correct Gist of the Provision

Some students rely on a general textbook, or their lecture notes or handouts, to explain what a statutory provision says. As a result, readers may be left with an incomplete picture of the provision and its content and scope:

---

**Example**

'Section 3 of the Human Rights Act allows the courts greater powers to interpret legislation in line with the Convention, and s. 4 allows certain courts to issue declarations of incompatibility.'

---

This statement is perfectly true, but if a question asks you to explain and analyse the provisions of the Human Rights Act, this answer fails to explain what the section says. The lecturer will note on your essay that you are being vague and ask, 'What is meant by 'greater powers?' **Which** courts have powers under s. 4? What **is** a declaration of incompatibility?'

## Make Sure That the Statutory Provision Is Not Out of Date and Has Not Been Repealed or Amended

- If you include out-of-date provisions, or fail to include new provisions, you are exposing your lack of knowledge and your inability to keep up with new law. In particular, you run the risk of making a clear error on the law.

- This type of mistake can be avoided in the vast majority of cases by relying on the most recent edition of the recommended textbook and by consulting the lecturer's handouts; lecturers often make student aware of recent developments in this way.
- The easiest way to check whether the provision is still in force is to use websites such as LAWTEL. You can simply punch in the provision and it will tell you its status – whether it is in force, if it has been repealed, amended, and so on.
- In addition, you should make a regular search of such websites and their current updates service to see whether any new statutory provisions have been passed or proposed.
- If a statutory provision has been amended by a later Act of Parliament, but is still in force, then you should use the original provision as amended and should not quote the amending provision as the primary source.

For example, Section 14A of the Public Order Act 1986 now covers the offence of 'trespassory assembly,' and this was introduced via s. 70 of the Criminal Justice and Public Order Act 1994. In this case, you would cite s. 14A of the 1986 Act and not s. 70 of the 1994 Act (although you can mention that s. 14 was amended by s. 70).

## Again, Use These Materials to Help You Answer the Question, to Get a Point Across, to Come to a Conclusion and So On

Do not just quote or use a statutory provision for the sake of it. Ensure that it serves a purpose and enhances your answer.

- You can use a statutory provision to provide simple authority.

**Or:**

'Clauses that seek to exclude business liability for death and personal injury caused by negligence are void.'[16]

---

[16]Section 2, Unfair Contract Terms Act 1977.

## Example

'The criminal law often reflects the view that certain conduct is morally wrong. Thus, s. 1 of the Theft Act 1968 (as amended) reflects society's disapproval of stealing by providing that it is an offence to commit an act of theft.'

## Example

'Most criminal offences require a specific mens rea, and are not committed unless the defendant has a guilty mind. For example, s. 1 of the Theft Act 1968 (as amended) provides that a person is guilty of theft if he *dishonestly* (italics added) appropriates property belonging to another.'

Note here that the student has stressed the word *dishonestly* to show that she appreciates which word in the section is relevant to the point she is making.

## Example

'It is fundamental that the law is prospective and not retrospective. Thus, s. 1 of the War Damage Act 1965, which retrospectively overruled the decision in *Burmah Oil v Lord Advocate*, thus depriving individuals of the right to compensation, is regarded as morally wrong and unconstitutional.'

## ● Using Law Journals

There are dozens of English legal journals and periodicals (and hundreds of international journals) that can assist you with your law study and the research and presentation of your work. Get used to reading these journals and using them as a secondary source for your work. You can use these journals for a number of purposes:

- Some journals, particularly the weekly and monthly trade journals, can be used to keep up to date with recent cases, statutory developments, and current legal and political debates. They also contain short articles on legal issues, which are of interest to both the practitioner and the law student. Get into the habit of reading these regularly, even if it is only to skim though them to check for relevant information. For example, consult the *New Law Journal*, *Solicitor's Journal*, *Legal Action*, *Justice of the Peace*, *Law Society Gazette*, *Legal Counsel* and *Legal Executive*.

- Academic legal journals contain articles, commentaries and analysis on recent cases and statutory developments. These articles explain a specific aspect of the law and its significance and can be used by the student in their work as a secondary source to address the question and back up any arguments.

- Soundly researched legal articles will contain references to a variety of primary and other secondary sources and can thus be useful in your general research of a legal area.

## Use Your Research Skills to Find Appropriate Journal Articles

You will need to use relevant journal articles in your work and you need to know how to research and locate them. You will need to employ the basis research skills that you have been taught in your Legal Method or Legal Skills course, but you may wish to follow this advice:

- Consult the lecture and seminar handouts to see if the lecturer has listed any journal articles in the area covered in the assessment.
- Consult your recommended textbooks and cases and materials books to see if they refer to any relevant articles.
- Conduct a search on the library facilities to see what journals they house and whether there are any articles in this area.
- Conduct a search on websites such as LAWTEL or WESTLAW to locate articles in the area.
- Ensure that your search is not too wide. If you are doing an essay on freedom of expression and the Human Rights Act, for example, don't just put in 'Freedom of Expression' or 'Free Speech' because you will get an unmanageable number of results. Instead, put in both terms together (or 'Section 12 of the Human Rights Act 1998').
- Read the abstract of the article before you download it or photocopy it and see whether it is relevant to your research.
- If the journal is in the library, look at the relevant issue and skim through the contents to check its relevance.
- Ensure that the journal is of an appropriate academic standard (see the next point).
- If your assessment is in a specialist legal area, you will need to research and use journals in that specific area (e.g., *Public Law* for constitutional and administrative law, *Criminal Law Review* for crime).

## The Quality and Status of Law Journals

Some journals may not be appropriate to your level of study; they may be too low or high level. Some journals are regarded as more authoritative than others. Leading academic journals, such as *Modern Law Review, Oxford Journal of Legal Studies, Law Quarterly Review, Legal Studies, Journal of Law and Society, Cambridge Law Review* – often referred to as 'weighty' journals, or the 'academic heavyweights' – are examples. Others are often aimed at a wider audience, including practitioners, and are referred to as trade journals (see the preceding section). There is also a wide range of journals in between, which cover either general legal issues or specific legal areas, such as employment, criminal law, property and so on.

- Trade journals serve a very useful purpose (see the preceding paragraph), but it is not always appropriate to use them in academic assessments. Articles and case notes in these journals can be used to keep up to date with the law and can be used in your work to draw attention to a new development. However, they should not be cited as leading academic authority, and you should use articles and case notes from weightier journals for this purpose.

- Articles and case notes in trade journals might not provide sufficient detail or academic analysis, and you might have to refer to weightier journals for this purpose.
- You will find more detailed articles in the weightier journals, such as *Modern Law Review*, *Cambridge Law Review* and *Law Quarterly Review*.
- You will find more detailed case and statute commentaries in the weightier journals, such as *Modern Law Review*, *Cambridge Law Review* and *Law Quarterly Review*, as well as in journals such as the *Law Teacher* and some specialist journals, such as *Public Law* or *European Human Rights Law Review*.
- Try to maintain a balance and include articles and case notes from both types of journal. This will show a wide research of the subject and an appreciation of a variety of sources: see Foster, 'Human Rights and Prisons' (2004) 67 MLR 66. For a useful account of the recent case of *Foster v Home Office*, *The Times*, 12 April 2005, see Foster, 'Prisons and Legal Correspondence' NLJ 2002 152 (7050) 1480.

## Do Not Cite or Refer to Journals That You Have Not Read

If you have not accessed and read a particular journal article, do not cite it in your bibliography; otherwise, your bibliography is misleading. Neither should you indicate in the text of the work that you have read and used an article when you haven't:

### Example

'This point is neatly summarised by Foster, 'Human Rights and Prison Life' ([2004] EHRLR 69, at 70).'

Many students employ this technique because they have seen the article cited in a book or a journal in that way, but it is usually quite clear that they have not read the article themselves. The lecturer will then comment on the script, 'What did Foster *actually* say in this article?'

## Do Not Use Articles that You Do Not Understand

Students should avoid using journal articles that contain views or language that they do not understand. Try to avoid using articles that are beyond the level that you studying at and do not use an author's view if you can't comprehend what he or she is getting at. It will usually be very clear that you do not really know what you are talking about:

### Example

'Judges are sometimes afraid to interfere with government decisions and it would not be very fair if they did this. Indeed, Foster notes that this judicial deference is most acute in cases involving sensitive policy decisions where the judicial decision-making is ill-equipped to second guess executive expertise. In such cases the court's interference lacks democratic legitimacy (Foster, 'Making Human Rights Complicated' (1995) OJLS 23).'

It is clear from the language used in the first sentence that the student is simply quoting the author and that he does not really appreciate what the author is getting at. If he did, he would probably simplify the author's words and provide a brief illustration. Again, the lecturer is likely to comment, 'What is Foster *actually* getting at here? Give a simple example.' The student should read the article again and see if he can simplify and illustrate the argument or avoid this source and use a plainer one that he does understand.

## Always Explain the Meaning and Significance of Views in Journals

When you have found and used journal articles in your work, your task is not complete. You must introduce the source at the relevant point in the work and ensure that the article assists you in making that point or supporting an argument. You can then comment on that view and see whether it is backed up by case or other authority, and whether you agree with it.

In the following example, the student is answering a question on the court's role in protecting human rights:

> ### Example
>
> 'If human rights are to be protected it is essential that the courts do not show too much respect to the administrative authorities, for Foster argues that this deference will compromise the court's constitutional role in protecting individual liberty.'[66] In particular, the courts might be reluctant to interfere where national security is an issue' (provide reference to a case).
>
> _____
> [66]Foster, Judicial Deference and the Protection of Human Rights [2003] PL 348, at 357.

This is quite a simple use of an author's view. The view is introduced at the relevant stage of the discussion, it is referenced and the student puts the statement in some sort of context.

Students answering the question at a higher level might adopt a more sophisticated style and show greater knowledge of various sources:

> ### Example
>
> 'If human rights are to be protected it is essential that the courts do not show too much respect or deference to the administrative authorities. In this respect, Foster argues that judicial deference will lead to a compromise of the courts' constitutional role and inadequate protection of individual liberty.[43] This is supported by a number of cases on national security, where the courts have refused to interfere with decisions which impacted on liberty and security of the person (refer to those cases in a footnote). However, as the recent case of *A v Secretary of State for the Home Department* (reference) suggests, the courts will not always decline to interfere, and Fosters views should be viewed in the light of the approach taken in that case.'[44]
>
> _____
> [43]Foster, Judicial Deference and the Protection of Human Rights [2003] PL 348, at 357. See also Williams, 'The Constitutional Role of the Courts' (2002) OJLS 1, and Johnson, 'Human Rights and the Separation of Powers' [2002] PL 98.
> [44]For an analysis of that case, see Jones, 'Belmarsh, the House of Lords and the Human Rights Act 1998' (2005) MLR 790.

Here the student is aware of relevant cases to support the author's views. (If the author has used them, then the student should say so: 'Foster cites a number of cases to support his contention.'). She has also used a more recent case to qualify the author's views and has provided a reference to an academic analysis of that new case, which could then be used to explore new views on the topic. There is also a reference to other articles on the same area, showing off the student's research.

## Do Not Use Journals and Views Expressed in Them as Primary Sources

Students often use articles as a source of cases, statutes and other primary sources. They do this because they read about the source in the article and think it is acceptable to cite the journal article rather than the primary source. You should not credit the author with the primary source and must cite the actual source. Thus, do not say:

- 'The leading authority is *Smith v Jones* (See Foster, 'Contract Terms' [2003] CLJ 20, at page 34)'; instead, put the reference to the case.
- 'There are a number of cases to illustrate this point (see Foster, 'Contract Terms . . . ')'; instead, refer to the cases and provide the reference.
- 'The Human Rights Act 1998 gives a power to the courts to interpret statutes in line with the Convention if at all possible (Foster, 'The Human Rights Act 1998' [2000] PL 678, at page 687)'; instead, refer to the statutory provision (s. 3 of the Act).
- 'The International Covenant on Civil and Political Rights 1966 protects freedom of expression. (Foster, 'The ICCPR and Democratic Rights' [2004] EHRLR 370, at 380)'; instead, refer to the article in the Covenant (Art 17).

In all these examples, the author has made a statement about the actual law; it is not his or her view on the law. In such a case do not credit the author as the source.

## ● Using Websites

You will be encouraged to access and use a variety of legal and other websites during your studies, and the modern student will rely very heavily on this source of information. However, it is essential that you cite them and use them appropriately.

- You can use some websites to carry out searches for both primary and secondary sources.

These websites (e.g. LAWTEL, WESTLAW) will have a search engine for cases, statutory provisions and articles. You can put in a keyword, and it will provide you with all the relevant cases and so on that it stores on that topic.

- Don't make your search too wide – put in 'statutory interpretation and the Human Rights Act 1998,' rather than 'statutory interpretation' or 'Human Rights Act 1998.'
- Look at the abstract of the case, article and so on to check for its relevance to your work before you download or print.
- Some cases, statutes and journal articles can be accessed in full, and you can use this facility to download or print off primary sources, particularly if your library doesn't have these resources.

If you access a primary source on this website, cite the primary source and not the website. (You can indicate that you have visited the website in a footnote or in your bibliography.)

- Some websites are very useful in accessing primary sources and specific information not available elsewhere.

Websites such as those attached to government departments or non-governmental organisations (e.g., Amnesty International) are particularly useful for accessing information and statistics relating to that organisation or its work. In this sense, the website is more useful that texts or articles, and you are advised to make full use of them.

- Some websites provide general textbook-style information on legal topics. They should be treated with great caution and should not be used as a substitute for standard textbooks.

Some of these websites are aimed at sub-degree students and are not suitable for undergraduate courses. They can be useful for grasping the basics but might be too superficial or simplistic to use for your assessments. Be careful not to cite them as academic authority unless they are written by experts in the area and are intended for academic analysis.

- Some textbooks and publishers provide regular updates on the law and can be used to keep up to date in the specific legal areas covered in the text.

You can access these websites by visiting the publisher's website or visiting an address in the book. Some update facilities are better than others, and they are obviously limited to the content of the book. You should not rely solely on this source to keep up to date with recent developments.

- Use websites to check for new cases and statutory developments and for new secondary sources such as articles, books and newspaper items.

As mentioned previously, some websites give you access to primary and secondary sources. This also allows you to check the website for recent cases and other developments and thus keep up to date with the law. This is much easier than looking through recent journals, law reports and so on in the library; however, note that a website might only let you search or access specific journals and law reports.

## ● Legal Referencing and Citation

There is a proper way of citing and referring to cases, statutory materials and journals, and as a law student you must get used to employing it. As an undergraduate you will be expected to acquire and employ those skills, and your marks will suffer if you fail to do so.

On an undergraduate course you will be required to employ either the Oxford method or the Harvard method of citation and referencing. Check with your lecturers which one you should use.

The Oxford method is commonly employed in law books and legal journals in Great Britain.

### Learn How to Cite Cases

You must employ the correct method of citing cases and providing the proper reference.

## The Oxford Method

The Oxford method is used at most institutions; check with your lecturer, but you will normally be expected to use this method, which is adopted in most texts and journal articles.

- The names of the parties to the action should come first (in italics preferably, but you can use bold or underline the names). This should be followed by the year of the law report in brackets (check whether the law report uses square brackets or parentheses) and then the volume of the report for that year. You should then refer to the relevant abbreviation of the law report, rather than the full name (e.g., WLR for Weekly Law Reports; All ER for All England Reports; AC for Appeal Cases). Finally, include the page reference – the page on which the report begins.

Thus:

*Foster v Jones* [1999] 2 All ER 555

*Foster v Home Office and another* [2004] 2 AC 300

Not: FOSTER ~v~ JONES (1999) All England Law Reports, July 5 1999. Here the student is using the information appearing on the front of the specific issue, which is there as part of the packaging. That information is *not* the correct reference.

- If you have already provided the full citation in your work, you can just refer to the case name subsequently:

### Example

This was decided in *Foster v Home Office*[72] .... Thus, in *Foster v Home Office* it was held that a prisoner who .... It is also acceptable to refer to just the claimant's name (It was held in *Foster*, Thus, in *Foster* ...)

---

[72][1990] 3 All ER 444.

- Some cases are more commonly known by a name other than the full case name. You can refer to this name instead of giving the full name, but ensure that you provide the full citation and reference somewhere.

### Example

'This was decided in the *GCHQ* case, . . .'[91]

---

[91]*Council of Civil Service Unions v Minister of State for the Civil Service* [1985] AC 374.

## The Harvard Method

The Harvard method is employed in a number of social science journals. In this case you give the full citation (as is done in the Oxford method) in the bibliography or your references, but not in the main text of your work. Instead you simply put the case name and then the date (in parenthesis). Thus:

*Smith v Foster* (1999)

# Citing Statutory Materials

## Acts of Parliament and Their Sections

- It is sufficient to refer to the short title of the Act and the year that it was passed by Parliament.

---

### Example

'The Human Rights Act 1998 gives further effect to . . . '

If the Act is mentioned in the middle of a sentence use lowercase for 'the.'

'The rights contained in the European Convention are given further effect by the Human Rights Act 1998.'

---

- If you are referring to a specific section of the Act, cite that section (s. for section, ss. for sections) and not just the Act itself.

---

### Example

'This duty is contained in s. 3 of the Human Rights Act 1998.'

---

- If you are referring to a sub-section of the act, you should put either sub-section 2 of section 3, or, preferably, s. 3(2).
- If an Act of Parliament is split into parts, then cite the part of the Act and the relevant sections.

---

### Example

'The offences concerned with racial hatred are contained in Part III of the Public Order Act 1986, in ss. 18-23.'

---

- If you are referring to a Schedule of an Act of Parliament, use the abbreviation Sch. and refer to the paragraph number of the schedule – Human Rights Act 1998, Sch. 2, paragraph 1. If the schedule has Parts, then include that information – Human Rights Act 1998, Sch. 1, Part II.
- If you have already referred to the title and year of the Act, you can abbreviate the Act, or shorten its title, in subsequent references. After you have given the full title, state in brackets how you are going to identify the Act during the remainder of the work.

---

### Example

'The Human Rights Act 1998 (hereafter 'the 1998 Act' or 'the Act' or 'HRA') provides . . .
'This is contained in s. 4 of the Act/the 1998 Act/HRA. . . .'

---

## Statutory Instruments

Statutory instruments are the commonest form of delegated legislation, passed by virtue of a parent Act of Parliament. For example, under s. 47 of the Prison Act 1952 the Home Secretary can make regulations for the control of prisoners, and those regulations (the Prison Rules 1999) are delegated legislation, added to by specific statutory instruments.

● You must identify whether the provision you are referring to is primary or secondary legislation.

In other words do not put 'Section 47 of the Prison Rules 1999.' Rather, you put 'this is contained in Rule 23 of the Prison Rules 1999 (reference, see below), passed under s.47 of the Prison Act 1952.'

● Note, the Prison Rules 1999 have a specific reference (SI 1999/728).
● Refer to the specific number of the (Prison) Rules – 'this is contained in Rule 23 of the Prison Rules 1999 (SI 1999/728).'
● If you are referring to a specific statutory instrument then cite that instrument by its title and its year, and then provide the reference (year passed followed by its number):

---

### Example

'These changes were introduced by the Prison (Amendment) Rules 2003,[57] and amend rules 35 and 43 of the Prison Rules 1999' (reference if required).

_____
[57]SI 2003/3301.

---

## International Treaties

● If you are referring to an international treaty you should put the title of the treaty and the year in brackets: The International Covenant on Civil and Political Rights (1966).
● Use the full title of the treaty: The European Convention For the Protection of Human Rights and Fundamental Freedoms (1950), not just the popular title: the European Convention.
● Once you have used the full title, you can then use an abridged form (the European Convention, the Convention or, commonly, the ECHR).
● Treaties provisions are known as articles, and you can use 'Article' 'article' or 'Art.'
● If the treaty has been incorporated into domestic law, do not confuse the treaty article with the statutory section.

---

### Example

'The right to a fair trial is guaranteed by section 6 of the Human Rights Act 1998.'

The student has confused s. 6 of the Act (liability of public authorities under the Act) with Article 6 of the European Convention. He should write:

'... guaranteed by Article 6 of the European Convention (as contained in s. 1 of the Human Rights Act 1998).'

---

HOW TO WRITE BETTER LAW ESSAYS

- For European Community (or Union) Law, you should refer to the name of the treaty and the article; for example, 'Article 25 of the EC Treaty, **or** EC Treaty, Art 25.'

- Note that some article numbers have changed following the passing of the Amsterdam Treaty 1997. In that case put – Article 25 of the EC Treaty (formerly Article 12), or, if referring to the old number, Article 189 (now article 239).

- For Directives, refer to the number and year of that provision, like this: 'This was contained in EC Directive 64/221/EEC.'

## Citing Journals

Under the Oxford system – the one preferred on most law courses and adopted by most English law journals – you put the author's surname, author's initial(s), title of the article, year of publication, volume number (if used), journal abbreviation, page number on which the article begins and the page number of the specific view (if you are highlighting or quoting a specific passage).

> **Example**
>
> If you are referring to an author's views you can write:
>
> 'See in particular Foster, S.H., 'How to Write a Lousy Essay' (1999) 62 MLR, 123, at page 140.'
>
> **Not:**
>
> 'Read Foster's article on lousy essays, summer edition of the *Modern Law Review* for 1999'.
>
> Here the student is referring us to the information on the front cover of the relevant issue of the journal and thus fails to give us the proper citation and reference.

Alternatively, you can use the Harvard method of citation and referencing for journals. This is often employed in social science journals, including some law journals. Check with your lecturer as to which system you should use, but for the Harvard system, put the author's surname and initial(s), the year of publication, the title of the article, the name of the journal (underlined), the issue number and the date of that issue (if given) and the page numbers from the start to the end of the article:

> **Example**
>
> Foster, S (2001) 'Human Rights and the Judges' <u>Modern Law Review</u>, 64, Issue No 4, September, pp 567–590.

You can put this reference in your bibliography (or references) at the end of the work, and then during the work you can refer to the article by referring to the specific page number, like this:

Foster, S (2001), 582.

If you are referring to more than article by that author, you can indicate which article you are referring to by including the date:

Foster, S (2004).

When using this method, ensure that you list this author's work chronologically in your bibliography. If there are two articles by that author from the same year, you can put this:

Foster, S (2004) (2).

That will refer to the order in which you referred to the author's work in your bibliography.

## Citing Specific Law Journals

You should learn how specific journals are cited and use that citation and referencing system. Articles in journals must be cited and referred to properly, especially if you are submitting work in the second and third year of your study, and for project work and on postgraduate courses. In particular you will be expected to get acquainted with and use accepted abbreviations:

| Abbreviation | Title of Journal | Example citation |
|---|---|---|
| BLR | *Business Law Review* | (2003) BLR 66 |
| Crim LR | *Criminal Law Review* | [2004] Crim LR 33 |
| CLJ | *Cambridge Law Journal* | [2004] CLJ 1 |
| ILJ | *Industrial Law Journal* | [2002] ILJ 33 |
| JBL | *Journal of Business Law* | [2005] JBL 66 |
| J Crim Law | *Journal of Criminal Law* | [2005] J Crim Law 33 |
| JLS | *Journal of Law and Society* | [2006] 27 JLS 234 |
| JP | *Justice of the Peace* | JP (2005) 169(23) 428 |
| LS | *Legal Studies* | (2004) LS 330 |
| LQR | *Law Quarterly Review* | [2000] 116 LQR 212 |
| MLR | *Modern Law Review* | (2002) 65 MLR 360 |
| NLJ | *New Law Journal* | NLJ (2002) 152 (7050) 1480 (or (2001) NLJ 1480) |
| NILQ | *Northern Ireland Legal Quarterly* | [2002] 53 NILQ 34 |
| OJLS | *Oxford Journal of Legal Studies* | (2004) OJLS 11 |
| PL | *Public Law* | [2005] PL 44 |
| SJ | *Solicitors Journal* | SJ 2004 148(41) 1226 |

In addition, you may need to become familiar with some international journals, such as the following:

| Abbreviation | Title of Journal | Example citation |
|---|---|---|
| CMLR | *Common Market Law Review* | [2000] CMLR 33 |
| *ICLQ* | *International and Comparative Law Quarterly* | [2004] ICLQ 222 |
| EHRLR | *European Human Rights Law Review* | [2005] EHRLR 56 |
| ELR | *European Law Review* | [2002] ELR 118 |

- You will notice that some journals use square brackets and others use parenthesis.
- Some journals use the volume number:
  For example, LQR: the reference '[2000] 116 LQR 212' refers to the year of publication, the volume number, the appropriate abbreviation for the journal and then the page number where the article starts.
- Some also use the issue number:
  For example, JP: the reference '(2005) 169(23) 428' refers to the year of the journal, the volume number and the issue number and then the page that the article starts on.
- You will soon acquire this information and if you are in doubt about how you cite these journals, see how they are cited in textbooks, journals and reading lists and so on. You can also look inside the journal itself – they will tell you how they should be cited.

## Citing Books

### The Oxford Method

The Oxford method is most commonly used for English law books and most commonly used on law courses in England and Wales. You should refer to the author's surname and initial(s), followed by the title of the book (in italics), then the publisher, year of publication and edition (if more than one edition).

For example:

  Foster, S.H. *The Law Relating to Football* (Sweet and Maxwell, 1998, 14th edition)

If you are referring to a specific page number, then use the preceding reference style, followed by ', at page(s) or p(p). 33(-37).'

### The Harvard Method

The Harvard method is used on many social science courses and is very often an acceptable way of citing law texts. Check with the lecturer to see which method is preferable. In this method, you give the author's surname and initial(s), the year of publication, the title of the book (in italics or underlined), and then the place of publication, the publishers and the edition.

For example:

  Foster, S.H (1998) *The Law Relating to Football,* London: Sweet and Maxwell, 14th edition

**Citing Websites**

- If you have accessed a website to find primary and secondary sources that are reported elsewhere, then cite those sources and not the website.
- However, you should indicate that you have visited that website in your bibliography by putting the web address (url) and the date you visited the site. For example,

  http://www.westlaw.com (last accessed 24.4.2005).

- You can also refer to the website if a case or statute and so on can be accessed on that site. For example:

  'See *Foster v Jones* [2004] AC 333. The case can be accessed on www.casesrus.com.'

- If the website provides you with an authoritative source or statistics, then cite that website as the source. For example:

  Department of Trade and Industry (2004) UK Energy Sector Indicators, http://dti.gov.uk.uk (followed by the address of the specific page of the website).

# ● References and Latin Words and Phrases

You can use a number of Latin words and phrases when referencing your work. It is not so essential that you do this in your first year, but you should use some for extended essays, projects and postgraduate work.

Many texts and journals are now abandoning the use of these terms, apart from *ibid*, (described next), so this text will refer to the more modern approach as well.

> *Ibid*:  If you have cited a reference in your previous footnote, then instead of giving the whole reference again you can use *ibid* and just refer to the actual page number.

---

**Example**

'The principle of proportionality was established in *Foster v United Kingdom*[45] and in that case European Court stressed that any measure that interfered with political free speech had to be strictly proportionate.'[46]

---

[45](1993) 27 EHRR 236.
[46]*ibid*, at para 45.

---

You can use this equally for books, journals and statutory materials that have been cited in the previous footnote.

> *Supra:* Rather like *ibid*, *supra* is used when you have already made reference to a particular source in your work, but not in the immediately preceding footnote.

---

**Example**

'The courts have adopted the doctrine of proportionality with respect to human rights violations.'[90]

Or:

'In *Foster v Home Office*[91] it was decided that . . .'

---

[90]*Foster v Home Office*, *supra* note 4, or note 4, above.
[91]*supra*, note 4, or note 4, above.

---

*Op cit: Op cit* is used to refer to a textbook or article that has already been referred to in your work and where you have already provided the full reference (e.g., Foster, *Human Rights*, (Hughes & Hughes, 1998)). It can be used instead of citing the whole reference again, leaving you the task of referring to previous reference (the footnote in which the reference first appeared) and then adding the page number of the already cited text.

**Example**

'The Human Rights Act 1998 has been criticised on grounds of its limited scope and the ambiguity of its central provisions.[99] 'Foster has argued that this provision is ambiguous.' [100]

***

[99]Foster, S *The Human Rights Act 1998* (OUP 2004), at page 12.
[100]*op cit*, note 1, at page 40, or note 1 above, at page 40.

If you are referring the reader to a footnote at a later stage of the work, then use the expression 'see note x below.'

**Example**

For example, 'As we shall see later, the courts have also shown deference to Parliament with respect to the regulation of obscene and indecent expression.'[29]

***

[29]*Post*, note 46 and the cases cited therein, or 'note 46, below.'

**Note**

**The use of referencing and citation skills, as with all the other skills, is acquired *gradually* and via regular *practise*. You can usually find out how to cite and refer by consulting your textbooks and good law journals. The more journals, books, law reports, Acts of Parliament and so on that you read, the quicker you will pick up these skills.**

## Summary

After reading this chapter you should be able to adopt the following good practice:

- always providing authority for any legal statement or academic opinion given in your answer;
- making sure you appreciate the difference between primary and secondary sources and knowing the rules on crediting such sources;
- using your library and research skills to locate relevant legal materials;
- using primary and secondary sources to illustrate your answer and to enhance your work;
- ensuring that the source is properly incorporated into your work and that the reader understands its significance;

- reading the source properly and ensuring that you understand it and its relevance before using it in your work;
- ensuring that the source is up-to-date and relevant to your answer;
- making proper use of legal and other websites;
- citing primary and secondary sources correctly and providing the correct and accepted references in your work.

You can test your skills by carrying out the relevant excercises on the Companion Website (www.pearsoned.co.uk/foster)

# 3    Good and Bad Essays

## ● Introduction

The purpose of this chapter is to examine good and bad techniques in writing law essays using two essay titles - one in contract law and the other in legal system and constitutional law. For each title, the chapter first provides a poor and flawed answer to the question and then a much improved and acceptable answer to the question.

Specifically, this chapter:

- allows students the opportunity to identify both good and bad essay writing techniques;
- enables them to examine specific essays in order to identify relevant errors and good practice;
- provides them with an indication of the lecturer's response to both types of essay;
- allows them to enhance their essay skills by following good and avoiding bad practice.

Thus, for Question 1, in part A, we examine a very poor answer to a question on offers and invitations to treat. The errors in this essay are exaggerated in order to identify the whole range of mistakes that can be made through poor research and presentation. The bad essay appears without any corrections, and the reader is asked to identify all that is wrong with it - the spelling, grammatical and typographical errors; the poor use of legal sources; the poor and unclear writing style; the inability to answer the question; plagiarism and poor referencing and citation skills - and to highlight any errors on the essay. To conduct this exercise, you will need to refer to Chapters 1 and 2 of the text and to measure the essay against the advice and the skills identified in those chapters. You will then be provided with a marked version of the essay - highlighting all the deficiencies and allowing you to compare notes with the author. In Part B the student revisits the question and studies a good answer to that question. The text highlights all the qualities of the answer, together with the author's advice on how to improve the answer further.

This exercise is then repeated with respect to Question 2 - a question on the Human Rights Act 1998, which tests the student's knowledge and appreciation of both constitutional law and the English Legal System. This question is used primarily to illustrate the relevant techniques in how to address and answer the question that has been set by the module leader. Part A contains a poor answer to the question, although the mistakes and style will not be as abject as that employed in Question 1. Again, you are invited to identify any shortcomings and mark them on the essay before consulting the author's criticisms and recommendations. A much improved answer is then provided in Part B, together with observations and recommendations for improvement.

It is hoped that at the end of this chapter, students will have a clear idea of how - and how not - to write an essay and what qualities are needed for a sound answer. The student should then be able to employ those skills in his or her law assessments for the remainder of the course, although it may take some time before many of these skills are perfected.

## ● Practice 1: Contract Law Essay

**Example Question**

By the use of case law explain the distinction between an offer and an invitation to treat. Why is the distinction so important?

This question could appear on a variety of undergraduate and sub-degree courses, although some undergraduate institutions might not offer such a basic question. The area should be familiar to most law students, and the question is a relatively straightforward one, although it does require the student to grasp the rationale of the legal area as well as the substantive rules. The word limit given for the question was 2,000 words (with a 10 percent leeway and excluding the front page, all references and citations and the bibliography), but such questions may be given a lesser word limit depending on the level of the course and the particular institution.

The student is on the first year of his LLB degree and is submitting this work as part of a module titled 100 LAW – Law of Obligations (Contract). The module leader is Maureen Williams, and his personal tutor is Janice Johnson.

The following guidance was given to all students:

Students are expected to display the legal and other study skills outlined in their student handbook. In relation to the particular question, the student must:

● Show an appreciation of the distinction made in the law of contract between offers and invitations to treat.
● Use case examples to illustrate how the courts make that distinction.
● Explain and appreciate the factors that are considered by the courts in distinguishing between offers and invitations to treat.
● Explain why the distinction is important in relation to that legal area.

## Part A: The Bad Essay

This essay highlights bad practice in writing legal essays. We then suggest how that practice might be improved so as to reflect the standard of skills and knowledge one is expected to display at undergraduate level.

What is wrong with the following essay? To what extent has the author addressed the question? Point out any irrelevant information and indicate where he has failed to clearly explain cases or concepts. Circle and correct any spelling and typographical mistakes, plagiarism and poor referencing and citation skills. With regard to any poor grammar, clumsy presentation and so on, suggest ways in which the work could have been presented in a more coherent and clearer fashion.

Explain briefly what you believe the question was asking and how you would have planned and approached the question.

**The Front Sheet**

First, here is the front sheet attached to the answer. How many errors can you spot?

---

<u>CoNtract ESSAY</u>

Submitted by Steve Foster

Year One law degree


Personal Tuter: Jane Jackson


Model Leader: Maxine Williamson

*'By the use of a case law explain the differnce between offers and invitations. Is the distinction important?*

Word count 2000 words


*October 21, 20006*

---

**The Answer**

**Answer**

### Offers and Invitations: A Conceptual Illusion?

Before answering the specific question asked by this question it is vital to outline the characteristics of a contract. All contracts don't have to be in writing but can be made not in writing, although some have to be in writing. They must all have consideration and if they are broken then the plaintiff (or as he is now known the complainer) can

▼

sue for damages or get monetary awards. A contract can come to an end by breach, frustration or agreement.

With that sorted out, there is a difference between an offer and an invitation to treat and it is a very important one. The courts employ a variety of conceptual tools to make this distinction, although at times they adopt a more elaborate conceptual structure.

Examples of invitations to treat are the advertising of goods for sale in a paper (SEE the case of Prtridge and Crittenden (1968) 1wlr 1204), goods being sold by tender (see the case of Garinger and SON VERSUS Gough (1896), or by an auction, the displey of goods in a shop window Fisher -v- Bell (1961) 1qb' and a bus company advertising the times of their busess.

It is sometimes difficult to distinguish between an offer and an invitation to treat and the courts have had a lot of trouble doing it. As the classification of any act or statement as being either an offer or an invitation to treat depends on intention to be bound rather than upon any a priori principle of law it is not easy to reconcile all the cases or there reasoning.

What needs to be done now is to look at some of the cases where the court have made the distinction between an offer and an invitation to treet. We will then be able to see how they make the distinction and how important it is to make a distinction between an invitation and an offer. As I have said before it is difficult to make a distinction and the courts find it very difficult as well, even though they do this sort of thing for a living.

Let us look at the case of Fisher and Bell (1961). Here a flicknife was displayed in a window and the shopkeeper was done under the Flicknife Act for trying to sell a flicknife without a license. In court he was founf not guilty because he hadn't offered the flicknife but merley invited a man (or woman) to buy it. Similarly in Pharmaceutical Society of Great Britain v Boots Cash Chemists Ltd (1952 QB 765) goods were dispayed on a supermarket shelf and the customer picked them upand took them to the cash desk. The Boots company were charged with selling drugs under the drugs law but again they were not convicted because they had never offered them for sale, only invited them to be sold.

So in cases of adverts there can never be an offer, only an invitation to treat. However the case of Carlill (1983) 1kb at page 256 is different. (See also the very important case of Bowerman versus ABTA [1995] 145 NLJR 1815) In that case a woman smoked a smokeball and still caught the flu, even though the Carbolic Smoke Ball Company said she would not. When she sued for the £100 the company said she had never accepted the offer because they had only invited her to smoke the ball and not offered her to smoke the ball. The judge held that there was an offer and she had accepted it by smoking the ball. The company had deposited money in the bank and sothey hade made an offer to smoke balls.

From this case we can see that the distinction between an offer and an invitation to treat is a very difficult one to make, but nevertheless it is an important one. But why should the courts have to make a disticnction and does it matter if they don't make a disticnction between an offer and an invitation to treat? In answering this we may wish to look at the case of Gibson V Manchester Council(1979) 1aLLer. In this case it was held that the Council had not made an offer, but only an invitation to treat therefore the council were not bound. Another illustrative case was that of Harvella Investments v Royal Trust of Canada 1985 2 all ER 966. In this case the vendors of a plot of land sought a single offer for the whole plot from each of the two interested parties, promising to accept the highest offer provided it made other conditions stipulated. Both parties submitted bids complying with the conditions, but while one merely stated a price it was prepared to pay, the other stated both a conctrete sum and a referential bid. The court held that the referential bid broke an implied condition of the offer and thus there was no contract. So we can see from this case that sometimes a request for a tender can be held to be an offer: see also the case of Spencer v Harding (1870) LR5CP561 which tells us that averts for tenders are not offers.

So where does that leave us with the question of whether there is a differnce between an offer and an invitiation to treat? It is quite clear that there is a diffenrce, and that the courts have adopted a variety of conceptual tools in order to assist them in their enquiry. However space precludes a full expalanation.

Why then is the distinction important? An offer is an expression of willingness to be bound by contractual relations if the offeree (the one who the offer is made towards) is willing to accept the essential conditions laid down in the offer (made by the offerror who makes the offer). An invitation to treat (made by an invitor to the invited) however is not an offer and can never form the basis of contractual relations because it is only an invitation to treat. It is merley inviting people to enter into a contract and cannot be an offer, the cases above clearly show this. Thus it is very important to make the distinction and that is why the courts want to make the distinction.

Obviously on many occassions offers and invitations to treat are easy to distinguish, like in the case of Carill which was obviously an offer because the woman smoked the smoke ball. On the other hand, the distinction is a very fine one and whilst some commentators prefer to speak in terms of rules, the courts tend to look at the individual facts of each case. In conclusion therefore it is probably safer to proceed on the basis of the single principle that an offer must be sufficiently specific and comprehensive to be capable of immediate acceptance and also as well made with an intention to be bound by the mere fact of acceptance.

If all things were offers then there would be absolute chaos, so the courts have to make a distinction. This is shown in the case of Crainger v Gough (see the page before) where the court held that it was only an invitation to treat and never an offer, otherwise the wineseller would have run out of wine. And in Gibson the council would have run out of houses. So adverts can never be invitations, but in Carlill it was different because they hade made an offer.

Again in conclusion a hidden element of discretion permits the courts to label the facts with the terminology of offer and acceptance, whenever they believe it is fair and reasonable to impose contractual liability. Consider for example the purchase of goods in a self service store. At what point is an agreement completed. Does the customer accept the offer when he or she places the goods in the wire basket? Or does acceptance take place when the customer presents the goods in the wire basket, or when they present the goods to the assistant, or when the assistant accepts the offer by ringing up the price? Or is that merly the offer? Each interpretation is plausible and thus we can see the distinction clearly.

▼

In this essat I have told you how the courts make the distinction between offers and invitations to treat and why they want to make the distinction. In conclusion then an offer is an offer which can be accepted, like in Mrs Carlills' case, wheras an invitation to treat does exactly that – it invites and it is not an offer. The difference is negligible and easy to make in every case apart from some difficult cases like in Gibson. An offer cannot be revoked after it has been accepted, see the very important case of Dikensian v Dodo (1840). An invitation can be revoked because it is not an offer, but merly an invitation. There would be commercial chaos if it was not so. An offer can crystallise in to a contract without further ado, but an invitation can't because it isn't an offer, although sometimes adverts can be offers as illustrated in Carlill.

To conclude therfore there is a clear difference, and indeed distinction between an offer and an invitation to treat and the courts have shown this to be true on a number of occassions. A contract needs an offer, an acceptance, consideration and an intention to create legal relations. Invitations don't need any of these as they are not offers. Terms can be implied into offers, but not invitations and Carlill displays this perfectly.

### AUTOBIBLIOGRAPHY

Lecture notes from Maxine Williamson

The Law of Contract by Hugh Collins

Textbook on Contract by Terry Downs

The Transformation Thesis and the Ascription of Contractual Responsibility by Collins

Hanson's Law of Contract, BY Hanson

Various articles in the New Law Journal, the Oxford and Cambridge Law Journal and International and Comparative Law Quarterly.

## Detailed Answer Criticism

Now let us examine what was wrong with that essay, beginning with his front page . . .

## FRONT SHEET WITH COMMENTARY

# CoNtract ESSAY

**(Not the module title, no module number and a mixture of lower and upper case)**

### Submitted by Steve Foster

### Year One law degree

**(No degree title identified)**

Personal Tuter: Jayne Jackson

(Wrong name for the tutor and tutor spelt incorrectly)

Model Leader: Maxine Williamson

(Model instead of module and wrong name of module leader)

*'By the use of a case law explain the differnce between offers and invitations. Is the distinction important?*

(Apart from the spelling/typographical error, this is not the question that was asked; he has rejigged the question and thus has little chance of answering the question properly.)

Word count 2000 words

(This is incorrect - his essay is about 1,300 words - and his count merely tallies with the word limit.)

*October 21, 20006*

(Italicised O and an extra O in the date.)

There are a dozen or so mistakes on this front page, and we haven't started the essay yet! The student has created a poor impression, showing carelessness, lying about the word count (risking a penalty) and displaying a lack of knowledge of the module, his course and the law staff.

---

Note
**At this stage, the marker is already expecting a sloppy, badly written piece of work.**

---

### Offers and Invitations: A Conceptual Illusion?

1. Before answering the specific question asked by this question (poor grammar - 'in order to address this question') it is vital to outline the characteristics of a contract. (it is not, because the question is only about formation of a contract) All contracts don't have to be in writing but can be made not in writing, although some have to be in writing. (poor and muddled grammar and in any case irrelevant to the question) They must all have consideration (wrong and, in any case, irrelevant) and if they are broken (again irrelevant) then the plaintiff (or as he is now known the complainer) (I think he means complainant) can sue for damages or get monetary awards. (damages and

▼

monetary awards are the same thing, and in any case, this is irrelevant) A contract can come to an end by breach, frustration or agreement. **(irrelevant to the question)**

2. With that sorted out, **(nothing has been sorted out)** there is a difference between an offer and an invitation to treat and it is a very important one. **(stating the obvious without saying anything of relevance)** The courts employ a variety of conceptual tools to make this distinction, although at times they adopt a more elaborate conceptual structure. **(Obvious plagiarism – he begins to write clear English after employing poor grammar. He also fails to explain what the author (Hugh Collins) means and has used a book and an idea that he clearly does not understand.)**

3. Examples of invitations to treat are the advertising of goods for sale in a paper (SEE **(incorrect use of upper case)** the case of Prtridge **(typo)** and Crittenden (1968) 1wlr 1204) **(should be [1968] 1 WLR 1204)**, goods being sold by tender (see the case of Garinger **(incorrect spelling)** and SON **(sudden use of upper case)** VERSUS **(should be v)** Gough (1896) **(no proper reference – although note that the year of the case is probably adequate in sub-degree courses and, of course, in exams)**, or by an auction, the displey **(incorrect spelling)** of goods in a shop window Fisher – v- Bell (1961) 1qb' **(Fisher v Bell [1961] 1 QB and page number)** and a bus company advertising the times of their busess. **(incorrect spelling)**

4. It is sometimes difficult to distinguish between an offer and an invitation to treat anfd **(typo)** the courts have had a lot of trouble doing it **(casual phrase that explains nothing – 'the courts have experienced some difficulty in making the distinction')**. As the classification of any act or statement as being either an offer or an invitation to treat depends on intention to be bound rather than upon any a priori **(Latin expression – should be in italics)** principle of law it is not easy to reconcile all the cases or there **(should be their)** reasoning. **(Clear plagiarism from a source the student does not understand – no effort to explain what the words mean.)**

5. What needs to be done now **(clumsy – 'we can now consider')** is to look at some of the cases where the court **(courts)** have made the distinction between an offer and an invitation to treet. **(should be treat)** We will then be able to see how they make the distinction and how important it is to make a distinction between an invitation and an offer. **(repetitive – 'to make such a distinction')** As I have said before **(clumsy – 'as mentioned earlier/above')** it is difficult to make a distinction and the courts find it very difficult as well, even though they do this sort of thing for a living. **(An immature and inappropriate remark. Some students believe they are being witty, but such comments are likely to irritate the marker – rather like saying 'all judges are old and out of touch with real life'.)**

6. Let us look at **(clumsy – 'Now let us examine')** the case of Fisher and **(v not and)** Bell (1961). **(full reference needed)** Here a flicknife was displayed in a window and the shopkeeper was done **('prosecuted/charged')** under the Flicknife Act **(wrong legislation – he has made it up)** for trying to sell a flicknife without a license **(not correct – he was charged with offering for sale)**. In court **(clumsy – if you are going to mention the court, state which court it was and which judge passed judgment)** he was founf **(typo)** not guilty because he hadn't offered **(what is an offer?)** the flicknife but merley **(incorrect spelling)** invited **(what is an invitation?)** a man (or woman) **(awkward – 'customers')** to buy it. Similarly in Pharmaceutical Society of Great Britain v Boots

Cash Chemists Ltd (1952 QB 765) **([1952] QB 765)** goods were dispayed **(typo)** on a supermarket shelf and the customer picked them upand **('up and')** took them to the cash desk. The Boots company **(the company)** were charged with selling drugs under the drugs law **(name the act and offence)** but again they were not convicted because they had never offered them for sale, only invited them to be sold. **(that merely tells us what was decided; it does not tell us why it wasn't an offer and why it was an invitation)**

7. So in cases of adverts **(non sequitur – he has been talking about shops)** there can never be an offer, only an invitation to treat **(this is wrong, as we will soon find out)**. However the case of Carlill [1983] 1kb at page 256. **(Carlill v Carbolic Smoke Ball Co [1893] 1 KB 256)** is different **(he has contradicted himself because he said adverts can *never be* (as opposed to are usually not construed as) offers)** (See also the very important case of Bowerman versus **(v)** ABTA [1995] 145 NLJR 1815) **(he does not explain *why* we should see it or given any impression that he has read it)** In that case **(which, Carlill or Bowerman?)** a woman smoked a smokeball **(smoke ball – what is that?)** and still caught the flu, even though the Carbolic Smoke Ball Company said she would not. **(poor explanation of the facts)** When she sued for the £100 **(what £100?)** the company said she had never accepted the offer **(they firstly pleaded that it was not an offer)** because they had only invited her to smoke the ball and not offered her to smoke the ball. **(confusing – what is the difference?)** The judge **(Bowen LJ)** held that there was an offer **(why, and what is an offer?)** and she had accepted it by smoking the ball. The company had deposited money in the bank **(first mention of this)** and sothey **(typo)** hade made an offer to smoke balls.

8. From this case we can see **(not from his explanation of the case)** that the distinction between an offer and an invitation to treat is a very difficult one to make, **(it wasn't that difficult in that case)** but nevertheless it is an important one. **(A pointless statement – why was it, and why is it generally, important?)** 'But why should the courts have to make a distinction and does it matter if they don't **(clumsy English – 'But why is it important for the courts to make this distinction'?)** make a disticnction **(typo)** between an offer and an invitation to treat? In answering this we may wish to look at the case of Gibson V **(v)** Manchester Council(1979) 1aLLer. **([1979] 1 All ER, page number)** In this case it was held that the Council had not made an offer, but only an invitation to treat therefore the council were **(was)** not bound. **(Confusing and incomplete account of the facts and decision – what had the Council done or said?)** Another illustrative **(his account of *Gibson* was not illustrative)** case was that of Harvella Investments v Royal Trust of Canada 1985 2 all ER 966. **([1985] 2 All ER 966)** In this case the vendors of a plot of land sought a single offer for the whole plot from each of the two interested parties, promising to accept the highest offer provided it made other conditions stipulated. Both parties submitted bids complying with the conditions, but while one merely stated a price it was prepared to pay, the other stated both a conctrete **(typo)** sum and a referential bid. The court held that the referential bid broke an implied condition of the offer and thus there was no contract. So we can see from this case that sometimes a request for a tender **(What *is* a request for a tender? In any case the account of the case does not address this issue. The student has explained *another* aspect of the case which is not relevant to our present discussion)** can be held to be an offer: see also the case of Spencer v Harding

▼

(1870] LR5CP561 (LR 5 CP 561) which tells us that averts (adverts) for tenders are not offers. (The student should have looked at this case first as a simple illustration of invitations for tender.)

9. So where does that leave us with the question of whether there is a differnce (typo) between an offer and an invitiation (typo) to treat? It is quite clear that there is a diffenrce, (typo) and that the courts have adopted a variety of conceptual tools in order to assist them in their enquiry. (that same plagiarism from Collins again) However space precludes a full expalanation. (Incorrect spelling, and space does not preclude a full explanation. He has seen the phrase used in academic journals when an author is writing on a specific issue, but has not the time to cover some aspect of the basic law. He falls short of the word limit by 700 words so he had plenty of space to explain it.)

10. Why then is the distinction important? An offer is an expression of willingness to be bound by contractual relations if the offeree (the one who the offer is made towards) (clumsy - to whom the offer is addressed') is willing to accept the essential conditions laid down in the offer (made by the offerror who makes the offer). (He asks the second question in the essay and then gives us the answer to the first question. He has in fact given us a decent definition of an offer here, but this is more than half way through the essay - this should have appeared in the first paragraph.) An invitation to treat (made by an invitor to the invited) (inappropriate words) however is not an offer and can never form the basis of contractual relations because it is only an invitation to treat. (Why can't it? - he must define an invitation and explain what it is, not just say it is not an offer) It is merley (incorrect spelling) inviting people to enter into a contract (that is quite a decent point, but it needs expanding) and cannot be an offer, the cases above clearly show this. (The cases might, but his account of them does not) Thus it is very important to make the distinction and that is why the courts want to make the distinction. (Again, this does not explain how and why the courts make the distinction)

11. Obviously on many occassions (incorrect spelling) offers and invitations to treat are easy to distinguish, (clumsy - 'it is relatively simple to make the distinction') like in (as in) the case of (delete the words 'the case of') Carill (Carlill) which was obviously an offer because the woman smoked the smoke ball. (A confusing explanation of the ratio of that case - does this mean to say that there can only be an offer when someone smokes a smoke ball? Anyway, the smoking of the ball was the acceptance) On the other hand, the distinction is (can be?) a very fine one (he has contradicted his first sentence - is it easy or is the distinction fine?) and whilst some commentators (which? - cite particular authors) prefer to speak in terms of rules, the courts tend to look at the individual facts of each case. (Quite a good point, but plagiarised - it needs crediting and explaining) In conclusion therefore it is probably safer to proceed on the basis of the single principle that an offer must be sufficiently specific and comprehensive to be capable of immediate acceptance and also as well (repetitive - delete 'as well') made with an intention to be bound by the mere fact of acceptance. (Another good point, but plagiarised and not expanded.)

12. If all things were offers then there would be absolute chaos, (inappropriate expression - 'there would be a good deal of disruption in the commercial world') so the courts have to make a distinction. (An obvious point that adds nothing.) This is shown

in the case of Crainger **(Grainger)** v Gough (see the page before) **(see above, or if using footnotes, supra note x. In fact, when we do 'see the page before', it tells us nothing about the case so he never explains the significance of that case)** where the court **(which court?)** held that it **(what is 'it'?)** was only an invitation to treat and never **(not)** an offer, otherwise the wineseller would have run out of wine. **(What wine seller, and what wine?)** And in Gibson the council would have run out of houses. **(What houses?)** So **(consequently)** adverts **(non sequitur)** can never be invitations, **(In fact they are normally invitations so of course they can be)** but in Carlill it was different **(contradiction because he used the word *never*)** because they hade made an offer. **(He is confused – he should have said adverts are normally invitations but in *Carlill* it was an offer, then explained *why* the advert in that case was an offer)**

13. Again in conclusion **(another conclusion)** a hidden element of discretion permits the courts to label the facts with the terminology of offer and acceptance, whenever they believe it is fair and reasonable to impose contractual liability. **(clear plagiarism and a failure to explain what this sentence means)** Consider for example the purchase of goods in a self service **(should be hyphenated)** store. At what point is an agreement completed. **(?)** Does the customer accept the offer when he or she places the goods in the wire basket? Or does acceptance take place when the customer presents the goods in the wire basket, or when they present the goods to the assistant, or when the assistant accepts the offer by ringing up the price? Or is that merly **(spelling)** the offer? Each interpretation is plausible and thus we can see the distinction clearly. **(Because each interpretation is plausible does not mean that we can see the distinction clearly, particularly if he has not explained it to us. What he has done is pose a number of (relevant) questions, but then failed to provide the answer)**

14. In this essat **(typo)** I have told you how **(clumsy – 'I have attempted to explain how')** the courts make the distinction between offers and invitations to treat and why they want to **(they need to/it is necessary to do so – in fact he has not explained this)** make the **(such a)** distinction. In conclusion **(yet another conclusion)** then an offer is an offer **(that does not tell us what it is)** which can be accepted **(that tells us the consequence of it being an offer, but does not tell us what it is)**, like **(as)** in Mrs Carlills' case **(Carlill)**, wheras **(incorrect spelling)** an invitation to treat does exactly that – it invites **(invites what? - explain)** and it is not an offer. **(But why? – explain)** The difference is negligible and easy to make in every case apart from **(contradiction because he has used the word *every*)** some difficult cases like in **(such as)** Gibson **(He does not explain why *Gibson* was a case where the distinction was difficult)**. An offer cannot be revoked after it has been accepted, **(this is a *consequence* of a proposition being an offer and in any case revocation is irrelevant to the question)** (see the very important case of Dikensian v Dodo (1840). **(Dickinson v Dodds, full reference)** An invitation can be revoked **(one does not revoke invitations; *offers* can be revoked)** because it is not an offer, **(why?)** but merly **(incorrect spelling)** an invitation. **(why?)** There would be commercial chaos if it was not so. **(Explain what his means)** An offer can crystallise in to **(into)** a contract without further ado, **(casual phrase)** but an invitation can't because it isn't an offer, **(what *is* it then?)** although sometimes adverts **(non sequitur)** can be offers as illustrated in Carlill. **(because. . . ?)**

▼

**15.** To conclude (another conclusion) therfore (incorrect spelling) there is a clear difference, and indeed distinction (there is no difference between difference and distinction)
between an offer and an invitation to treat and the courts have shown this to be
true (clumsy - 'have been called upon to make that distinction') on a number of occassions. (Spelling - the courts might have, but he hasn't told us how, or why, they did it) A
contract needs an offer, an acceptance, consideration and an intention to create
legal relations. (This is not relevant to the question and is merely taking up a few more
words) Invitations don't need any of these as they are not offers. (He is confused as
to the context of making the distinction between offers and invitations) Terms can be
implied into offers, (irrelevant) but not invitations and Carlill displays this perfectly.
(That case does not illustrate anything of the sort)

---

### AUTOBIBLIOGRAPHY(Bibliography)

Lecture notes from Maxine Williamson (Never quote lecture notes during the essay or in your
bibliography. Also the lecturer's name is wrong)

The Law of Contract by Hugh Collins (wrong citation - author, title of the text, publisher, year,
edition. Also, he should never have used this text when he has not yet grasped the basics
of the subject)

Textbook on Contract by Terry Downs (ditto regarding citation, the book is now written by Jill
Poole)

The Transformation Thesis and the Ascription of Contractual Responsibility by Collins (wrong
citation - author, title of article, year, issue and title of the article (Law Quarterly Review
(LQR) and page number)

Hanson's Law of Contract, BY Hanson (It is Anson, not Hanson - in fact it is now written by
Jack Beatson. There is also no proper citation)

Various articles in the New Law Journal, the Oxford and Cambridge Law Journal and
International and Comparative Law Quarterly. (All articles must be specifically and sepa-
rately cited - he is trying to give the impression that he has read so many that it would
be futile to cite them all. In addition, some of these journals are not relevant to the legal
area and the 'Oxford and Cambridge Law Journal' does not exist - does he mean the
*Oxford Journal of Legal Studies* and the *Cambridge Law Journal*?)

## Summary of Errors

- The student does not appear to have any knowledge of the subject matter, of what has
  been taught during the academic session or of the module itself and the people who
  teach it.
- The piece lacks any of the legal skills necessary to tackle a law essay.
- The introduction is irrelevant and garbled.
- The writing style is too casual and the grammar is very poor.
- The piece is repetitive and unstructured (caused mainly by ignorance of the subject
  matter).
- The essay is full of typographical and spelling mistakes.
- The student is careless with his choice of words and, as a consequence, confuses the
  reader and contradicts himself.
- The student does not know how to cite and refer to legal authorities and shows incon-
  sistency in style.

- The student does not know how to use cases and other legal materials to support his answer; he never explains the significance or ratio of the case and gives a confused account of the facts and decision. Instead of enhancing his answer, his use of cases makes the essay worse.
- He is guilty of plagiarism on several occasions and tries to use words and ideas that he simply does not understand.
- He makes about four attempts to conclude, and his conclusion(s) contains new information.
- His bibliography is not properly cited and contains lecture notes as a source; furthermore, he attempts to mislead the marker into believing that he has actually read a number of sources.

This is an essay written by a student who lacks strong academic skills and who has an insufficient grasp of the demands of undergraduate study in law. He clearly has not (for one reason or another) engaged with the module and the subject and has not in any sense acquired any of the necessary legal and academic skills to write law essays or survive on the course.

### What Is It Worth?

The piece would struggle to pass at sub-degree level, but is clearly a very bad fail at undergraduate level. The student would lose substantial marks for the poor grammar and the typographical and spelling mistakes, but essentially it is muddled and unstructured – because he is completely confused on (or indifferent to) the relevant law. A mark of between 10 percent and 20 percent could be suggested, but certain lecturers would give even less.

### What Could Be Done to Improve It?

- The student needs to go back to the textbooks and learn the basics of the subject.
- He needs to learn how to cite and refer to legal materials and how to compile a bibliography.
- He needs to plan the answer and to know exactly what he is going to say before he puts pen to paper.
- He needs to read the cases properly and use them to illustrate the answer.
- He needs to learn how to write in a clear and formal style – reading texts, law reports and articles and listening to how the lecturer talks will be of the greatest assistance in this respect.
- The piece should be checked for typographical, spelling and grammatical errors.
- The conclusion needs rewriting so that it excludes irrelevant information and relates to the relevant legal area.
- He needs to begin engaging with the module and his law studies and to realise that he simply has not got the ability to write an essay without first learning the subject matter.

## Part B: The Good Essay

Below is a reworking of the bad essay. Examine this essay and consider the remarks made at the end of each paragraph and at the conclusion of the essay itself.

100 LAW – Law of Obligations (Contract)

Assessment One

*By the use of case law explain the distinction between an offer and an invitation to treat. Why is the distinction so important?*

Submitted by Steve Foster

Course: LLB, Year One

Module Leader: Maureen Williams

Personal Tutor: Janice Johnson

Word Count: 2,089 (excluding all references and citations, front page and the bibliography)

Submitted on October 10, 2006

The student has placed the question at the top of the sheet, which acts as a guide for when he starts his introduction. He should check whether this could count towards the word count before including it.

### Answer with Commentary

**By the use of case law explain the distinction between an offer and an invitation to treat. Why is the distinction so important?**

1. To answer this question one has to appreciate the basic rules relating to the formation of a contract. A contract is a legally binding agreement[1] and in most cases results from the agreement of the parties.[2] This agreement usually takes the form of a specific offer made by one person (the offeror) to another (the offeree), which that other person accepts. An offer has been defined as an expression of willingness to be bound, made with the intention that it shall become binding as soon as it is accepted.[3] To constitute an offer, therefore, the proposition needs to be firm enough to be

---

[1] See Treitel, G *The Law of Contract* (Sweet and Maxwell 2003, 11th edition) page 1: an agreement giving rise to obligations which are enforced or recognised by law.

[2] Some contracts are explainable on a basis other than pure agreement. See *Clarke v Earl of Dunraven and Mount Earl; The Satania* [1897] AC 59, where a contract came into existence by implication – a person entering his ship for a race impliedly entered into a contract to be bound by the rules.

[3] Treitel, G *The Law of Contract* (Sweet and Maxwell, 11th edition) at page 8.

capable of acceptance, and there needs to be sufficient evidence that the offeror is ready, at that stage, to accept liability should the other accept his proposition.

*In paragraph 1 the student has made a good start, first by identifying what area of law the question is concerned with, and second by giving the reader a clear and useful definition of an offer. As the question directs the student to make a distinction between and offer and an invitation to treat, his definition provides him a reference point whenever he has to make the distinction or explain why a particular case was decided as it was. The student also makes good use of secondary sources and footnotes and writes in a clear, uncomplicated and appropriate way. He shows quite clearly that he has read and understood the texts and appreciates what the question is asking.*

2. In this area the courts attempt to draw a distinction between an offer, which is capable of creating a contract on its acceptance, and an invitation to treat, which merely invites the other person (or persons in general) to make an offer, and which in turn can be accepted or rejected by the other party. This essay will seek to illustrate how the courts make this distinction, identifying some guiding principles that they use in making the distinction. It will then explore *why* such a distinction is important, although, as we shall see, the two questions may be linked as the importance of the distinction will often be relevant to the actual outcome of a particular case.

*The second paragraph is useful for two reasons: First, it explains what the legal dilemma is all about and what effect the distinction between offers and invitations means in contractual practice; and second, it informs us what he is going to tell us in the essay – how he is going to approach it and in particular how he is going to split and interrelate the two parts of the question.*

3. As mentioned above, an offer has two characteristics: it is capable of acceptance; and the offerors' intention is that he or should be bound at the point of acceptance by the person to whom the offer was addressed. Thus, Poole states that an offer must be (i) sufficiently specific and comprehensive to be capable of immediate acceptance; and (ii) made with an intention to be bound by the mere fact of acceptance.[4] If the court is not satisfied that the proposition in question has these characteristics then it will decide that there exists no offer capable of being transformed into a contract.

*There is some repetition in paragraph 3, and had he not been given 2,000 words as a limit, this paragraph might have had to be deleted. In any case, some of the material could have been merged within the second paragraph. However, he does stress the essential issues, and this paves the way for a discussion on the cases.*

4. To assist the courts in this function the law may presume that certain actions are not to be treated as formal offers. This presumption may be made on the basis that the proposition simply lacks the certainty so as to constitute an offer. Thus, in *Harvey v Facey*,[5] in reply to a question whether the defendant was willing to sell certain property and a request to telegram his lowest price, the defendant replied that the lowest price would be £900. It was held that the defendant had not made an offer. He had

---

[4]Poole, J *A Textbook on Contract* (Blackstone Press/OUP 2006 8th ed), at page 64.
[5][1893] AC 552. See also *Gibson v Manchester City Council* [1979] 1 All ER 972. Here the council's invitation to local people to buy their council houses by completing an application form was held not to be an offer.

responded to the plaintiff's question, but showed no willingness to be bound should the plaintiff find the price acceptable. Presumably, he was saying that that was the price with which he would begin negotiations, *should* he wish to sell the property.

**In paragraph 4, the student begins by making a good and relevant point that goes a long way to explaining how the courts make the distinction in practice (which is the whole point of the question). He also makes very good use of the case – by making a relevant point to introduce the case, by giving the briefest account of facts and the decision and, finally, by concluding on its relevance and its ratio. In particular, he uses italics to stress the real rationale of the case, giving the strong impression that he understands the case and the way it was decided.**

5. Applying this principle, the courts may in similar cases conclude that the person making the initial proposal was looking for a more concrete proposition from the other party. This can be seen in the area of tenders. A company, or local authority, might wish certain work to be done, or goods delivered. They will invite people to make offers (tenders) and then accept only the tender that they find most attractive. In most cases this invitation for tenders is considered as just that. Thus, in *Spencer v Harding*[6] it was held that a circular distributed to potential customers offering the defendant's stock for sale was not in fact an offer, but merely an invitation to buyers in general to make their offers, which could then be accepted or rejected by the defendant. This was despite the defendants using the word offer in the circular. However, certain requests for tenders may be regarded as offers. In *Harvella Investments Ltd v Royal Trust Co of Canada (CI) Ltd*[7] the defendants had invited two persons to make a bid for a certain plot of land. They had instructed them to make a sealed bid and had intimated that the highest offer would secure the shares. It was held that that the invitation to apply for the shares was an offer capable of acceptance. Here the defendants had *clearly indicated* that they were prepared to accept the highest bid and the general rule was thus displaced.

**Paragraph 5 follows on neatly from the preceding one and provides a good, clear illustration of the principle in action. He use the area of tenders to explain the rationale of the law and how the courts approach the problems in hand, giving us just enough detail on the facts and the decision of each case. The use of Harvella as an exception to the rule clearly shows his understanding, and he stresses the real ratio by putting the relevant words in italics.**

6. A similar rationale is used in the case of auctions. The seller of the goods, via the auctioneer, does not, by putting the goods in an auction, offer to sell the goods to the highest bidder, and can normally withdraw the goods before the bidder's firm offer is accepted by the auctioneer.[8] The courts have thus concluded that the offer is made by the bidder, and can be accepted or rejected by the auctioneer.[8A] This type of case, and others such as those involving bus and train time tables[9], can be

---

[6](1870) LR 5 CP 561. See also *Grainger and Sons v Gough* [1896] AC 325: a wine merchant's catalogue with price list held to be an invitation to treat, inviting offers via customer orders.

[7][1985] 2 All ER 966. However, it was held on the facts that the offer had been improperly accepted.

[8]See *Harris v Nickerson* (1873) LR 8 QB 286: an advertisement that an auction was to take place was not an offer to hold the auction and to sell to highest bidder.

[8A]*Payne v Cave* (1789) 3 Term Rep 148.

[9]*Wilkie v London Passenger and Transport Board* [1947] 1 All ER 258.

HOW TO WRITE BETTER LAW ESSAYS

explained either on the basis that the placing of goods in an auction is too vague an act to constitute a firm offer – in other words the terms of the contract are, as yet, too vague or that the vendor does not *at that stage* wish to commit him/herself to selling the goods at an unknown price. This presumption, however, can be rebutted by a clear indication that the auctioneer will accept the highest bid.[10]

*In paragraph 6, the student gives the reader further illustrations of the principle, drawing on examples that he has found in textbooks and in lectures. He gives us a number of illustrations and makes good use of authority and his footnotes to give the impression that he could have provided much more detail had time allowed. Equally importantly, he tells us the rationale of this general principle and uses italics to stress that he fully understands the cases and the rules. Note that he does not have the space to devote an equal amount of time to all these examples, instead using tenders as his main example. He could as easily have chosen auctions as the main vehicle, but chose tenders – this generally will be a matter of personal choice and the student should choose an example that he or she understands and can explain simply and fully.*

7. In making the distinction the courts may presume that a person wishes to avoid the harsh or absurd consequences of his or her proposition being held to be an offer. Thus, in the following cases there is a presumption that the proposition is not an offer, but simply an invitation for offers. This is the case even though the proposition is, theoretically, capable of immediate acceptance. One example is the advertising of goods for sale in a newspaper or catalogue. Thus, in *Partridge v Crittenden*[11] it was held that a notice placed in a periodical that a person had bramblefinch cocks and hens for sale at 25 shillings each was not an offer so as to constitute an offence of offering for sale a wild live bird under the Protection of Birds Act 1954. Explaining the decision Lord Parker said:

> "I think that when one is dealing with advertisements and circulars, unless they indeed come from manufacturers, there is business sense in their being construed as invitations to treat and not offers"[12]

*In paragraph 7, the student moves the essay on by looking at how commercial sense might dictate the outcome of the law and the cases. This explains the second require-ment of an offer – that the offeror wishes to be bound at that stage if the other party accepts. He makes good use of the decision in Partridge and uses a quotation from the case to illustrate its ratio. This quotation shows that he has read the case prop-erly, perhaps in a law report (or at least in a good text book or cases and materials book). The quotation is relevant and neatly explains the principle in question. It is also properly referenced, displaying good referencing and citation skills.*

8. In this type of case, the proposition might have one of the characteristics of an offer – certainty of terms – yet not possess the other characteristic: a willingness to be bound once someone accepts the proposition. For instance, an advert in the news-paper that I wish to sell my specific car for a specific price and on specific terms might have the characteristics of a firm offer, yet still be classed as an invitation to

---

[10]See *Warlow v Harrison* (1859) 1 E and E 309, where it was held (obiter) that an auction advertised 'with-out reserve' imposes an obligation to sell to the highest bidder once the auction begins. See also the more recent case of *Barry v Davis (Heathcote Ball Co)* [2001] 1 WLR 1962, which upholds this principle.
[11][1968] 2 All ER 421.
[12]*ibid*, at page 424.

▼

treat because, presumably, I do not intend to be bound by every person who purports to accept that proposition. If I were to be so bound, I would be bound to *everyone* who accepted that proposition, and would, somehow, have to notify all the other interested parties of the concluded contract.

**Paragraph 8 follows neatly on from the last, pursuing the relevant argument. More importantly, the author uses a hypothetical example in illustration. This displays his understanding by proving that he is confident enough to use his own examples to explain the law and its rationale. Note that if the student has seen this specific example in a textbook, he should credit the author with the idea by citing and referencing the source. Alternatively, as in this case, if the example is the student's own, he or she can use it as such even though it has been inspired by one noticed in lectures or texts. In such a case, the student may wish to create a footnote and say something like 'Treitel gives a similar example,' citing the text and the page number.**

9. Another example is the display of goods in a shop window. Here the courts have concluded that (generally) the display of goods is merely inviting offers, and is not an offer in itself. For example in *Fisher v Bell*,[13] when a flick-knife was displayed in a shop window and the shopkeeper was charged with offering for sale an offensive weapon, it was held that the defendant had not *offered* the flick-knife for sale as required by the statute. The display merely invited the potential customer to make an offer to the shopkeeper, who could then accept or reject it. Otherwise, the shopkeeper would be bound to sell the goods even though, for example, the display item had been already sold, or had been incorrectly priced. This principle was applied to self-service supermarkets in *Pharmaceutical Society of Great Britain v Boots Cash Chemists (Southern) Ltd*.[14] Here goods were displayed on a supermarket shelf, and the customer was invited to pick them up and take them to the cash desk. A registered pharmacist had been placed at the cash desk, but not at the shelf where the customers were able to help themselves to the goods. The company was charged with selling listed drugs without the supervision of such a pharmacist. It was held that the point of sale was the cash desk. The display of goods on the shelf was not an offer capable of acceptance and merely invited the customer to place the goods in their basket and make an offer at the cash desk. The court reasoned that to hold otherwise would prevent the customer from changing their mind after they had taken the step of placing goods in the basket.

**In paragraph 9, the student works through other, well-known examples in which the law presumes that certain actions are merely invitations. He makes good use of this well-established case law and is careful to explain the rationale of each case rather than merely reciting the facts and decision. Note that, had he be given a shorter word limit, he would have to provide this information in brief and in footnotes, although he has the choice of which illustrations to use and could have spent more time on circulars and adverts.**

10. In the above cases, therefore, the courts seem to be ruled by some form of commercial sense and presume, generally, that the person making the proposal did not intend to be bound at that point in time. This presumption can, of course be rebutted. As a consequence it is wrong to conclude that adverts or circulars (or indeed shop window or supermarket displays) can *never* be offers. The famous case of *Carlill v Carbolic*

---

[13][1961] 1QB 394
[14][1953] 1 QB 401.

*Smoke Ball Co*[15] illustrates this in the area of advertisements. In this case the company placed an advert in a newspaper stating that they were prepared to pay £100 to any person who used their product (a smoke ball) and yet still contracted influenza. The company stated that they had deposited £1,000 in their bank as a mark of their sincerity. The plaintiff tried the product yet still contracted influenza and sued the company for the promised £100. In rejecting the company's claim that their advert was a mere invitation to treat, and not intended to be legally binding, the court held that the advert was clearly an offer. It was couched in clear terms, was capable of acceptance, and the company had shown its intention to be bound by depositing the money in its bank account. Thus there is no rule of law that adverts, invitations for tenders or shop (window) displays are merely invitations to treat. Provided they are certain enough, and there is a clear intention to be bound at the point of acceptance, then the courts will declare that the (advert) was in deed an offer.

The student begins paragraph 10 by stressing the importance of commercial sense in this area and then makes it clear that this presumption is only that, and not a hard and fast rule. He has allowed himself to do this and to bring in exceptions to the general rule because he has been careful in the words that he has employed and has never presented this presumption as a rule without exception (as the bad essay writer often did). He then makes extensive use of the decision in Carlill to make his point. This case is always a good one to use, as almost every student knows the facts and decision and, more importantly, understands the ratio. It makes much more sense to use examples that one understands – only use more complicated ones if the nature of the question asks for it (For example, 'Explain how the traditional rules of agreement have been modified to meet complex and modern commercial relationships') or if it is necessary (because of the level at which you are studying or to ensure a higher grade) to show more than a basic understanding of the traditional cases.

11. With regard to the question *why* such a distinction is important, it will have become clear that the finding of the court in each of the above cases was significant to the parties involved in the legal action. In cases such as *Fisher v Bell*, the court had to decide whether an offer had been made for the purposes of determining criminal liability for making an offer to sell certain prohibited products. Here the defendant was found not guilty because the offence was to make an *offer*, and *inviting* persons to offer did not, therefore, attract liability.[16] In the context of contractual liability, the court's decision will be important in establishing the point, if any, at which the contract came into existence. Thus in cases such as *Harvey v Facey*, above, the court will have to decide whether one party had made an offer to another, or whether the parties were still at the stage of preliminary negotiations. If the court concludes that an offer exists, then the other party may accept the offer at that juncture; if not, then that other party needs to put forward a firm proposition which in turn is then capable of acceptance. The finding that the proposition is an offer means that the offer can be accepted immediately, whereas a finding that the act was merely inviting offers will at the very least delay liability until the time when the firm offer is accepted. We have also seen that the court's decision *whether* an offer has been

---

[15][1893] 1 QB 256.
[16]The particular legislation had to be amended so as to make it an offence to *display* offensive weapons; see now s. 1 Restriction of Offences Weapons Act 1961.

▼

made is also tied to the *consequences* of them holding such. In other words, the courts presume that a person does not wish to suffer the harsh consequences of his or her actions, unless they have made it clear by specific words or actions.

**In paragraph 11 the student begins to tackle the second part of the question and appears to have left himself little time to do it. However, he explains that the two questions are interrelated and that in fact by answering the first part he has been addressing the issues raised by the second part. This is an acceptable tactic provided the student gives advanced warning of this (which he does in the second paragraph of the essay) and the two parts are indeed interrelated (which in this case they are). He then proceeds to illustrate why the distinction is important by referring to case examples employed in the first part of the question, making some good observations about how the courts use the reason for the distinction as the basis of their decision.**

12. In conclusion the courts appear to make the distinction between an offer and an invitation to treat by looking at the essential elements of an offer and considering whether the parties' actions are consistent with such a definition. Thus, in those cases where it has been held that the proposition was not in fact an offer but only an invitation to treat, it is apparent that the proposition either lacked the certainty of an offer, or failed to display a sufficient intention to be bound at that stage of negotiations. Although the courts may presume that certain acts are invitations, their minds are not closed on this issue; adverts and invitations for tenders, for example, may be construed as offers provided there is sufficient evidence of the party's intention. The contractual or criminal consequences of the court's finding make the distinction between an offer and an invitation important, and in general the courts have devised guidelines in order to make that distinction sufficiently clear and predictable.

**The student's conclusion is neat and relevant. It recaps the main points made during the main body of the essay. It does not introduce any fresh information (as the bad essay attempts to do) and concludes with a suitably intelligent and open-ended comment with respect to the current state of the law.**

---

### BIBLIOGRAPHY

Adams, J and Brownsword, R; *Understanding Contract Law* (Sweet and Maxwell 2004, 4th edition)
Beatson, J: *Anson's Law of Contract* (Oxford 2000, 28th edition)
Furmston, MP: *Cheshire, Fifoot and Furmstone's Law of Contract* (Butterworths 1996, 13th edition)
Poole, J; *Textbook on Contract* (Blackstone Press/OUP 2006, 8th edition)
Treitel, GH: *The Law of Contract* (Sweet and Maxwell 2003, 11th edition)

**The bibliography is properly cited and there is evidence throughout the essay that he has actually read and understood some of the texts. However, he has not used all the texts cited in the bibliography and could have shown off his reading to better effect in this respect. The bibliography is also missing one or two good academic articles and could have referred to a more theoretical textbook such as Hugh Collins' *Law of Contract* (a book that the bad essay writer plagiarised from).**

**Summary of Good Points**
- It was clearly written, employing a simple yet legal style that one would find in most good textbooks.

- His introduction was direct and to the point and contained useful legal definitions of relevant legal concepts.
- The author made it clear what the question was about and how he was going to tackle it, and having done that he followed that format.
- It was clear that he had researched the area and had planned the answer to the question *before* he set pen to paper.
- The author made good use of case authority, always introducing the reader to the relevance of the case, its facts and decision (where relevant), and always displaying his appreciation of the case and its rationale.
- The piece was professionally constructed, contained good reference and citation skills and made good use of footnotes.
- The conclusion was direct and related to the most salient points he had made in the main body of the answer.
- The bibliography displayed reasonably wide research and was properly cited.

In general, it was a very competent piece of work written by a student who has paid attention to the lectures, has attended seminars, has read the books and cases and has ensured that he understood the area before attempting to write the answer.

### What Is the Essay Worth?

Given that the essay was directed at a first-year law student and that the area of law and the title was fairly basic, we might consider that he has done as well as he possibly could in providing this answer. Consequently, *some* markers might regard this as a first-class answer, albeit with some reservations. This might be the case particularly if the course is sub-degree. Other teachers might regard the answer as lacking academic rigour and any theoretical analysis – it lacks one or two meaty articles and does not make use of the more theoretical texts such as Collins' *Law of Contract*; in which case a mark of between 60 and 68 might be more appropriate. It is a very competent, although rather functional, piece, and the mark might depend on what particular contract lecturers are looking for from the student.

### How Could the Essay Have Been Improved?

- For a degree-level student, the piece might be regarded as a little pedestrian and functional, and some teachers might see it as lacking real academic rigour.
- In some teachers' view, the author could have employed a more theoretical approach, looking at authors such as Hugh Collins.
- There was some repetition, particularly early on in the essay.
- The essay did not refer to some of the sources quoted in the bibliography.

## ● Practice 2: Legal System and Constitutional Law Essay

**Example Question**

'The passing of the Human Rights Act 1998 has had a profound effect on both the British Constitution and the English Legal System.' Discuss.

This question is likely to appear in one form or another on most undergraduate courses, either on a public (constitutional and administrative law) course, or one on legal system or legal process. The question is a relatively straightforward one and requires the student to possess a sound knowledge of the Act and its central provisions as well as an appreciation of the impact of the Act on both the constitutional system and certain aspects of the English legal system.

The main difficulty with the question is that it requires a lot of issues to be raised and for the student to have a very broad knowledge of the Act, its provisions and any relevant case law. The student must focus on the actual question and find room to include a lot of information in the answer without omitting relevant points. The answer requires very careful planning.

The word limit given for the question was 2,000 words (with a 10 percent leeway and excluding the front page, all references and citations and the bibliography), but other word limits are possible, depending on the particular institution.

The student is on the first year of her LLB degree and is submitting this work as part of a module titled Legal and Constitutional System.

The following guidance was given to all students:

> Students are expected to display the legal and other study skills outlined in their student handbook. In relation to the particular question, the student must:

> - Display a sound knowledge of the provisions of the 1998 Act as they affect both the British Constitution and the English Legal System.
> - Appreciate the potential impact of those provisions on the central features of both the British Constitution and the English legal system.
> - Analyse the truth of that statement by reference to relevant case law or other evidence.

## Part A: The Bad Essay

Below is a poor answer to the question. It does not suffer from the very poor grammar and style witnessed in the bad essay in Question 1; most of the defects are related to the problem of not answering the question. For this reason, there is no detailed marked-up essay to examine as with the preceding question. Read through the essay and make criticisms as you are doing so. Then you can compare your notes with the appraisal at the end.

---

**Answer**

**'The passing of the Human Rights Act 1998 has had a profound effect on both the British Constitution and the English Legal System.' Discuss.**

1. The Human Rights Act 1998 was passed to incorporate the European Convention on Human Rights into domestic law. Before the Act was passed the European Convention had no role to play in domestic law and if an individual's human rights were violated the only redress was to take the case to the European Court of

---

HOW TO WRITE BETTER LAW ESSAYS

Human Rights in Strasbourg. Since October 2000[1] an individual may bring a claim for breach of their human rights in the domestic courts and thus they do not have to take the long journey to Strasbourg.

2. The European Convention contains a list of human rights which can be described as civil and political rights, and these rights are incorporated into domestic law by the Human Rights Act 1998.[2] These rights include the right to life (Article 2), freedom from torture (Article 3), liberty and security of the person (Article 5), the right to a fair trial (Article 6), the right to private and family life (Article 8), freedom of expression (Article 10), freedom of peaceful assembly (Article 11) and the right to marry (Article 12). We can see, therefore, that these rights are civil and political rights and that the Convention does not include any social, economic and cultural rights. This has been criticised and it has been proposed that the Human Rights Act be expanded to include such rights.[3]

3. These rights are enforced by the European Court of Human Rights who hear cases of human rights violations by member states to the Convention. Thus under Article 34 to the Convention it may hear applications from individuals claiming to be a victim of a violation of the Convention and may award just satisfaction to that person under Article 41 of the Convention. Many cases have been brought under this process against the United Kingdom and the Court has ruled in favour of individuals with respect to matters such as censorship of prisoners' correspondence (*Golder v United Kingdom*[4]), freedom of expression (*Sunday Times v United Kingdom*)[5], corporal punishment (*Tyrer v United Kingdom*)[6] and the right of peaceful assembly (*Steel v United Kingdom*).[7]

4. The rights are either conditional, in which case they can be violated if there is a legitimate reason for their interference, or absolute, in which case there can be no justification for their violation. For example, freedom of expression (under Article 10) can be compromised provided the restriction is prescribed by law, and necessary in a democratic society for the protection of things such as public safety, health or morals, or national security. Thus, In *R v Shayler*[8] it was held that a prosecution under the Official Secrets Act 1989 was not in violation of Article 10 of the Convention. On the other hand, in *Chahal v United Kingdom*,[9] the European Court held that Article 3 could not be violated whatever the circumstances and whatever risk the individual posed to society.

5. The passing of the Human Rights Act has been described as having great constitutional significance.[10] For the first time individuals will be able to seek a remedy for

---

[1] The Act's implementation was delayed to allow for fuller training of the judiciary and thus came into force on that date.

[2] See section 1 and Sched. 1 of the Human Rights Act 1998

[3] Van Beuren, Including the excluded: the case for an economic, social and cultural Human Rights Act [2002] PL 456.

[4] (1975) 1 EHRR 524

[5] (1979) 2 EHRR 245

[6] (1978) 2EHRR 1

[7] (1999) 28 EHRR 603.

[8] [2002] 2 WLR 754

[9] (1997) 23 EHRR 413

[10] See Ewing and Bradley, *Constitutional and Administrative Law* (Longman 2003), at page 416.

▼

violation of their human rights before the domestic courts. Thus, if an individual is tortured by the police he or she will be able to bring an action before the domestic courts under the Human Rights Act and the courts can, under section 8 of the Act, provide just satisfaction for that breach. No longer will the individual have to take an action under the European Convention. Thus, in *Napier v Scottish Ministers*,[11] a prisoner brought a successful claim under Article 3 when he was subjected to 'slopping out' in prison. Also, in *Campell v MGN*,[12] the House of Lords held that a model's privacy had been invaded when the newspapers printed stories about her drug habit, and she was awarded compensation. More significantly, in *A v Home* Secretary[13] the House of Lords held that the power to detain persons suspected of terrorism under the Anti-Terrorism, Crime and Security Act 2001 was incompatible with Article 5 of the Convention and thus declared the Act incompatible under section 4 of the Human Rights Act 1998.

6. As we can see from the above cases, the Act has had a substantial effect on both the legal and constitutional system of the United Kingdom. Under section 2 of the Act the courts can now take into account the case law of the European Court and Commission of Human Rights when adjudicating upon human rights disputes in domestic law. In addition, they have the power to interpret legislation in line with the European Convention (under section 3 of the Act), and the power to declare both primary and secondary legislation as incompatible with the Convention (under section 4). Thus, in *R v A (Sexual History)*[14] the House of Lords held that the Youth Justice and Criminal Evidence Act 1999 could be interpreted so as to allow a defendant to cross-examine a rape victim wherever that was necessary to ensure the right to a fair trial under section 6 of the Act. The courts have also used their new power under section 4 of the Act to declare legislation incompatible with the European Convention. For example, in *A v Home Secretary* (above), section 26 of the Anti-Terrorism, Crime and Security Act 2001 was declared incompatible with Article 5 of the European Convention, which guarantees the right to liberty and security of the person.

7. Before the Act was passed domestic courts could not take the European Convention into account. For example, in *Malone v Metropolitan Police Commissioner*[15] it was held that the plaintiff could not rely on Article 8 of the European Convention when the police had tapped his telephone because it was pointed out that the Convention had not been incorporated into domestic law and that any remedy the plaintiff had under the Convention would have to be pursued before the European Court of Human Rights. In that case *Malone* took his case to Strasbourg (*Malone v United Kingdom*)[16] and the European Court held that the telephone tapping was in violation of his right to private life and correspondence. As a consequence Parliament enacted the Interception of Communications Act 1985, which put telephone tapping on a statutory footing, and this power is now contained in the Regulation of

---

[11] *The Times*, May 13 2004.
[12] [2004] 2 AC 457.
[13] [2005] AC 68.
[14] [2002] 1 AC 1546.
[15] [1979] Ch 344.
[16] (1984) 7 EHRR 14.

Investigatory Powers Act 2000. In another case, *R v Ministry of Defence, ex parte Smith*,[17] the Court of Appeal held that Article 8 of the Convention could not assist armed forces personnel who had been expelled from the armed forces because of their sexual orientation. On appeal, the European Court of Human Rights held that such expulsions were contrary to Articles 8 and 14 of the Convention and that the expulsions were disproportionate.[18] Following that decision the armed forces replaced the blanket ban with a conduct-based policy so as to comply with the judgment of the European Court.

8. Under the Act the courts have got the power to interpret legislation compatibly with the European Convention, although this does not mean that they can refuse to apply clear legislation that is in breach of the Convention. In *Mendoza v Ghaidan*[19] the House of Lords held that the words 'living together as husband and wife' could be interpreted as 'as if they were living together as husband and wife'. Accordingly same sex partners were given equal treatment and this was re-enforced by the Civil Partnership Act 2004. On the other hand in *Bellinger v Bellinger*[20] the House of Lords refused to interpret the words man and woman to include a person who had undergone gender re-assignment. This was despite the European Court's decision in *Goodwin v United Kingdom*[21] that discrimination against transsexuals was in violation of Articles 8 and 14 of the Convention. As a result of the decision in *Goodwin* Parliament has enacted the Gender Reassignment Act 2004, which recognises the rights of transsexuals to change their sexual identity and to marry a person of their choice.

9. The courts have also got the power under the Act (section 4) to declare primary and secondary legislation incompatible with the European Convention, although again this does not empower the courts to overrule legislation. For example, in *R (Anderson and Taylor) v Home Secretary*[22] the House of Lords held that the Home Secretary's power to fix the minimum terms of life sentence prisoners was incompatible with Article 6 of the European Convention, which guarantees the right to a fair trial, including the right to a fair sentence. This decision followed the decision of the European Court of Human Rights in *Stafford v United Kingdom*,[23] where it was held that the Home Secretary's powers were inconsistent with the rule of law and the separation of powers and thus in breach of the Convention. Interestingly, the Court of Appeal in *Anderson* refused to declare the power of the Home Secretary as incompatible until the European Court had made its decision in *Stafford*, because before that decision the European Court had held that such a power was lawful with respect to mandatory life sentence prisoners.[24]

10. The Human Rights Act 1998 may also have a horizontal effect and thus apply to disputes between private individuals. Normally the Act only applies between individual

---

[17] [1996] 1 All ER 257.
[18] *Smith and Grady v United Kingdom* (2000) 29 EHRR 493.
[19] [2004] 2 AC 557.
[20] [2003] 2 AC 467.
[21] (2002) 35 EHRR 18.
[22] [2002] 3 WLR 1800.
[23] (2002) 35 EHRR 32.
[24] *Wynne v United Kingdom* (1994) 19 EHRR 333.

▼

victims and public authorities (as defined in section 6 of the Act). However, because the courts are public authorities under section 6 they have the duty to safeguard and uphold Convention rights and as a consequence the Act has been applied horizontally in the law of confidentiality in cases such as *Campbell v MGN*[25] and *Douglas v Hello!*[26] However, the House of Lords has held recently that the Act cannot be used to create a separate law of privacy, and that the decision in *Hello!* was confined to the law of confidentiality. Nevertheless the courts have gained extensive powers under the Act and can now apply the principles of proportionality when adjudicating upon disputes that raise Convention rights. Thus, any interference with a Convention right must now be necessary in a democratic society and be proportionate to any legitimate aim being pursued (R *(Daly) v Home Secretary*).[27] Furthermore, this test of proportionality is stricter than the previous test of *Wednesbury*[28] unreasonableness and will require the courts to take a more active approach to defending civil liberties.

11. Since the Act came into force there have been a number of cases brought against public authorities claiming that Convention rights have been violated. For example, in *R v DPP, ex parte Pretty*[29] it was held that the European Convention was not violated when domestic law (the Suicide Act 1961) outlawed assisted suicide. The House of Lords held that the right to life guaranteed by Article 2 of the Convention did not include the right to die with dignity. This decision was upheld by the European Court of Human Rights in *Pretty v United Kingdom*[30] where it was confirmed that Article 2 was principally concerned with preserving life. Another example of the Act's use was in *A v Home Secretary* (above) where the House of Lords held that the indefinite detention of foreign person suspected of acts of terrorism was in breach of Article 5 of the European Convention. The House of Lords held that although there was an emergency threatening the life of the nation within Article 15 of the Convention, the measures within the Anti-Terrorism, Crime and Security Act 2001 were both discriminatory and disproportionate and thus incompatible with the Convention. As a result the government introduced the Terrorism Bill 2005 into Parliament.

12. In conclusion, the Human Rights Act 1998 has had a profound effect on the protection of human rights and has thus impacted on both the legal and constitutional system in the United Kingdom. The courts can now take the Convention and its case law into account and thus must apply European principles to human rights cases. Further, the courts have new powers of interpretation under section 3 of the Act and under section 4 can declare legislation incompatible with the Convention. Since the implementation of the Act the courts can use the Convention in domestic law and the individual no longer has to make use of the procedure under the European Convention. This will save considerable time and expense, although it should be pointed out that the victim can still make use of that procedure if they

---

[25]See above, note 12.
[26][2001] 2 WLR 992.
[27][2001] 2 WLR 1622.
[28]*Associated Provincial Picture House Ltd v Wednesbury Corporation* [1948] 1KB 223.
[29][2002] 1 AC 800.
[30](2002) 35 EHRR 1.

HOW TO WRITE BETTER LAW ESSAYS

are unsuccessful under the Human Rights Act. These new powers, therefore, have had a profound effect on the legal system and the constitution in the United Kingdom, bringing rights home to domestic law.

BIBLIOGRAPHY

Ewing K and Bradley A, *Constitutional and Administrative Law* (Longman 2002)
Foster, S *Human Rights and Civil Liberties* (Longman 2003).

## What Was Wrong With the Essay?

**Answer with Commentary**

**'The passing of the Human Rights Act 1998 has had a profound effect on both the British Constitution and the English Legal System.' Discuss**

1. The Human Rights Act 1998 was passed to incorporate the European Convention on Human Rights into domestic law. Before the Act was passed the European Convention had no role to play in domestic law and if an individual's human rights were violated the only redress was to take the case to the European Court of Human Rights in Strasbourg. Since October 2000[1] an individual may bring a claim for breach of their human rights in the domestic courts and thus they do not have to take the long journey to Strasbourg.

   In the introductory paragraph the student uses the word *incorporate* rather than the phrase 'give further effect to,' which is technically correct. She makes an incorrect statement about human rights before the Act, suggesting that there were no remedies at all apart from the Convention machinery. The introduction does not refer to any of the constitutional and legal issues highlighted in the question.

2. The European Convention contains a list of human rights which can be described as civil and political rights, and these rights are incorporated into domestic law by the Human Rights Act 1998.[2] These rights include the right to life (Article 2), freedom from torture (Article 3), liberty and security of the person (Article 5), the right to a fair trial (Article 6), the right to private and family life (Article 8), freedom of expression (Article 10), freedom of peaceful assembly (Article 11) and the right to marry (Article 12). We can see, therefore, that these rights are civil and political rights and that the Convention does not include any social, economic and cultural rights. This has been criticised and it has been proposed that the Human Rights Act be expanded to include such rights.[3]

   The second paragraph simply lists some of the Convention rights given effect to by the Act rather than addressing the Act's provisions. The student does not explain the difference between the two sets of rights or the consequence (if any) of that distinction on the impact of the Act.

---

[1] The Act's implementation was delayed to allow for fuller training of the judiciary and thus came into force on that date.
[2] See section 1 and Sched. 1 of the Human Rights Act 1998
[3] Van Beuren, Including the excluded: the case for an economic, social and cultural Human Rights Act [2002] PL 456.

3. These rights are enforced by the European Court of Human Rights who hear cases of human rights violations by member states to the Convention. Thus under Article 34 to the Convention it may hear applications from individuals claiming to be a victim of a violation of the Convention and may award just satisfaction to that person under Article 41 of the Convention. Many cases have been brought under this process against the United Kingdom and the Court has ruled in favour of individuals with respect to matters such as censorship of prisoners' correspondence (*Golder v United Kingdom*[4]), freedom of expression (*Sunday Times v United Kingdom*)[5], corporal punishment (*Tyrer v United Kingdom*)[6] and the right of peaceful assembly (*Steel v United Kingdom*).[7]

**This information relates to the role of the European Court of Human Rights under the Convention, rather than to the terms and impact of the Human Rights Act 1998. The cases mentioned towards the end do not appear to be relevant in answering the question and thus can be regarded as background information at most.**

4. The rights are either conditional, in which case they can be violated if there is a legitimate reason for their interference, or absolute, in which case there can be no justification for their violation. For example, freedom of expression (under Article 10) can be compromised provided the restriction is prescribed by law, and necessary in a democratic society for the protection of things such as public safety, health or morals, or national security. Thus, In *R v Shayler*[8] it was held that a prosecution under the Official Secrets Act 1989 was not in violation of Article 10 of the Convention. On the other hand, in *Chahal v United Kingdom*,[9] the European Court held that Article 3 could not be violated whatever the circumstances and whatever risk the individual posed to society.

**The explanation that some rights are absolute and some conditional does not appear to be relevant to the question and the issues it raises. Thus, whilst the information is true, without some explanation of the provisions of the Act itself the content of the paragraph is largely irrelevant. The fact that some rights are conditional and some absolute will impact on the domestic court's role, but the student does not identify this.**

5. The passing of the Human Rights Act has been described as having great constitutional significance.[10] For the first time individuals will be able to seek a remedy for violation of their human rights before the domestic courts. Thus, if an individual is tortured by the police he or she will be able to bring an action before the domestic courts under the Human Rights Act and the courts can, under section 8 of the Act, provide just satisfaction for that breach. No longer will the individual have to take an action under the European Convention. Thus, in *Napier v Scottish Ministers*,[11] a prisoner brought a successful claim under Article 3 when he was subjected to 'slopping

---

[4] (1975) 1 EHRR 524.
[5] (1979) 2 EHRR 245
[6] (1978) 2 EHRR 1.
[7] (1999) 28 EHRR 603.
[8] [2002] 2 WLR 754.
[9] (1997) 23 EHRR 413.
[10] See Ewing and Bradley, *Constitutional and Administrative Law* (Longman 2003), at page 416.
[11] *The Times*, May 13 2004.

out' in prison. Also, in *Campell v MGN*,[12] the House of Lords held that a model's privacy had been invaded when the newspapers printed stories about her drug habit, and she was awarded compensation. More significantly, in *A v Home Secretary*[13] the House of Lords held that the power to detain persons suspected of terrorism under the Anti-Terrorism, Crime and Security Act 2001 was incompatible with Article 5 of the Convention and thus declared the Act incompatible under section 4 of the Human Rights Act 1998.

**The student does not explain why the Act has been described as having great constitutional significance, or what constitutional, rather than legal, significance might be. She repeats the error about the Act providing a remedy for the first time, ignoring the pre-Act position. She mentions section 8 but has not put that section into any context because she has not yet explained the central provisions of the Act (including sections 6 and 7, which allow Convention rights actions against public authorities to be brought in legal proceedings). The case examples she uses would then have been useful had they been placed in that context.**

6. As we can see from the above cases, the Act has had a substantial effect on both the legal and constitutional system of the United Kingdom. Under section 2 of the Act the courts can now take into account the case law of the European Court and Commission of Human Rights when adjudicating upon human rights disputes in domestic law. In addition, they have the power to interpret legislation in line with the European Convention (under section 3 of the Act), and the power to declare both primary and secondary legislation as incompatible with the Convention (under section 4). Thus, in *R v A* (*Sexual History*)[14] the House of Lords held that the Youth Justice and Criminal Evidence Act 1999 could be interpreted so as to allow a defendant to cross-examine a rape victim wherever that was necessary to ensure the right to a fair trial under section 6 of the Act. The courts have also used their new power under section 4 of the Act to declare legislation incompatible with the European Convention. For example, in *A v Home Secretary* (above), section 26 of the Anti-Terrorism, Crime and Security Act 2001 was declared incompatible with Article 5 of the European Convention, which guarantees the right to liberty and security of the person.

**The paragraph opens with a claim that the previous paragraphs have addressed and illustrated the relevant legal and constitutional issues, which they have not. The student then gives information relating to some provisions of the Act that do have such an impact, but she does not explain the significance of those sections vis à vis issues such as precedent, the separation of powers and parliamentary sovereignty. Consequently the information via the cases adds little to the debate and does not assist in answering the question.**

7. Before the Act was passed domestic courts could not take the European Convention into account. For example, in *Malone v Metropolitan Police Commissioner*[15] it was held that the plaintiff could not rely on Article 8 of the European Convention when the police had tapped his telephone because it was pointed out that the Convention had not been incorporated into domestic law and that any remedy the plaintiff had under

---

[12][2004] 2 AC 457.
[13][2005] AC 68
[14][2002] 1 AC 1546
[15][1979] Ch 344.

▼

the Convention would have to be pursued before the European Court of Human Rights. In that case *Malone* took his case to Strasbourg (*Malone v United Kingdom*)[16] and the European Court held that the telephone tapping was in violation of his right to private life and correspondence. As a consequence Parliament enacted the Interception of Communications Act 1985, which put telephone tapping on a statutory footing, and this power is now contained in the Regulation of Investigatory Powers Act 2000. In another case, *R v Ministry of Defence, ex parte Smith*,[17] the Court of Appeal held that Article 8 of the Convention could not assist armed forces personnel who had been expelled from the armed forces because of their sexual orientation. On appeal, the European Court of Human Rights held that such expulsions were contrary to Articles 8 and 14 of the Convention and that the expulsions were disproportionate.[18] Following that decision the armed forces replaced the blanket ban with a conduct-based policy so as to comply with the judgment of the European Court.

**This paragraph contains some useful content, but again it is not put into context. The case examples could have been used early on to illustrate how the Act now allows the Convention to be used directly in domestic law, thus illustrating the change brought about by the Act to the old system. Instead, the student concentrates on the facts and the measures taken by the domestic authorities in response to the judgements, failing to mention the significance of the absence in domestic law of substantive human rights and doctrines such as proportionality.**

8. Under the Act the courts have got the power to interpret legislation compatibly with the European Convention, although this does not mean that they can refuse to apply clear legislation that is in breach of the Convention. In *Mendoza v Ghaidan*[19] the House of Lords held that the words 'living together as husband and wife' could be interpreted as 'as if they were living together as husband and wife'. Accordingly same sex partners were given equal treatment and this was re-enforced by the Civil Partnership Act 2004. On the other hand in *Bellinger v Bellinger*[20] the House of Lords refused to interpret the words man and woman to include a person who had undergone gender re-assignment. This was despite the European Court's decision in *Goodwin v United Kingdom*[21] that discrimination against transsexuals was in violation of Articles 8 and 14 of the Convention. As a result of the decision in *Goodwin* Parliament has enacted the Gender Reassignment Act 2004, which recognises the rights of transsexuals to change their sexual identity and to marry a person of their choice.

**This is the fist mention of section 3 and the courts' new interpretative powers. The section and its scope and wording are not properly examined, and there is no real mention of the legal and constitutional issues that might arise from that provision – for example, whether it gives the courts the power to legislate. Thus, the cases, which are very relevant, are simply presented as bald examples and reference is made to the background and the follow-up to the cases without exploring the legal and constitutional impact of the cases.**

---

[16](1984) 7 EHRR 14.
[17][1996] 1 All ER 257.
[18]*Smith and Grady v United Kingdom* (2000) 29 EHRR 493.
[19][2004] 2 AC 557.
[20][2003] 2 AC 467.
[21](2002) 35 EHRR 18.

9. The courts have also got the power under the act (section 4) to declare primary and secondary legislation incompatible with the European Convention, although again this does not empower the courts to overrule legislation. For example, in *R (Anderson and Taylor) v Home Secretary*[22] the House of Lords held that the Home Secretary's power to fix the minimum terms of life sentence prisoners was incompatible with Article 6 of the European Convention, which guarantees the right to a fair trial, including the right to a fair sentence. This decision followed the decision of the European Court of Human Rights in *Stafford v United Kingdom*,[23] where it was held that the Home Secretary's powers were inconsistent with the rule of law and the separation of powers and thus in breach of the Convention. Interestingly, the Court of Appeal in *Anderson* refused to declare the power of the Home Secretary as incompatible until the European Court had made its decision in *Stafford*, because before that decision the European Court had held that such a power was lawful with respect to mandatory life sentence prisoners.[24]

Section 4 is very relevant to the question, but the student does not highlight the relevant constitutional problems associated with it – for example, does it impact on parliamentary sovereignty? Instead, she provides a paraphrased account of the section's wording. This is followed by a rather long-winded account of the Anderson case, which does not really assist in addressing the relevant issue. The case is useful in illustrating parliamentary sovereignty and the status of European Court decisions, but the student doesn't really explain these points, providing instead some unnecessary detail about life sentences.

10. The Human Rights Act 1998 may also have a horizontal effect and thus apply to disputes between private individuals. Normally the Act only applies between individual victims and public authorities (as defined in section 6 of the Act). However, because the courts are public authorities under section 6 they have the duty to safeguard and uphold Convention rights and as a consequence the Act has been applied horizontally in the law of confidentiality in cases such as *Campbell v MGN*[25] and *Douglas v Hello!*[26] However, the House of Lords has held recently that the Act cannot be used to create a separate law of privacy, and that the decision in *Hello!* was confined to the law of confidentiality. Nevertheless the courts have gained extensive powers under the Act and can now apply the principles of proportionality when adjudicating upon disputes that raise Convention rights. Thus, any interference with a Convention right must now be necessary in a democratic society and be proportionate to any legitimate aim being pursued (*R (Daly) v Home Secretary*)[27] Furthermore, this test of proportionality is stricter than the previous test of *Wednesbury*[28] unreasonableness and will require the courts to take a more active approach to defending civil liberties.

The student mentions section 6 of the Act for the first time; this provision is absolutely central to the scope of the Act and the effect of the Act on the legal system! Because

---

[22][2002] 3 WLR 1800.
[23](2002) 35 EHRR 32.
[24]*Wynne v United Kingdom* (1994) 19 EHRR 333.
[25]See above, note 12.
[26][2001] 2 WLR 992.
[27][2001] 2 WLR 1622.
[28]*Associated Provincial Picture House Ltd v Wednesbury Corporation* [1948] 1KB 223.

those issues are not properly explored, she loses the impact of mentioning some of the relevant cases under that heading. There is then a non sequitur when she moves on to the doctrine of proportionality (again mentioning it for the first time). She fails to define proportionality and explain its significance and also fails to distinguish it from the Wednesbury test. Consequently, she finishes the paragraph by making a general and unsupported statement about civil liberties protection.

11. Since the Act came into force there have been a number of cases brought against public authorities claiming that Convention rights have been violated. For example, in *R v DPP, ex parte Pretty*[29] it was held that the European Convention was not violated when domestic law (the Suicide Act 1961) outlawed assisted suicide. The House of Lords held that the right to life guaranteed by Article 2 of the Convention did not include the right to die with dignity. This decision was upheld by the European Court of Human Rights in *Pretty v United Kingdom*[30] where it was confirmed that Article 2 was principally concerned with preserving life. Another example of the Act's use was in *A v Home Secretary* (above) where the House of Lords held that the indefinite detention of foreign person suspected of acts of terrorism was in breach of Article 5 of the European Convention. The House of Lords held that although there was an emergency threatening the life of the nation within Article 15 of the Convention, the measures within the Anti-Terrorism, Crime and Security Act 2001 were both discriminatory and disproportionate and thus incompatible with the Convention. As a result the government introduced the Terrorism Bill 2005 into Parliament.

This paragraph contains some useful cases, but the student wastes them by not explaining their significance and by failing earlier to explain the basic provisions of the Act and its constitutional and legal scope and impact. The decision in A has now been used three times, but the student doesn't really explore the significance of that decision with respect to the question.

12. In conclusion, the Human Rights Act 1998 has had a profound effect on the protection of human rights and has thus impacted on both the legal and constitutional system in the United Kingdom. The courts can now take the Convention and its case law into account and thus must apply European principles to human rights cases. Further, the courts have new powers of interpretation under section 3 of the Act and under section 4 can declare legislation incompatible with the Convention. Since the implementation of the Act the courts can use the Convention in domestic law and the individual no longer has to make use of the procedure under the European Convention. This will save considerable time and expense, although it should be pointed out that the victim can still make use of that procedure if they are unsuccessful under the Human Rights Act. These new powers, therefore, have had a profound effect on the legal system and the constitution in the United Kingdom, bringing rights home to domestic law.

The conclusion presumes that the student has covered the central issues raised by the question, which she has not. Thus, there is no firm basis for any of her conclusions, and she ends up summarising the provisions of the Act and making an unsupported and vague statement that the Act has had a profound effect in those areas.

---

[29][2002] 1 AC 800.
[30](2002) 35 EHRR 1.

HOW TO WRITE BETTER LAW ESSAYS

---

### BIBLIOGRAPHY

Ewing K and Bradley A, *Constitutional and Administrative Law* (Longman 2002)

Foster, S *Human Rights and Civil Liberties* (Longman 2003)

---

## Summary of Errors

- In general, the student did not address or answer the question, and the information that she did provide was sometimes irrelevant. Thus, although she includes some reasonable information on the Act, the European Convention and the protection of human rights, little of it addresses the issue of whether and to what extent the Act has impacted on the constitutional and legal system. In addition, when she does mention information that is relevant to those issues, she does not take the opportunity of highlighting the significance of that information, or case, to the question.

- She does not appear to have understood the question or the issues that it raises. She does not seem able to identify the potential impact of the Act on the legal system and the Constitution and perhaps is confused on how the two issues can be distinguished or might overlap.

- A lot of the information relates to the machinery and case law of the European Convention on Human Rights, rather than the provisions and effect of the Human Rights Act itself.

- She deals with some relevant cases but rarely makes the relevant point, failing to extract the real issue of the case and providing instead unnecessary detail on the facts of and decision in the case.

- She omits discussion of some provisions of the Act that are relevant to the question, such as the effect of the Act on the legislative process (sections 10 and 19 of the Act).

- Many of the points the student makes are repetitive, such as that there is no longer the need to go to Strasbourg.

- Most of the cases are not explained clearly, and some of her explanations of the Act's provisions are general and vague.

- The content (where relevant) would have been improved by a closer reading of the Act, the cases and the secondary sources.

- The bibliography was limited and did not contain any texts on legal system or recent articles on the relevant legal and constitutional issues.

- In the conclusion, the student professes to have raised the constitutional and legal issues raised by the question, but in truth she hasn't.

## What Is the Essay Worth?

One would expect the marker to reply with comments such as the following:

### Marker's Feedback

The essay is reasonably well written, although a little general at times. You have raised some relevant points about the Act and the Convention, but you do not address the question. What legal and constitutional issues **are** raised by the Act, and **how** has the

Act impacted on those issues? You need to explore the scope of the Act's provisions and the powers of the courts under the Act, and then assess their impact on the legal and constitutional system. For example, how has the Act impacted on matters such as precedent, the public/private law divide, the separation of powers, the constitutional role of the courts, sovereignty of parliament and the provision of legal remedies for human rights violations? You do not really address any of these issues, but rather provide some unfocused information about the Convention, the Act and some case law under both.

You have wasted a lot of your research and some very useful case law by not discussing the law in the context of the question. Read the question and address the issues raised by that question!! **34%**

## How Could This Essay Be Improved?

The student needs to look at the question carefully and to make a careful plan of her answer, identifying the central thrust of the question, the issues that she is going to raise and the specific provisions of the Act and any case law that she is going to use in support of her answer.

She should have identified the following:

- The question suggests that the Act has had a profound constitutional and legal effect; therefore, the answer should concentrate on either substantiating or refuting that suggestion.
- The question mentions the impact on both the British Constitution and the English Legal System, so the answer must identify the potential and actual impact on both. To do this, the student must appreciate the difference between the legal system and the constitution and be able to identify relevant statutory provisions and case law that may have, or have had, an impact on both.
- To examine whether the Act has had a profound effect, the student must examine the pre-Act as well as the post-Act situation and consider carefully the aims of the 1998 Act.

A plan for the answer would, therefore, look something like this:

- a general explanation of the role of human rights protection in a constitutional and legal system;
- an examination of the reasons why the Act was passed, including a summary of the pre-Act position and any defects of that system;
- an examination and explanation of the central provisions of the Act as they affect the British Constitution and any of its basic principles (e.g., the separation of powers, the rule of law, sovereignty of power and the constitutional role of the courts), along with an examination of any statutory or case developments to support the contention that the Act has had a profound impact;
- an examination of the same with respect to the impact of the Act on various aspects of the legal system (e.g., judicial precedent, judicial law-making, the parliamentary law process, statutory interpretation, the development of the common law);
- general conclusions as to the truth of the statement in the question.

# Part B: The Good Essay

**'The passing of the Human Rights Act 1998 has had a profound effect on both the British Constitution and the English Legal System.' Discuss**

1. The protection of human rights and civil liberties is a principal function of any state's legal system, providing as it does an effective method of redress when fundamental rights are transgressed. In addition, such protection will impact on the state's constitution, addressing questions such as the constitutional role of the courts, the separation of powers and, particularly within the British Constitution, the sovereignty of Parliament.[1] The passing of the Human Rights Act 1998 ('the Act'), under which rights are to be brought home, and the European Convention on Human Rights is to be given further effect in domestic law,[2] appears to raise a number of legal and constitutional questions, some of which, as we shall see, overlap. This essay will examine the Act's content and operation in order to assess the impact of it on the United Kingdom's constitutional and legal system.

   *The student has identified the central thrust of the question and the relevant aspects of the 1998 Act that should be concentrated on. She has identified that the Act gives rise to issues with respect to both the constitutional and the legal system and tells the reader how she is to tackle those issues and the extent to which they might overlap.*

2. According to the long title, the Act was passed to give further effect to the rights and freedoms guaranteed by the European Convention on Human Rights 1950. As this will involve the partial incorporation of the Convention into domestic law, the Act is bound to have some effect on the constitutional arrangements for the protection of human rights in domestic law, which in turn will impact on both the constitutional role of the courts as well as the sovereignty and autonomy of, respectively, Parliament and executive government.[3] The 'incorporation' of the Convention into domestic law questions whether the United Kingdom would follow many other states in establishing an entrenched and supreme bill of rights, which will protect fundamental rights from the general law. This would indeed fundamentally alter the traditional common law system of rights protection, favoured by writers such as Dicey, whereby such rights were protected within the traditional law.[4] Furthermore, the idea that these rights could be upheld by the courts despite conflicting legislation would be contrary to the doctrine of the sovereignty of Parliament, thereby clashing fundamentally with the central principle of the British Constitution.[5]

   *The student begins to identify and address the potential impact of the Act on the Constitution by explaining the traditional constitutional position and by identifying*

---

[1]See Foster, S *Human Rights and Civil Liberties* (2003), at pages 15-17.

[2]Home Office, *Rights Brought Home: The Human Rights Bill*, Cm 3782. See also Wadham and Mountfield, *Blackstone's Guide to the Human Rights Act* 1998 (OUP 2003), pages 6-11.

[3]See Feldmam, The Human Rights Act and Constitutional Principles (1999) LS 195.

[4]Dicey, AV *Introduction to the Law of the Constitution* (Macmillan 1965).

[5]For general discussion on the constitutional effect of the Act, see Bradley, A and Ewing, K *Constitutional and Administrate* Law (Longman 2003), chapter 19).

the potential constitutional changes brought about by the passing of the Act. There are also good references to secondary sources.

3. However, both of these fears remain largely unfounded. First, the Act does not create a domestic bill of rights as such, but instead allows the traditional domestic law to be informed by the rights contained in the Convention, and for the domestic courts to enforce the Convention in legal disputes which raise Convention rights. Secondly, the Act makes it quite clear that the new powers of the courts to enforce Convention rights do not disturb the validity and application of conflicting legislation, where such provisions are clearly in conflict with the Convention.[6] Thus, the sovereignty of legislation passed and authorised by Parliament is preserved under the Act and the domestic courts do not have the general power to overrule legislative and executive acts that violate human rights, as does, for example, the US Supreme Court.[7] This principle is also reflected with respect to the potential supremacy of the European Convention over domestic law. Whilst the European Communities Act 1972 incorporates relevant European Community law into domestic law and attempts to give supremacy of such law when it is in conflict with domestic law, the Human Rights Act does not create a direct conflict, and instead preserves parliamentary sovereignty when compatibility with the Convention cannot be achieved by the domestic courts via interpretation.[8] Thus, the constitutional principle whereby international law does not override domestic law is maintained, despite the duty of the courts, under s. 2 of the Act, to take into account the case law of the European Court and Commission of Human Rights when adjudicating upon disputes that raise Convention rights.

The student displays a keen awareness of the true nature of the Act and its potential impact on the Constitution, explaining very clearly the nature and scope of the Act and the cautious method of incorporation adopted by the Act. Relevant references are made to key provisions of the Act to illustrate these observations.

4. Despite the retention of parliamentary sovereignty, the Act does provide the courts with powers to enforce Convention rights, which might create a shift of power from the legislative and the executive to the courts. Thus, s. 3 of the Act empowers the courts, *so far as it is possible to do so*, to interpret both primary and secondary legislation in a manner which is compatible with the European Convention. This section allows the courts to find a Convention-friendly interpretation even where the legislation in question is not truly ambiguous.[9] Although the section makes it clear that this power does not affect the validity of legislation (primary or secondary) which is incompatible with the Convention,[10] this new power of interpretation, if abused by the courts, might lead them to giving a strained interpretation to clear legislative provisions and thus blur the distinction between interpretation and law-making. In the post-Act era, although the courts have stressed that their role is one of interpretation, and

---

[6]See ss. 3 and 4 of the Act.

[7]See Feldman, *Civil Liberties and Human Rights in England and Wales* (OUP 2002), at page 60.

[8]See ss. 3 and 4 of the Act, discussed below.

[9]See Lester, A The Act of the Possible: Interpreting Statutes under the Human Rights Act [1998] EHRLR 665, and Stychin, C and Mulcahy, D *Legal Method: Text and Materials* (Sweet and Maxwell 2003), pages 251-282.

[10]Section 3(2)(b) and (c) of the Act.

does not entitle them to legislate, there have been instances where the courts have taken a robust and inventive approach. For example in *R v A (Sexual History)*[11] the House of Lords held that the niceties of statutory language could be subordinated in the desire to achieve a Convention-compliant result, thus making it possible to read up or read down legislation which appeared on its face to be in conflict with the Convention. Similarly, in *Mendoza v Ghaidan*[12] the House of Lords held that it was possible to depart from the traditional meaning of the Act so as to make it compliant with Convention rights. On the other hand the courts have been reluctant to re-interpret legislation when to do so would clearly conflict with the aims and policy of the Act, and where repeal or amendment of such legislation would be more appropriately carried out by Parliament.[13] Further, s. 3 cannot be used where that would amount to 'judicial vandalism' of clear legislative provisions.[14]

**The student now balances the observations made in the previous paragraph with some discussion of the courts' increased powers under the Act, as well as an appraisal of their likely and actual impact on issues such as the constitutional role of the courts. She uses several good case examples to illustrate the points she makes and provides a balanced account of the cases with respect to their constitutional impact.**

5. Further, s. 4 of the Act allows the higher courts to issue a declaration of incompatibility with respect to both primary and secondary legislation that cannot be read consistently with Convention rights. Although this does not allow the courts to strike down or refuse to apply such legislation, it does allow them to pass judgment on the compatibility of legislation passed or authorised by Parliament.[15] For example, the courts have issued declarations of incompatibility with respect to legislation which imposed disproportionate criminal penalties,[16] which denied transsexuals the right to marry,[17] and which gave the Home Secretary the right to fix sentences for mandatory lifers.[18] It should be noted, however, that in such cases the relevant legislation remains in place and that Parliament is left with the power to amend or repeal such legislation,[19] or, indeed, to ignore the court's ruling altogether.

**Again, the student explains a central provision of the Act in a manner that provides the basis for a balanced argument as to the likely effect of that provision on the Constitution. She offers a range of case examples, which illustrate their impact without giving unnecessary detail of their facts and decision.**

6. In particular, the Act, by allowing the domestic courts to take into account the jurisprudence and principles of the European Convention on Human Rights, has

---

[11] [2002] 1 AC 1546.
[12] [2004] 2 AC 557.
[13] *Bellinger v Bellinger* [2003] 2 AC 467 See also Lord Millett in *Medoza* (above) who felt it was inappropriate to interpret a statute inconsistently with its original aim when its amendment was a matter for Parliament.
[14] *R (Anderson and Taylor) v Home Secretary* [2002] 3 WLR 1800.
[15] See, in particular the decision of the House of Lords in *A v Home Secretary*, discussed below.
[16] *International Transport Roth GmbH v Home Secretary* [2002] 3 WLR 344.
[17] *Bellinger v Bellinge*, above, note 13.
[18] *R (Anderson and Taylor) v Home Secretary*, above note 14.
[19] The Minister will probably use the procedure under s. 10 of the Act, discussed later.

▼

impacted on the separation of powers and the level of deference expected of the judiciary towards both the executive and Parliament.[20] Since the Act's coming into force the courts are free to apply the principle of proportionality when assessing the balance between the achievement of a legitimate aim (such as national security or public safety) and the protection of Convention rights. In *R (Daly) v Home Secretary*[21] Lord Steyn warned that proportionality allowed the courts to conduct a more intensive review of acts that infringe fundamental rights, going beyond the traditional *Wednesbury* unreasonableness test,[22] which only allowed the courts to interfere if there was strong evidence of irrationality. Although Lord Steyn stressed that this did not allow a merits-based review, subsequent case law shows that the courts will be prepared to take a robust approach in the defence of human rights. For example, in *A v Home Secretary*[23] the House of Lords declared detention powers under the Anti-Terrorism, Crime and Security Act 2001 incompatible with the right to liberty of the person, despite the powers being authorised by Parliament, and despite the government lodging a derogation under the Act to accommodate the threat of terrorism. Such an approach appears radically different from the traditional principles of judicial review, although as Lord Bingham stated in that case, this approach has been sanctioned by Parliament itself, by passing the 1998 Act.

The student places greater emphasis on a central aspect of the courts' new powers – the use of proportionality. She is careful to explain the significance of this power and to contrast it with the traditional position before the Act. She also uses the 'Belmarsh' case as a stark example of the courts' new approach and justified the use of such power in the context of the aims of the Act itself.

7. In addition to the constitutional ramifications, the Act also impacts on the general legal system in areas such as precedent, legal process and remedies. For example, the court's duty to take into account the case law of the European Court and Commission of Human Rights (under s. 2), coupled with its new powers of statutory interpretation under s. 3 (above), affects the traditional principles of judicial precedent. Accordingly, if a previous decision of a higher court is now inconsistent with a ruling of the European Court of Human Rights, that decision can now be departed from, even by a lower court. This reflects Parliament's intention that the domestic courts should follow the Convention case law, although it has been held that unless the European decision deals specifically with the domestic law issue, the courts should wait until the House of Lords rules on that point before departing from earlier authority.[24] Similarly, with respect to s. 3 of the Act, domestic courts are now allowed to depart from previous interpretations of primary and secondary legislation. This again reflects Parliament's intention that statutory provisions are, wherever possible, to be compatible with the enjoyment of Convention rights.

The student now begins to address the effect of the Act on the legal system and identifies a number of aspects of the system that might be so affected. She then moves

---

[20]See Edwards, R Judicial deference under the Human Rights Act (2002) MLR 859.
[21][2001] 2 WLR 622.
[22]*Associated Provincial Picture Houses Ltd v Wednesbury Corporation* [1948] 1 KB 223.
[23][2005] 2 AC 68.
[24]*Price v Leeds County Council* [2005] 1 WLR 1925.

HOW TO WRITE BETTER LAW ESSAYS

swiftly to the first aspect (judicial precedent), clearly and succinctly explaining the effect of ss.2 and 3 on the traditional doctrine of precedent and providing clear general examples. She also makes an effort to explain the rationale of those provisions.

8. The Act also addresses the duty of the legal system to provide redress for violations of human rights. Formerly, the legal system provided redress thorough traditional private law remedies,[25] but the 'incorporation' of the Convention into domestic means that specific procedures and redress will be available for human rights cases in addition to existing public and private law remedies. Under s. 6 of the Act it is now unlawful for a public authority to act in a way that is incompatible with a Convention right, and under s. 7 the victim of any violation may either bring proceedings for such under the Act or rely on the Convention rights in any legal proceedings. This will affect how the traditional criminal and civil courts deal with cases which raise Convention rights, because whether the Convention issue is raised in direct proceedings under the Act or in other public, criminal or civil proceedings, the court will need to consider its powers under the Human Rights Act. This will include its power under s. 8 of the Act to grant just and equitable orders for the commission of unlawful violations by public authorities, including the power to award just satisfaction in the form of compensation, and in this respect the courts must be informed by the case law of the European Court of Human Rights.[26]

*The student now moves to the next issue, summarising the main effect of the Act on the provision of legal remedies for human rights violations, contrasting it with the previous position and explaining how such remedies will be addressed and provided in practice. Again, good use is made of references to either case examples or statutory provisions.*

9. More specifically, the Act creates a further public/private law divide with respect to the bringing of legal actions against public bodies. In general, the Act only applies to violations committed by 'public authorities' (s. 6) and this has required the courts to apply the distinction previously employed in determining the availability of judicial review proceedings.[27] Thus, in the post-Act era, the courts have had to distinguish between pure public authorities, which are liable under the Act, and bodies who despite carrying out functions affecting the public, are nevertheless essentially private.[28] However, as the courts are public authorities under the Act,[29] it is possible for the Act to have a 'horizontal' effect and thus inform disputes in the private law domain. Thus, the case law and principles of the Convention have been used to develop the law of confidentiality,[30] although the House of Lords has stressed that the Act largely applies to public authorities and that it is not necessary to develop a private common law action in privacy.[31]

*This aspect of the Act follows on neatly from the previous paragraph and deals with a more specific concern – the effect of the Act on the public/private law divide. Having*

---

[25]For example, in the law of trespass: see *Entick v Carrington* (1765) St Tr 1030.
[26]See section 8(4) of the 1998 Act and article 41 of the European Convention on Human Rights (1950).
[27]*O'Reilly v Mackman* [1983] 2 AC 237.
[28]Contrast the decision in *Heather, Ward and Callin v Leonard Cheshire Foundation* [2002] 2 All ER 936 with *Poplar Housing Association v Donogue* [2001] 2 WLR 1546.
[29]See s. 6(3) of the Act.
[30]See *Douglas v Hello!* [2001] 2 WLR 992 and *Campbell v MGN Ltd* [2004] 2 AC 457.
[31]*Wainwright v Home Office* [2004] 2 AC 406.

▼

identified the particular concern, the student then refers to relevant case law with respect to the definition of public authorities and then introduces the possibility of the Act applying in the private sphere, again referring to relevant authority. The paragraph provides a good and balanced account of the legal position in this area.

10. Finally, the Act has impacted on the general legislative process.[32] For example, under s. 19 of the Act the relevant Minister must, before the Second Reading of any Bill, either make a statement of compatibility of the Bill with the Convention, or make a statement that the Bill is incompatible, but that nevertheless he wishes the House to proceed with the Bill.[33] This seeks to ensure that Parliament passes compatible legislation, although such a declaration of compatibility would not stop the courts using its powers under ss. 3 and 4 of the Act (above). In addition, s. 10 of the Act provides a fast track procedure for the amendment of incompatible legislation, thus re-iterating that the ultimate power of legislative amendment lies with the government thorough Parliament.

The student now winds up her discussion of the Act and the legal system by considering the impact on the legislative process, identifying two central provisions of the Act in this respect. The description of the provisions is coupled with a balanced and intelligent commentary on their rationale and potential impact.

11. In conclusion, the Act has provided the courts with new powers of interpretation and review, and allows victims a more structured system for redressing human rights violations. The 'incorporation' of the European Convention allows European Convention case law and principles to inform domestic law and for individuals to seek redress more akin to the system applied by the European Court of Human Rights. However, the Act simply gives 'further effect' to the Convention, and retains the essential constitutional and legal structure of the United Kingdom, in particular the concept of the sovereignty of Parliament. Accordingly, given the method of incorporation adopted by the Act, together with the relatively cautious approach taken by the judiciary in enforcing the Act, it would be incorrect to suggest that the Act has had a *profound* effect on the constitutional and legal system.

The conclusion reflects the approach taken by the student in the main body of the essay. Thus, it neatly summarises the central issues raised in the main text and contains a reasoned and balanced conclusion on the truth of the statement within the question. Note that she stresses the word *profound* to display the careful conclusion, illustrating that she is always addressing the question.

## BIBLIOGRAPHY

Bradley, A and Ewing, K *Constitutional and Administrative Law* (Longman 2003) 13th edition

Feldman, D *Civil Liberties and Human Rights in England and Wales* (OUP 2003) 2nd edition

Feldman, D The Human Rights Act and Constitutional Principles (1999) LS 195

Foster, S *Human Rights and Civil Liberties* (Longman 2003)

Lester, A The Act of the Possible: Interpreting Statutes under the Human Rights Act [1998] EHRLR 665

Nicol, D The Human Rights Act and Politicians (2004) LS 451

---

[32]See in particular, Nicol, D 'The Human Rights Act and Politicians (2004) LS 451.'

[33]Thus far, the Communications Bill 2003 has been the only Bill stated to be incompatible with the European Convention, with respect to its ban on political advertising.

Slapper, G and Kelly, D *The English Legal System* (Cavendish 2004), 7th edition

Stychin, K and Mulcahy, D *Legal Method: Text and Materials* (Sweet and Maxwell 2003), 2nd edition

Wadham, J and Mountfield, H and Edmundson, A Blackstone's *Guide to the Human Rights Act 1998* (OUP 2003) 3rd edition

## Summary of Good Points

- The student has looked at the question very carefully and has decided which issues need to be raised with respect to the Act. The answer is well structured and appears to correspond to a clear plan.

- She has distinguished between issues relating to the constitution and those relating to the legal system, whilst identifying that the issues may well overlap.

- Given the word limit and the wide scope of the question, she covers a wide range of issues in the essay, choosing the most controversial and pressing concerns relating to the Act and its impact.

- She displays a sound understanding of the relevant law and a confidence with the various legal and constitutional issues raised by the question.

- She refers to a variety of statutory provisions and relevant case law, being careful to exclude unnecessary detail.

- Her consideration of each issue is reasoned and balanced, always addressing the question and making way for her conclusion.

- Her conclusion is neat and covers the salient points that she has made during the essay. It concludes with an intelligent and reasoned comment on the truth of the statement contained in the question, which is backed up by the content of the essay.

- Her bibliography contains a sound selection of texts and articles and displays wide reading in the area considering the level at which she is studying.

## What Is It Worth?

Given the broad range of the question and the amount of issues that needed to be raised and addressed by the student, the answer is a very good one. It shows evidence of a wide knowledge of, and wide reading in, the area and is well written and very well structured. In particular, it shows expertise in including so much information in the answer whilst retaining a critical and analytical approach. It could, perhaps, have been a little more critical, and the student could have made more use of some of the academic opinion contained in her bibliography, as well as some further extracts from judges. All in all, it is a very good essay and may be regarded as a 'bare first.'

## Summary of Points on Good Essay Techniques

- Read the question thoroughly the moment you get it so that you can pick up on any clues in lectures and seminars and do your basic research and reading as soon as possible.

- Always ensure that you know the legal area thoroughly before attempting to write out your answer; this will help you understand the question and locate relevant sources. Read the set text very carefully and then advance to further and more specialist texts and articles.

- Never leave the research and planning of your answer until the last minute, even though you may write it up at the eleventh hour.
- Always plan your answer to ensure that you are answering the set question. Carefully plan what you are going to say and how it is to be structured in individual paragraphs.
- Always follow the three-stage pattern: Say what the question is about and what you are going to say, say it and then conclude by saying what you have said.
- Follow the academic *style* (not the actual content) adopted in good textbooks and journals and adopt that style in your essays.
- Make sure that when you include legal authority in the form of statutes, cases and so on that they enhance your answer.
- Make the most of your research and ensure that you use the appropriate parts of books, articles, cases and statutes in your essay.
- Avoid plagiarism and ensure that you have displayed your own understanding.
- Always ensure that you read through your answer to check for typographical and spelling mistakes, to ensure that the essay makes sense and to confirm that you have answered the question.

Remember: It is much easier to apply these skills if you engage with your law studies and with the individual modules. By undertaking regular and in-depth study you will witness and then acquire the necessary writing skills in addition to substantive legal knowledge.

You can test your skills by carrying out the relevant exercises on the Companion Website (**www.pearsoned.co.uk/foster**)

# 4  Answering Problem Questions

## ● Introduction

This chapter looks at the particular skills required of the student when tackling problem type questions.

Specifically, it:

- provides simple advice on how to plan answers to problem questions;
- enables students to identify central issues raised in such questions;
- provides advice on how to apply the relevant law to the facts of any given scenario;
- advises students on how to avoid bad practice when tackling such questions, such as ignoring the scenario and writing general essay answers, failing to give advice to the concerned parties or allowing for a number of possible answers and solutions.

The chapter contains two examples of problem-type questions and a good and bad answer to each question. It also contains an appraisal of each answer, highlighting the strengths and weaknesses of each answer and providing hints as to how they could have been improved, and what marks each answer might receive.

## ● Understanding Problem Questions

### What Are Problem Questions?

Problem questions are based around a hypothetical scenario, which raises a number of legal issues that require the student to give advice to the parties affected by the situation. They are set in almost all legal subjects but are particularly evident in subjects such as contract, tort, criminal law and property law, although they can often appear in constitutional and administrative law assessments, particularly in the areas of human rights and administrative law.

### Why Are They Set?

Problem questions are set in order to test the student's ability to *apply* the relevant legal principles that they have studied to a set of facts. This will test the student's knowledge and appreciation of the law that they have been taught, but more specifically will require them to explain how the law will be applied in a given factual situation. Such questions will thus test the student's ability to identify the relevant legal issues, to digest legal material including case law, and to decide whether and how that law can be applied to the given facts. By setting problem questions, the lecturer will be able to identify whether the student has fully appreciated the law and cases that have been explained to him or her. They will also test the student's ability to explain the law and its application to another person (usually a layperson) in a simple, clear and professionally legal style.

## How Are They Different From Essay Questions?

Unlike essay questions, problem questions do not simply ask the student to explain and analyse the relevant legal principles and case law in a given area. Specifically, they ask the student to advise the parties as to how the law will apply to them. Thus, although the student will need a thorough knowledge of the law and the cases, they will not be expected to give a detailed account of those principles or to supply an academic analysis or critique of the law. Rather, the student must concentrate on giving advice to the parties after explaining the law in as simple a fashion as possible and only in respect of the specific issues raised by the scenario.

## Why Are They More Difficult Than Essay Questions?

As stated previously, the problem question not only tests the student's ability to learn legal principles and cases but also asks the student to apply that law to a factual situation. To do this the student needs to:

- appreciate and understand what he or she has learnt;
- identify which legal issues are raised by the given scenario;
- decide which cases and other materials are relevant to the given scenario;
- identify possible legal arguments so as to apply established law to the facts, or to distinguish such law on the facts;
- explain the law clearly to the interested parties;
- consider all possible arguments and to assess their respective strengths;
- draw sensible, logical and supportable conclusions.

With some essay questions, the student can provide a reasonable answer simply by learning the relevant law, even where they do not really appreciate what they are saying. Even where the essay question asks for a critical analysis, the germ of the answer can usually be located in the student's text or other sources.

With problem questions, however, students are to a great extent on their own. They will need to know the law, but to advise someone as to how it applies requires the student to truly understand what that law is saying and what its significance is. Consequently, students who have gone through the course without truly engaging with the subject will find problem questions especially difficult because they do not provide one with anywhere to hide. Students cannot simply write about the general legal principles and the cases they have read about in the book; they must be able to identify the relevant legal area (essay titles at least give students that clue) and then apply this general knowledge to the facts.

However, we should not go away with the idea that problem questions are insurmountable and that they should be avoided if at all possible. Some students prefer problem questions to essay questions, perhaps because they like the constraints of a specific scenario and often cannot determine what an essay question is getting at. In addition, the problem question tests different skills that some students might excel at, such as the structuring and ordering of legal issues, the ability to explain the law to a layperson and the ability to spot potential legal arguments within the factual scenario. Although problem questions do not allow students to waffle, they can pick up valuable marks by identifying a particular legal argument and by putting together a cogent argument in favour of one of the parties. Thus, some students are good at remembering massive amounts of legal information and providing academic commentary and criticism, whereas others have more practical skills and prefer to apply the law to the facts of a hypothetical problem.

Whatever skills you have as a student – and you may have both – you must acquire the basis skills in order to answer problem questions; you are not going to survive on your law course if you cannot do this. Below are a number of points about tackling problem questions, which you should find useful when faced with this type of question. But remember, you cannot exercise these skills before you learn the relevant legal principles. A good, sound knowledge of the legal principles and the cases is a prerequisite of tackling problem questions, so do not go away with the idea that they are the type of question you can answer with pure common sense and good problem solving skills.

## ● Tackling Problem Questions

### Identifying the Legal Areas and the Specific Problems

This aspect of problem questions is perhaps the one that students experience most difficulty with. Many students will look at a factual scenario and fail to identify what legal issue is raised. Inevitably, therefore, the student will provide an inappropriate answer by including the wrong law and cases and missing out the central issues.

There is no easy mechanism for solving this issue other than saying that you must know your law before you attempt any problem question. If you have engaged with the lectures, (and particularly the seminars) in the relevant module, the likelihood is that you will recognise the legal issues raised in the scenario. The chances are that you will have gone through similar scenarios in seminars; in addition, there are a number of self-test questions included in your textbooks and examples given in question and answer books, which will be reasonably similar to the scenario you are now faced with. This will help you identify the specific issues raised in the question, and along with a good knowledge of the cases studied on the specific module, you should now be ready to start answering the question.

You should thus identify the legal areas immediately and include these in your plan and, briefly, in your introduction. You can then begin your answer by saying something like the following: "This question is concerned with the area of misrepresentation and whether a person can avoid a contract when a misrepresentation has been made to her during negotiations leading up to the conclusion of the contract." Note that at this stage you should avoid launching into a long explanation of the law (of misrepresentation); the preceding introduction merely identifies the area of law and explains the importance of that area to the parties concerned.

More importantly, you must identify the specific legal arguments that will need to be raised in the answer. Again, you need to make a plan of these points:

1. Did X make a statement of fact, rather than future intention?
2. Was Y induced to enter into that contract because of that statement?

3. More specifically, did Y rely on X's statement, or rather on his own investigations and experience?

4. If he did, can he recover the loss that he is claiming?

In addition, in your plan, but not necessarily in your introduction, you can include the cases and other legal sources that you are going to use when answering these specific points.

These points can then form the basis of the introduction to your answer, and such questions can be asked every time you begin addressing each issue in turn. Such an introduction will provide a focus for your answer and a guide for you as to which point to deal with next.

## Giving Clear, Simple but Full Advice

Remember, with problem questions you are giving advice to the interested parties. They want to know what the relevant law is but are only interested in the specific legal issues that are raised in their dispute. Ensure that your advice is:

### Clear

Your answer must deal with the relevant points in a structured and ordered manner. You also need to take the advised parties through the law and its application clearly. If your answer lacks this cohesion and structure, the person you are advising will become confused, and more importantly, the marker will think that *you* are confused as to the law, the relevant issues and the application of the law to the facts.

### Simple

This does not mean that your client is simple, or that you can use a casual and unprofessional style. Rather, it means that the interested parties do not want a complicated and academically analytical answer that you might write in an essay question. You will often be asked to advise laypersons (e.g., a businessperson, a consumer) as to the law, and they will not appreciate it if your answer is riddled with academic jargon. You should write in plain and simple English, avoiding overly complex legal language wherever possible. However, the lecturer will expect you to write like a lawyer (or at least a law student) and not a layperson. Your style should combine clarity that would appeal to the lay person and legal professionalism. In other words, you are writing the answer for *both* the parties involved and the module leader. Study the following styles:

---

**Examples**

1. "Your problem is about the law of misrepresentation, which is where one party tells the other a lie and the other is tricked to enter into a contract."

   This is far too informal and unprofessional.

2. "The scenario raises the possibility that the apparent agreement has been vitiated by misrepresentation, a factor which will allow the innocent party to rescind the contract." Professor Treitel has noted that the difference between a misrepresentation and a contractual term is often an illusory one and . . ."

   This is too academic and complex. Your client does not want an academic analysis or the views of academic authors on conceptual matters that do not really concern him or her. If you are going to use words such as rescind and vitiating, provide a simple translation and, perhaps, example to illustrate.

---

3. 'The scenario faced by John concerns the law of misrepresentation, whereby a person may seek to avoid a contract if during the negotiations a false statement of fact has been made to him or her, which then induces that person to enter into that contract. An actionable misrepresentation therefore consists of . . . (a simple definition)'

This introduction is both simple and legally professional. It avoids academic jargon or complex conceptual arguments and issues, and provides the person to be advised with a straightforward explanation of the legal area involved. It also shows the marker that you are familiar with relevant and appropriate legal phrases and concepts, but that equally you can explain them simply to the lay person.

### Full

The client will want you to cover every angle and to provide as many feasible solutions as possible. A good answer will think of a number of possible interpretations and outcomes, but at the very least you need to cover the essential arguments.

## Do Not Just State the Law

Many students fill out their answers to problem questions with a general account of the law and do not address the facts of the given scenario or apply the law to those facts. Thus, they show that they understand the law, or at least that they are able to locate the relevant legal issues and cases in their texts, but fail to address the facts and apply those principles and cases to the given facts.

Many students fail problem questions because they simply state the relevant law (and often include some irrelevant law) and do not make any real effort to address the issues or to give advice. As a consequence, students can receive low marks even though they have a good knowledge of the law and have written a well structured answer, displaying sound research and writing skills.

## Use Only Relevant Cases and Statutes and Apply Them to the Facts

- Remember, the person you are advising has no interest in the general law, how it is developing and what people think about it, *unless* it has a bearing on the outcome of their dispute. Thus, discuss legal principles or cases to assist you in giving advice on the particular facts, and concentrate on those principles and cases as they affect the possible outcome of that dispute.
- Students tend to give a general explanation of the law or of a specific area because the information is contained in their notes or textbooks. Avoid this mistake and only include principles and cases if they are relevant to the factual situation.
- Once you have raised a relevant legal point, apply it (and the case law) to the facts and consider its possible application to those facts *before* you move on to the next point.

## Do Not Give Vague and Open Advice

- You will not be expected to give the definitive answer to the legal issues raised by the scenario. Often the law and its application are unclear, and it will not be certain whether the rules apply to a given set of facts.

- However, you will be expected to come to a logical and feasible conclusion on the facts based on your knowledge and appreciation of the law and its potential application.
- You cannot avoid the task of giving advice to the concerned parties by either ignoring the possible application of the law to the facts altogether or by providing vague or open advice. Look at the following example.

This fails to inform Jack as to the likely outcome of his dispute. In effect, the student is saying 'Well, I have given you the law and the cases, now sort the rest out yourself.' This is not only unhelpful to Jack, but it shows that the student is unable to apply the relevant law and cases to the facts and that he does not really appreciate the law and its application. The student is thus failing in the central task, even though his knowledge of the general law is sound.

## Always Read the Facts Carefully

It is amazing how many students, when asked in a seminar 'Do you think Jack intended to accept John's offer in the seminar question before us?' start looking for the answer in their lecture notes or textbooks! The notes and books will give you information on the general law, but that question can only be answered by looking carefully at the facts of the scenario in the seminar question and discovering whether what he said or did amounts to acceptance in the legal sense.

You must, therefore, look at the facts very carefully before answering the question: Make a list of factual as well as legal problems raised in the scenario (see the plan to the good answers in the next section) and ensure that you address those factual issues. You will then be able to offer constructive advice on the basis of the similarity, or otherwise, of the facts in the case with previous cases.

## Don't Repeat the Facts

Too many students pad out their answers by reciting the facts of the scenario. This is not helpful and is taking up time better spent on addressing the issues raised by those (already established) facts.

## Consider All Options

- Your advice should include your consideration of all the legal possibilities and solutions to the problem. You must address all possibilities, even if you ultimately opt for one conclusion and reject the others.

For example, if the question posed is whether X has accepted Y's offer, you should consider both possible arguments – that his conduct *was* evidence of acceptance, or that his reply was too conditional to be regarded as an acceptance. Problem questions are usually phrased in a way which admits of alternative constructions and you will gain extra marks by considering both possibilities.

- Furthermore, you must consider the legal effect of alternative conclusions.

For example, if the question is whether an advertisement was an offer or merely an invitation to treat, you need to consider the effect of either construction. Thus, you would say '*If the advert was an offer, then Y was at liberty to accept that offer and thus X would be bound to supply the goods to Y. If, on the other hand the advert was an invitation to treat, it appears Y has made an offer and X can reject that offer and thus no contract will have come into existence*'. You can then consider the most likely construction and conclude accordingly.

## Do Not Invent Facts, but Consider Every Possibility

- You should not introduce hypothetical facts in order to consider other possibilities. Generally, therefore, you must stick to the established facts given to you in the problem.
- However, if the facts are unclear, you should consider all the factual possibilities, followed by the legal consequence of each.

### Example Question

**Fred is serving a prison sentence and is sharing a cell with Peter. Peter threatens to attack Fred because he discovers that he has burgled Peter's mother's house. Fred asks the prison warden to move Fred to another cell and this request is refused. The next day Peter attacks Fred, causing him head injuries. Discuss.**

From the facts it is not clear whether Fred informed the warden of the reason for his request. If he did, the warden should have appreciated the risk of attack and moved him; if he didn't, the warden might have no reason to appreciate such a risk. This will have an effect on the liability of the prison in negligence, and you must consider the legal effect in either contingency.

Moreover, it is not made clear why the request was refused. Whether it was for a sound operational reason or for an unsatisfactory reason impacts on the liability of the prison, and again you must consider the legal impact in both possible scenarios, in addition to providing examples of satisfactory or unsatisfactory reasons.

- Consequently, the facts may be sufficiently unclear that you have the task of asking further questions, rather like a lawyer advising a client.

## Ensure That Your Conclusions Are as Clear and Full as Possible

- After you have considered all the possible factual and legal permutations, you should provide clear and full advice, considering all *possible* conclusions (disregarding highly unlikely answers), and settling on the most likely solution.

- Do not simply state several possible outcomes and leave the client to choose the most likely:

'The advert could be an offer, or indeed it could be construed as an invitation to treat. Equally, Y's conduct might suggest that he accepted the offer (if indeed it was an offer), but his actions could also be construed as a counter offer.'

This is largely unhelpful and again shows the author's uncertainty as to the law and its application to particular facts.

- If the state of the law is uncertain, or the potential decision of the court on the facts is difficult to predict, then warn the client of that fact, but still comment on the most likely outcome:

'This area of law (the privacy of public figures) is still being developed and the case law is far from consistent. However, given the fact that the celebrity in our case had a high public profile, had admitted committing certain anti-social or criminal acts in the past, and had indicated a desire to become a Member of Parliament, it is submitted that it is unlikely that he could successfully sue for the disclosure of his past sexual activities by a public newspaper.'

## ● Practice 1: Contract Problem

Below is a fairly straightforward problem question on the formation of a contract. The topic is dealt with at the beginning of any contract law module and thus should not be beyond the ability of any first-year law student. The word limit for the answer is set at 1,500 words, indicating that the answer should be succinct and simple and will not require extensive or in-depth analysis. First, we look at how to tackle the question. Then we examine both good and poor answers.

Easy Sell Ltd, a company selling various household goods, placed the following advertisement in the local newspaper:

Exclusive Offer! Hundreds of fridges to be sold at discount prices. For example, we have 200 ElectroBest 250s at just £150 each. All you have to do is to telephone in your order and we will deliver the next day.

Sam saw the advertisement and immediately telephoned the company, ordering 150 ElectroBest 250s, but was told that that product was now out of stock.

The next day Ella telephoned the company and asked whether they had any BVS fridges and was told that there were 100 left in stock priced at £125 each. Ella said that she would have 50 of them, and was then told to fill in an application form at the company's office, in which case the fridges would be delivered to her the next day. When she travelled to the office to complete the form she was told that the company had sold out of that particular product.

Advise Sam and Ella as to whether they can sue Easy Sell Ltd for breach of contract.

## How to Tackle This Question

### Identifying the Legal Area and the Relevant Legal Issues

- Formation of a Contract – offer and acceptance. The scenario is clearly about whether a contract has come into existence, which of the parties has made an offer and whether any offer has been accepted. The student thus needs to be aware of the basic rules on offer and acceptance and the relevant case law in this area.

- Nature and status of advertisements. The answer must assess the legality and status of the company's advertisement and decide whether it is an invitation to treat or a true offer. The student must be aware of the relevant case law in this area.

- Study of the words of this particular advert. The student will need to look at the wording of the advert and the surrounding circumstances to decide its true status.

- Was the advert an offer or an invitation to treat? By answering this question the student can then assess the significance of the parties' subsequent actions in deciding whether or at what point a contract came into existence.

- Was Sam's order an offer or acceptance? The answer to this question is determined by whether the student feels the advert is an offer or an invitation to treat.

- Was Ella's order an offer or acceptance, or neither? Again, the answer will depend on how the student has classified the advert, but in addition it needs to be asked whether Ella's initial inquiry is an offer or indeed a preparatory inquiry, whether the company's reply is an offer or merely the supply of information, or whether the offer is made when she says that she will have 50 fridges.

- Did the company accept Ella's offer on the telephone? Assuming Ella has made an offer for the fridges, it must be considered whether that offer is accepted on the telephone, or whether the company has postponed the formation of the contract until Ella fills in an order and form and they accept that order.

- Was the requirement to complete the application form a condition of formation, or a mere formality? The essential issue is whether the agreement on the telephone is subject to contract, or whether the subsequent written order is a mere formality confirming the already existent contract.

### Giving Legal Advice to Sam and Ella

- Identify the central legal arguments (see the preceding section) and explain the relevant law clearly and simply, explaining the significance of any findings.

- Apply the relevant legal principles and case law to the facts of each situation, carefully considering the facts and the actions of the parties and deciding whether such actions are consistent with established principles and any previous case law.

- Give advice on the basis of such principles and on the likely outcome. Do not simply give an account of the law and cases, but rather give clear and direct advice to the parties as to the probable, or possible, legal outcome. Be careful to consider all possible outcomes, but stress the most likely result.

**Use of Relevant Legal Authority**

Students need to use relevant case law with respect to:

- Advertisements and circulars - *Spencer v Harding, Partridge v Crittenden, Carlill v Carbolic Smoke Ball Company*
- Certainty of Offers - *Harvey v Facey, Carlill* (see the preceding section)
- Fact of Acceptance - *Brogden v Metropolitan Railway Co, Gibson v Manchester City Council, Branco v Cabarro*

## Part A: A Good Answer

Below is a good and appropriate answer to the question, displaying all relevant problem-solving skills and identifying the essential issues as outlined previously.

---

**Answer**

### Introduction

The scenario raises the question of whether Easy Sell Ltd has entered into a valid contract with Sam and/or Ella. For a contract to come into existence, a valid offer must be made by one person, which is then accepted by another person. An offer must be firm and capable of acceptance and must imply that the person making it intends to be bound if that offer is accepted, whereas an acceptance must accept the terms of the offer unconditionally,[1] and then be communicated to the person making that offer.[2] If both an offer and acceptance are found to exist then the contract will be complete and both parties will be bound to fulfil their respective promises.

### Sam

Sam will argue that the company made an offer when it placed an advert in the newspaper, and that he accepted that offer when he placed an order for 150 named fridges. On the other hand, the company will argue that the advert was not an offer, but merely an invitation to treat, inviting people such as Sam to make an offer by placing an order and leaving the company free to accept that order.

In law, advertisements, and circulars distributed by traders, are usually construed as invitations to treat. This is because they usually lack the certainty of terms necessary to make them offers; for example, they may not contain specific terms (such as price and description) and require the customer to provide such details on making the order. Thus in *Spencer v Harding*[3] it was held that a circular advertising the defendant's goods for sale and distributed to the general public was an invitation to treat rather than an offer. Equally in *Partridge v Crittenden*[4] it was held that an advertisement placed in a magazine that certain birds were for sale was held to be an invitation to treat and in that case Lord Parker LJ held that there was business sense in construing

---

[1] *Hyde v Wrench* (1840) 3 Beav 334.
[2] *Entores v Far Eastern Miles Corp* [1955] 2 QB 327.
[3] (1869-70) LR 5 CP 561.
[4] [1968] 1 WLR 1204.

such advertisements as invitations to treat. This would reflect business practice and hence allow the company to inform the customer that the goods are out of stock or have already been sold. Consequently, there is a presumption that the advert in our case is merely an invitation to treat and that Sam has made an offer, which has been rejected by the company.

However, this is merely a presumption and if the court finds that the terms of the advertisement are clear enough to constitute an offer, then they will construe the advert as an offer capable of acceptance by Sam. For example, in *Carlill v Carbolic Smoke Ball Company*[5] it was held that the defendant's advert, stating that it would pay £100 to anyone who contracted flu after they had used its herbal remedy was not an invitation to treat but indeed a clear offer, made to anyone who was capable of and willing to perform the conditions of the offer. In that case it was stated that the terms of the offer were certain and capable of clear acceptance by anyone who wished to perform the conditions.

Thus, whether the advert in our case is an offer on an invitation to treat depends on an examination of its wording and whether the company intended, by the words it used, to make a certain offer capable of acceptance. On one interpretation, it could be concluded that by stating that all that the customer had to do was to telephone in their orders, the company had indeed made a clear offer and that Sam had accepted the offer by placing his order. Sam would thus argue that the company had made a unilateral contract, which was binding on the company if Sam followed the instructions in the advert and binding on Sam only when he placed such an order. However, on another interpretation, it could be held that the advert was only an invitation to treat and that the use of the words "Exclusive offer" and the instructions to simply telephone your order were not sufficiently certain to rebut the normal commercial rule that such adverts merely invite offers in the form of orders. The wording of the advert is not as clear as the one in *Carlill*, and in *Carlill* the finding of the court that the advert was an offer appeared to be the only sensible explanation of the company's actions (particularly as they had deposited £1,000 as a mark of the company's good faith).

In our case, although the company has stated that all the customer needs to do is to telephone his or her order, and promised that it will deliver the next day, the most likely interpretation of the advert is that the company is inviting people to make an offer over the telephone and then promising in good faith that delivery will be made the next day once that offer is accepted. It is suggested that this is the case even though the goods ordered by Sam have been identified and priced in the advert. Thus, although the terms of the agreement between Sam and the company appear certain, it is likely that the courts will construe the advert as a general invitation for potential customers to make their offers.

### Ella

In Ella's case, if a court was to construe the original advert as an open and definite offer, then Ella's order could be regarded as an acceptance of that offer and the contract could have been concluded the moment she placed that order. However, as has

---

[5] [1893] 1 QB 256.

been stated above, it is unlikely that the advert will be construed in that manner and that the more likely possibility is that a court will find that the company has merely invited Ella to make an offer. In addition, even if the words used in the advert did intend to bind the company, the fact that the advert did not contain any details of the particular fridges that Ella was interested in would preclude a court from labelling the advert as a firm offer in her case.

Consequently, the negotiations begin with the telephone call and Ella's inquiry regarding the BSV fridges will be regarded as merely a preliminary inquiry, which will bind neither her nor the company. The company's response that it had 100 of the fridges left and that they were priced at £150 per machine, would appear to be no more than the provision of essential information, rather than any definite offer to supply those goods to Ella. Thus, in *Harvey v Facey*,[6] when the claimant asked the defendant what was the lowest price he would accept for his property and the defendant replied £900, it was held that the defendant had not made an offer, but had merely indicated a price at which he might sell, should he sell at all. Using that case in our scenario, it is likely that a court would conclude that the company is still awaiting a definite offer from Ella.

If that is the case, the next question is whether the contract came into existence over the telephone, or whether the contract's formation was suspended until Ella made a formal offer via the official application form. In this case the company would argue that Ella had been asked to make a formal offer via the application form at the office, and that until that formal offer was made, and accepted by the company, then no contract would come into existence. Thus, in *Gibson v Manchester City Council*[7] it was held that the council had not made an offer to the plaintiff when it had requested him to fill in an order form if he wished to buy. On the other hand, Ella would argue that her offer had been impliedly accepted by the company,[8] and that the request to fill in an application form should be regarded as a mere formality or a formal record of an already completed bargain. Thus, in *Branco v Cabarro*,[9] where the parties had described a contract as a provisional agreement, to be replaced by a more formal arrangement, the court held that the contract was already in existence, and that the more formal agreement was not a condition of the contract's formation.

Ella's claim could be supported by the fact that the advert stated that all one had to do was to place an order and the goods would be delivered the next day. Although the advert is probably not a clear offer (see above), its terms could be used to discover the intention of the parties. Ella could argue that the terms of the advert led her to believe that the company was willing to complete the contract over the telephone, and that the completion and acceptance of the order form were to act as a formal record of that agreement. However, the company would claim that it had made a clear counter offer to Ella by insisting on new conditions of acceptance,[10] and that because

---

[6][1893] AC 552.

[7][1978] 1 WLR 520.

[8]See, for example, *Brogden v Metroplotcan Railway Co* (1876-87) LR 2 App Cas 666, where one party accepted the terms by placing an order for the goods.

[9][1947] KB 854.

[10]See *Brogden* (above, note 8).

the majority of terms had not been settled over the telephone, a formal order form was needed to clarify the exact terms of their agreement. On balance, it is likely that the courts would conclude that the completion of the order form was a prerequisite of the formation of the contract and that no contract was completed between Ella and the company.

## Conclusion

In conclusion, Sam would probably fail in any action for breach of contract. The advert is more likely than not to be construed as an invitation to treat, and his offer appears to have been rejected by the company by stating that the goods are no longer in stock. In Ella's case, although there are grounds for arguing that Ella's specific offer has been accepted by the company's conduct, and that the filling in of the order form is a mere formality to act as a record of an already concluded agreement, the court is more likely to find that no agreement was reached over the telephone and that the company had notified Ella of the fact that they had sold out in good time.

### What Was Good About This Answer?

- The introduction immediately identifies the general legal area and the specific legal issues that are relevant to resolving any dispute.
- Separate advice is given with respect to both potential contracts so that the author can deal specifically with each dispute.
- The author identifies the arguments that would be put forward to both parties before applying the relevant legal principles and coming to any conclusion.
- The author uses relevant and useful authority before attempting to reach any conclusions.
- Cases are explained briefly and simply and are illustrated in the context of the dispute.
- The author at least considers all possible arguments before coming to a conclusion.
- The conclusion is sufficiently certain and appropriately guarded, and is based on sound reasoning and a knowledge and appreciation of the case law.
- It is written in a style that could be readily understood by a business client, but with appropriate legal skills expected of those giving legal advice.

### What Is It Worth?

One would expect the marker to make the following comments:

### Marker's Feedback

The piece is well written and structured and you deal with the points in a logical and clear fashion. You also make good use of relevant legal authority, and consider a number of alternatives. However, some of the possibilities you considered were not entirely feasible and could have been dismissed at an earlier stage, leaving you more room to discuss the relevant legal principles and cases in detail

Overall a good effort **65%**

# Part B: A Poor Answer

Below is an inappropriate and poor answer to the problem involving Sam, Ella and the company. Identify the mistakes that the author has made throughout the answer and advise him as to how he could improve the answer. **Do not consult the guidance points discussed in the text after the essay before you carry out the exercise yourself.** You can check your comments with the text afterwards to see whether you have spotted the same errors.

---

**Answer**

Easy Sell Ltd have not made an offer by putting the advert in the paper so Sam and Ella cannot accept by telephoning the company and placing their order. Consequently it is unlikely that either of them can sue the company for breach of contract. If they can sue the company then they can either sue for damages, which would be the difference between the price that they would have to pay in the open market and the price that they had contracted to pay Easy Sell Ltd. Alternatively, they could bring an action for specific performance, ordering Easy Sell Ltd to deliver the goods. This would be unlikely because the goods are not unique, and in any case the company no longer has them in stock.

A contract is a legally binding agreement that must contain the following elements. First, there must be agreement between the parties in the form of an offer and acceptance. Secondly, the parties must intend the agreement to have legal effect. Thirdly, both parties must show consideration.[1] Fourthly, the agreement must be legal and finally, the parties must have the capacity to enter into the contract in the first place. In our case only the first element – offer and acceptance – appears relevant.

An offer is a firm proposition put by one person (an offeror) to another person (the offerree) that is intended to be legally binding if the other person accepts that proposition. For an offer to be valid, therefore, it must be firm in the sense that it contains sufficient certainty. Thus if the proposition lacks information on the fundamental terms of the contract it will not be considered an offer. For example, if X said that he was willing to sell a car, that proposition could not be an offer as we do not know what car he is selling and so if Y said 'yes' to that proposition it could not result in a contract as X and Y would not know which car was being referred to. There would be no meeting of the minds, no *consensus ad idem*. Similarly, in *Harvey v Facey*,[2] there was held to be no offer because when the plaintiff asked what the lowest price for Bumper Hall Pen was and the defendant said £900 it was held that the defendant had not made a certain offer but had only indicated a price at which he might start negotiating.

In contrast to a firm offer, the law regards some propositions to be mere invitations to treat. These invite a person to make an offer, rather like the advert in our case, and do not amount to offers themselves. Examples of these invitations to treat are

---

[1] *Currie v Misa* (1875) LR 10 Exch 153.
[2] [1983] AC 552.

shop window displays and the placing of goods on a supermarket shelf. In these cases the law says that a shop window display is an invitation to treat, so in *Fisher v Bell*[3] it was held that the display of a knife in a shop window was not an offer but merely an invitation to treat. Similarly, in *Pharmaceutical Society of Great* Britain v *Boots Cash Chemists*[4] it was held that the display of goods on a supermarket shelf was not an offer and that the customer makes the offer when he or she goes to the checkout and places the goods on the belt for the cashier to accept. Other examples of invitations to treat are invitations for tenders and, as in our case, general advertisements, where the courts have held that the person placing an advert does not intend to make a definite offer, but rather wants to invite others to make offers.[5]

The company's advert in our case is very similar to this as it is merely inviting Sam and Ella to make an offer by placing their order. When the order is placed, therefore, Sam and Ella make an offer and the company can accept or reject the offer. It would only be different if the company had made a clear offer to Sam and Ella, which was capable of acceptance by them placing the order with the company. This happened in *Carlill v Carbolic Smoke Ball Company*.[6] In this case a company had placed an advertisement in a newspaper promising everyone that if they sniffed their product and still caught influenza the company would pay £100. Mrs Carlill used the product as instructed and still caught influenza and then claimed the £100 from the company. The company claimed that it had not made an offer, and that Mrs Carlill had not accepted that offer, that there was no intention to create legal relations, and that Mrs Carlill had not provided any consideration for the £100. The court rejected all the company's claims and held that the company had made a firm offer to the whole world, that Mrs Carlill had accepted that offer by using the product, which was also her consideration, and that the company did intend to create legal relations as the advert was not a mere advertising puff but was on the other hand a firm proposition capable of acceptance.

This case shows that an advert can be an offer if there are exceptional cases. However, in *Carlill* the company had placed £1000 in the bank as a mark of its sincerity and thus were bound by its advert. In our case the company has not done anything like that, they have simply said all you need to do is to telephone your order, which will then be the offer, and we will deliver. It does not suggest that they intend to be bound. Thus, the company have made an invitation to treat and not an offer and Sam and Ella cannot claim that they accepted when they telephoned the company with their orders.

A contract also requires an acceptance for it to be binding. First of all there must be a fact of acceptance, which means that the offeree must unconditionally accept the term of the offer. Thus, if the offeree rejects the offer or makes a counter offer in response to the offer, that counter offer will destroy the original offer and no contract

---

[3][1961] 1 QB 394.
[4][1953] 1 QB 401.
[5]*Partridge v Crittenden* [1968] 1 WLR 1204.
[6][1893] 1 QB 256.

comes into existence. This was seen in *Hyde v Wrench*,[7] when the plaintiff made a counter offer to the defendant, and then tried to accept the original offer. However, in *Stevenson v McClean*[8] it was held that a mere request for further information was not a counter offer and that such a request does not destroy the original offer. Secondly, there must be communication of the acceptance – the offeree must clearly communicate the acceptance to the offerror.[9] Actual communication does not have to take place if the offeror has waived the requirement of acceptance, as in the *Carlill* case, or where the acceptance is made by post, in which case the acceptance is valid once the letter is sent. However, the postal rule does not apply to telexes or, probably e-mails, and it cannot apply where the parties have made it clear that they want a different method of acceptance.[10] It must also be stressed that silence cannot amount to acceptance.[11]

In our case the acceptance does not appear to have taken place at all. Sam telephoned in his offer and the company immediately rejected it by saying the goods were out of stock. The company can do this, as there was no obligation to accept this offer in the first place. In Ella's case she made an offer by ordering the fridges but was then told that she would have to fill in a form. This amounts to a counter offer as it is introducing new terms into the agreement, and before the new agreement is signed the company inform Ella that the goods are no longer for sale as they have sold out. Although this appears unfair and contrary to what the company said in the advert, I think they can do this because there was no contract in existence at that point and an offer can be revoked at any time before acceptance.[12]

In conclusion, therefore, there appears to be no contract in existence between the company and Sam and Ella. Their offers have been rejected by the company, and without a clear acceptance there can be no contract. Perhaps Ben and Ella could ask the company to sell them some fridges when it gets some more in stock. Although they will not necessarily be on special offer then, perhaps the company can give them a discount to make up for the fact that it treated Sam and Ella unfairly.

---

[7](1840) 3 Beav 334.
[8](1879-80) LR 5 QBD 346.
[9]*Entores v Far Eastern Miles Corp* [1955] 2 QB 327.
[10]*Holwell Securities v Hughes* [1974] 1WLR 155.
[11]*Felthouse v Bindley.*
[12]*Routledge v Grant.*

## What Was Wrong With the Answer?

- The student gave his conclusions right at the start of the answer without considering the law or the cases.
- The first paragraph considers possible remedies for breach of contract before deciding whether there has been a breach of contract.
- The student lists all the requirements of a legally binding contract and then admits at the end of the paragraph that only one of those requirements is relevant to the question.
- Although the next paragraph defines an offer, he gives hypothetical and case examples that do not appear to be relevant to the scenario.

- His paragraph on invitations to treat is too general and does not concentrate on advertisements, merely mentioning them as one example without explaining the rationale of the rule and the relevant case law.
- He concludes that the advert in this case was only an invitation to treat without fully considering the possibility that it might be a unilateral offer.
- He mentions *Carlill* but fails to see that that case might be relevant and then distinguishes it on the spurious ground that this company did not deposit money as a sign of good faith.
- His treatment of the acceptance issue is again too general, and he does not deal with the specific issues raised by the scenario, or the relevant cases such as *Clifton v Palumbo*. He fails to recognise that the contract with Ella might already be in existence before the completion of the order form.
- His conclusion is very one-sided, and he finishes by giving vague and meaningless advice as to what Sam and Ella might do to ease their disappointment.

Overall, the student was on the right lines and had basically identified the relevant legal areas. However, he had failed to spot most of the specific factual and legal arguments raised by the scenario. As a result, his answer was general and largely unhelpful to the parties concerned. His use of cases was also rather poor. He mentioned many cases that were not particularly relevant to the question and failed to pick up on the importance of many other cases. He lacked the ability to analyse the law and the cases and to apply those principles to the facts before him. In particular, he made his conclusions early on in the essay and refused, or was unable to, consider other possibilities.

### What Is It Worth?

One would expect the marker to make the following comments:

> **Marker's Feedback**
>
> You were in the right area and you used some very relevant cases. However, you also included some irrelevant material and failed to apply the really relevant cases and principles to the facts in hand. Your conclusions were not based on the application of the strict contractual principles or the cases and you failed to consider a number of possible arguments. Do not conclude at the start of your essay, instead work through the facts considering every possible solution before coming to a firm conclusion. I think the parties would have been somewhat confused with the advice you gave and would have expected you to address further legal possibilities. In addition, your concluding advice was legally unhelpful. Look at the facts closely and try to apply the law and the cases clearly to the scenario. **33%**

## ● Practice 2: Statutory Interpretation/Judicial Review Problem

The following problem question is on judicial review and is a typical example of one set on many constitutional and administrative courses, requiring the student to comment on the possible unlawful or unfair use of power by someone acting under an imaginary Act of Parliament. This sort of question may also appear on legal system and skills courses, because they involve the interpretation of statutes and require the student to display interpretation skills.

This type of question has been chosen because, generally, students can find them particularly difficult for a number of reasons:

1. They require the student to study the words of an imaginary Act of Parliament and then to offer a plausible interpretation of those words.
2. They require the student to apply quite abstract and complex concepts such as irrationality, abuse of discretion and proportionality to factual situations.
3. They are perceived by students (sometimes wrongly) as requiring an appreciation of political matters.

To answer the question the student must concentrate on the words of the imaginary Act of Parliament and or any imaginary secondary legislation. The ultimate answer to the question, therefore, lies within the words of those imaginary provisions, and not the textbooks or the cases - although you will need to apply the legal principles and the case law to the factual situation provided. Consequently the student must examine those words very carefully and always keep them in mind when giving advice.

## Pre-Practice Question

Before we tackle our specific problem, take this example as an illustration of the above problems.

### Example Question

In June 2005 Parliament passed the Local Authority (Provision of Resources) Act 2005, section one of which provides as follows:

> If the Secretary of State is of the opinion that a local authority requires resources to deal with an exceptional contingency affecting the duties of any local authority, he may order that such sum as he thinks fit to meet such a contingency be given to that authority.

Acting under that provision, the Secretary of State decided to give £25,000 to assist every County Council to erect an appropriate statue outside the council buildings to commemorate the Queen's birthday. Grumpy, a resident of Coventry, claims that the Secretary of State has acted unlawfully and has applied for permission (leave) to apply for judicial review on the following grounds:

1. That the power to order payment under section 1 only applies if the contingency relates to the duties of a public authority, the erecting of memorials not being such a duty as envisaged under the Act;

2. That the words 'exceptional contingency' only apply to a situation faced by a particular local authority and not one faced by all authorities;

3. That the Secretary has abused his discretion by giving an identical sum to each local authority irrespective of their needs and resources and, specifically, by ignoring the fact a statue of the Queen was erected in 1954 to mark her coronation.

Advise Grumpy as to the possible success of his action in judicial review.

The question requires the student to address issues that have been specifically identified in the question (in points 1-3). Thus, the format of the question has performed one essential task for the student – rather than simply saying 'Discuss,' leaving the student the task of identifying the potential grounds for review, it has listed the arguments that the applicant is making. Nevertheless, many students will still find it difficult to identify what the claims are getting at and what specific grounds (and cases) are relevant in answering the question.

The student must address and answer the following questions:

- Is erecting memorials *a duty* of a local authority? (What *are* the duties of a local authority?) If that is a duty, is it the sort of duty that was envisaged by this act? This depends on the construction of the words of the Act, and the intention and purpose of the Act. Students must look in the area of illegality and *ultra vires* and use cases such as *A-G v Fulham Corporation* and *Padfield v Ministry of Agriculture*.

- Does the Act apply to an exceptional contingency faced by *all* local authorities, or only ones faced by specific authorities? Can it be *exceptional* if faced by all? Again, the answer depends on the interpretation of the words of the Act – '*a* local authority requires resources to deal with an exceptional contingency affecting the duties of *any* local authority' – and the application of the *ultra vires* doctrine.

- Has the Home Secretary fettered his discretion by awarding the same sum, irrespective of each local authority's resources and needs? Explain the concept of fettering of discretion and include relevant case law (e.g., *Roberts v Hopwood*). Also, could the allocation of such funds be *Wednesbury* Unreasonable?

Note that there can be no definite answer, the Act is imaginary, students do not have access to Hansard and so on. However, students should be able to identify the possible arguments and can apply the general principles that they have found from the relevant case law.

## Main Practice Question

Now let us look at our specific example:

---

**Example Question**

Under s. 1 of the (imaginary) Public Order (Emergency Powers) Act 2005 the Secretary of State may pass such regulations as he thinks fit for the purpose of protecting the public from serious public disorder and for restoring stability to the community. Section 2 of the Act requires the Secretary to lay the regulation before the House of Commons for its approval and s. 3 states that the Secretary shall consult with such persons as he considers appropriate before acting under any regulation approved by Parliament,

In November 2005, following a serious disturbance at a Gay Rights meeting in Bognor Regis, the Secretary laid the following regulation before the House:

▼

---

> If the Secretary of State is of the opinion that there has been an instance of serious public disorder in a locality, he may order police officials and local authorities to take such action as he thinks necessary.

Two days after receiving approval, and acting under the regulation, the Secretary ordered the local authority and the local police force in Bognor Regis to prohibit and disperse any political meeting which in their opinion may lead to serious public disorder. Although he did not consult with anyone before making and laying the regulation, he did consult with the local authority and police before issuing the order; however, he refused to hear representations from several groups who had their planned meetings cancelled.

Advise the local Amnesty International Group, which has always held its rally in the town, and fears that it may be cancelled, whether and how they can challenge the Secretary of State's regulation and his order.

The question has been set in Constitutional and Administrative (Public) Law in the second term of the first year. Thus, the students are well into their legal studies, are expected to have acquired a reasonable understanding of the constitutional and legal system, and should be able to tackle a question in this specific area of Public Law.

The word limit is 2,000 words (with a 10 percent leeway), excluding references and citations.

## How to Tackle This Question

### The Relevant Points

The making and passing of the regulation and the subsequent order give rise to a number of factual and legal problems, which students should identify in their plan before embarking upon the answer.

### The Regulation

- Does the regulation have to protect the public from serious public disorder *and* restore stability to the community?
- Does 'the public' mean the general public, or a section of the public? In other words. can the regulation be passed to deal with the situation in Bognor Regis or must it apply to the whole country?
- Can the Secretary give himself a power to deal with *an instance* of serious public disorder or does there have to be a general breakdown in public order?
- Does the regulation interfere with Convention rights of free speech and peaceful assembly? And, if so, did the Act authorize such and is the regulation lawful and proportionate?
- Does the regulation effectively delegate public order powers to the police and the local authorities?

- Can the Secretary give himself a discretionary power to decide whether there has been an instance of serious public disorder?
- Does the fact that there was no consultation make the regulation invalid? In other words, does there have to be any consultation before the regulation is made?

### The Order

- Does the order attempt to protect the public from serious public disorder and to restore stability?
- Was it ever intended by the Act or the regulation that the Home Secretary would interfere with the Convention rights of expression and assembly?
- If so, does the order unlawfully or disproportionately interfere with those rights?
- Has the order delegated the public order powers to the police and the local authorities? In particular, how are the police and local authorities to decide whether to take action, and might this lead to bias?
- Was there any duty on the Secretary of State to hear representations from the groups who had their meetings cancelled?

### The Relevant Law

Students require a sound knowledge of the grounds of judicial review, and a general awareness of procedure and remedies. In addition, as seen in the sample answer, the scenario raises a variety of legal areas and issues. Accordingly, students must ensure that each point is dealt with directly and succinctly and that the answer does not include any unnecessary detail with respect to the law or particular cases.

More specifically, students must discuss the following:

- the availability of judicial review and whether the applicants are eligible to claim it;
- the doctrine of *ultra vires* and the ground of illegality with respect to the legality of the regulation and order;
- wrongful delegation and the consequent legality of the Secretary's regulation and order in granting discretion to the police and local authorities;
- abuse or non use of discretion with respect to the Secretary's regulation and order, and in particular whether the regulation and order are *Wednesbury* unreasonable;
- the possible breach of convention rights by the regulation and the order and the relevant powers of the court under the Human Rights Act 1998;
- the legality and proportionality of the regulation and order with respect to any breach of convention rights;
- any possible breach of the rules of natural justice and the duty of consultation, including the effect of the Human Rights Act 1998 on such.

## Part A: A Good Answer

Below is a good and appropriate answer to the question, displaying relevant problem-solving skills and identifying the essential issues as outlined previously.

### Introduction

The regulation and the order can be challenged via the process of judicial review, regulated by the Supreme Court Act 1981 and the Civil Procedure Rules (CPR) 1999. Under that procedure Amnesty International would need to apply for permission to apply for review within three months of the decision[1] and must show that they have sufficient interest in the matter.[2] The court would also need to be satisfied that this was a public law matter brought against a public body[3] and that if the applicants are to raise Convention rights under the Human Rights Act 1998, they are victims or potential victims of any violation.[4] The applicants in our case have a direct interest in the regulation and the order, and the Home Secretary is clearly a public body, acting under a public law power under the 2005 Act. However, the court would need to consider whether the group has been affected by the regulation and order (or whether they are victims for the purpose of s. 7 of the Human Rights Act 1998) *before* the local authority or police have made any decision with respect to their particular rally. Given the fact that the regulation and order have a real and potential effect on the rally, and that it might be unjust for the group to have to wait for the rally to be affected, the court should consider the challenge to the regulation and order's validity at this stage.[5]

The task of the courts in the present case is to see whether the Home Secretary's regulation and order are *intra* or *ultra vires* the powers given to him via the 2005 Act and the traditional grounds for judicial review have been classified as illegality, irrationality and procedural impropriety.[6] However, as the applicant's convention rights might be at issue in this case, we will also need to consider any claim for breach of convention rights as well as any claim that the regulation and order is disproportionate.[7]

### The Secretary's Regulation

We must firstly examine the regulation to see whether it is *intra vires* the powers under the parent Act. Section 1 of the Act allows him to pass regulations for the purpose of protecting the public from serious public disorder and restoring stability to the community. It would need to be established therefore that the regulation was passed for, and was capable of achieving, that statutory purpose, as all discretion needs to be

---

[1] Section 31 Supreme Court Act 1981 and CPR 54.5.

[2] Section 31(3) Supreme Court Act 1981; see also *R v IRC, ex parte National Federation of Self-Employed and Small Businesses* [1982] AC 617.

[3] *O'Reilly v Mackman* [1983] 2 AC 286.

[4] Section 7 of the Human Rights Act 1998.

[5] It has been held that a statutory instrument that was allegedly in violation of the European Communities Act 1972 could be challenged before it came into operation: *R v HM Treasury, ex parte Smedley* [1985] 1 All ER 589.

[6] *Council of Civil Service Unions v Minister for the Civil Service* [1985] AC 374. Illegality is defined as the misinterpretation or misapplication of the legal power, irrationality refers to *Wednesbury* Unreasonableness (see below) and procedural impropriety is either a breach of a statutory procedure or a breach of the rules of natural justice.

[7] Under s. 7(3) of the Human Rights Act 1998 the provisions of the Act apply to judicial review proceedings provided the applicant is a victim for the purpose of s. 7 of the Act.

exercised within the scope of the statutory provision.[8] One initial question is whether any regulation must seek to achieve *both* the protection of the public from serious disorder *and* the restoration of stability to the community, or whether it is sufficient that it is passed for one of those purposes. The secretary's regulation does not mention the latter purpose and might be challenged on that basis, although it could be argued that any measure intended to protect the public from serious disorder will, by its very nature, restore stability to the community, and that the Minister's regulation appears to achieve both purposes.

Further, the regulation appears to have been passed in response to trouble in one particular location (Bognor Regis), and the resultant order applies to that area only. The parent Act talks of protecting *the public* and it could be argued that any regulations and orders should apply nationally and not locally. It is possible therefore that the Minister did not have the jurisdiction to make the regulation in this case.[9] As the Act talks of restoring stability *to the community* it appears to envisage the Home Secretary dealing with local issues. However, it doubtful that the Secretary has the power to initiate his powers, which he intends to use nationally, on the basis of disorder which has occurred in one locality only. This could make the regulation *ultra vires* on this ground. Further, Amnesty International could argue that a regulation inspired by a serious disturbance at a specific meeting, and which then provides the basis of interference with all meetings, is *ultra vires* and that Parliament did not intend such a wide power to be given on such flimsy evidence. Specifically, it could be argued that the Home Secretary has acted irrationally by passing the regulation and that no reasonable Home Secretary would have made such a wide-ranging regulation on the basis of such evidence.[10]

Turning to the wording of the actual regulation, it could be argued that the Secretary has acted *ultra vires* in a number of other respects. First, the regulation appears to give him a wide discretion to make orders *if he is of the opinion* that there has been sufficient evidence of public disorder. This is acceptable provided that discretion is exercised for the correct lawful purpose and used rationally and proportionately (see below). Further, such discretion will have been countenanced by Parliament when the laying procedure under s. 3 was carried out, and although Parliamentary approval is not determinative of the regulation's legality, the regulation should not be declared invalid on the ground that it allows the Secretary some discretion.

There is also the possibility that the Secretary of State has abused his discretion under the parent Act by wrongfully delegating his powers and discretion to bodies that have not been authorised by the Act. Under the principle of *delegatus non potest delegare* a person charged with statutory powers must not unlawfully delegate those powers to another body, and consequently an act carried out by that body will be *ultra vires*.[11] Further, if it can be shown that the Secretary has abused, or failed to

---

[8] *Padfield v Ministry of Agriculture, Fisheries and Food* [1968] AC 997.
[9] *Anisminic v Foreign Compensation Commission* [1969] 2 AC 147.
[10] *Associated Provincial Picture House Ltd v Wednesbury Corporation* [1948] 1 KB 223.
[11] *Vine v National Dock Labour Board* [1957] AC 488.

exercise, his discretion by passing on his statutory power and duty to the local authorities and the police, then it could be claimed that the regulation was unlawful for that purpose.[12] In the present case it was obviously not the intention of Parliament that the Secretary deals with public disorder on his own, and any Secretary would need to employ the assistance of bodies such as the local authorities and local police to ensure that his policies were carried out lawfully and effectively. Government ministers may certainly devolve powers to officials within their own department,[13] provided such a power is exercised rationally,[14] and equally the courts would expect that the Secretary would use other bodies to effect his actions and policies. In the present case the regulation makes it clear that the actions of the police and the local authority are subject to what the Secretary regards as necessary to deal with the situation. Such delegation does not, therefore, authorise the transfer of policy-making and appear *intra vires*.[15]

### The Secretary's Order

For the Secretary of State's order to be valid, it must be *intra vires* both the parent Act and the regulation passed under that Act, assuming that the regulation is valid. In our case, it could be argued that the order, like the regulation, was not passed in order to restore stability to the community, but simply to protect the public from serious public disorder and the success of this claim will depend on the success of the similar claim with respect to the regulation (above).

In addition, the order appears to impact on the enjoyment of convention rights, thus bringing into play the Human Rights Act 1998. Under that Act it is unlawful for a public authority to act in breach of Convention rights,[16] and in our case the order affects the applicant's rights under articles 10 and 11 of the European Convention, which guarantee, respectively, the rights to freedom of expression and peaceful assembly. In such a case the courts have a duty under s. 3 of the 1998 Act to interpret any primary and secondary legislation in line with the Convention, if that is at all possible.[17] This does not give the courts the power to ignore the clear wording of the Act or the regulation,[18] but the Act, the regulation and the order can be interpreted with the assumption that Parliament did not intend to give the Secretary a power to violate Convention rights when acting under the Act.[18A] In particular, the court could ensure that any interference with the applicant's Convention rights of speech and peaceful assembly are prescribed by law and necessary in a democratic society for the purpose of achieving a legitimate aim,[19] which in our case would be to achieve public safety and the prevention of disorder and crime.[20] Although the order, and

---

[12]*Lavender v Minister of Housing* [1970] 3 All ER 871.
[13]*Carltona v Commissioner of Works* [1943] 2 All ER 560.
[14]*R v Home Secretary, ex parte Oladenhinde* [1991] 1 AC 254.
[15]See *Barnard v National Dock Labour* Board.
[16]Section 6 Human Rights Act 1998.
[17]*R v A* [2002] 1 AC 45.
[18]*Re S and W* [2002] 2 WLR 720.
[18A]*R v Home Secretary, ex parte Simms* [2000] 2 AC 115.
[19]*R v Home Secretary, ex parte Farrakhan* [2002] 3 WLR 481.
[20]See articles 10(2) and 11(2) of the European Convention on Human Rights.

the regulation, was passed for the legitimate aim of protecting public safety, it could be argued that the order is so wide and discretionary that it provides an unfettered and unclear power to interfere with Convention rights. Further, because such a power was given on the basis of isolated trouble in one locality, it could be argued that the measure is disproportionate to the aim which the Secretary hopes to achieve.[21]

That claim is supported by the argument that the Secretary's order unlawfully and unreasonably bestows on the local authority and the police a power to prohibit and disperse meeting which *in their opinion* may lead to serious public disorder. This raises the question whether he has unlawfully delegated his discretionary powers to those bodies instead of exercising such discretion himself. As stated above, he would be allowed to employ the services of the local authority and the police to assist him in carrying out *his* policy and discretion. However, it would be unlawful for him to divest himself of his statutory powers and duties and allow such bodies to make decisions on which meetings to disperse. This would appear to be contrary to the main aim of the parent Act and the regulation passed under that Act, which states that he may order these bodies to take such action as *he* thinks necessary. For example, in *Vine v National Dock Labour Board* (above) it was held that the Board could delegate powers to a committee to gather evidence for subsequent dismissal proceedings, but could not allow the committee to make the actual decision. In addition, by allowing these bodies to make such decisions, the Secretary appears to be creating an arbitrary power to interfere with people's convention rights, which would be relevant to the legality and proportionality of that order with respect to any claim under the Human Rights Act 1998.

Finally, the order may be challenged because the Secretary failed to hear representations from groups who had been affected by it. Section 3 of the 2005 Act states that the Secretary must consult with such persons as *he considers appropriate* before acting on any regulation, and although this provides him with a reasonably wide discretion to choose who he is to consult, such discretion must be exercised reasonably and within the purpose of the parent Act. Thus, in *Agricultural, Horticultural and Forestry Industry Training Board v Aylesbury Mushrooms*[22] it was held that the Minister had acted unlawfully in not consulting with the Mushroom Growers Association, who, in the court's view, were a group who were 'representative of a substantial number of persons employed in the industry' as defined in the parent Act. The argument for consulting with potentially affected parties may be strengthened given that the order might impact on the applicant's Convention rights, and in such a case consultation with the police and local authority might be regarded as insufficient. Although consultation with such groups might be impracticable it could be argued that the Secretary should have provided for consultation between the police and any affected group. Further, the group may claim

---

[21]See *R v Home Secretary, ex parte Daly* [2001] 2 AC 532, where Lord Steyn held that any interference had to meet a specific and pressing social need and had to be proportionate to the legitimate aim being pursued.

[22][1972] 1 All ER 280.

▼

that the Minister has acted unlawfully in not consulting anyone before laying the regulation before Parliament. However, as the parent Act does not prescribe any consultation process before laying the regulation before Parliament, and specifically prescribes a process before acting on the order, it may be difficult to imply a duty of consultation before the regulation comes into force.[23]

## Conclusion

Although the Secretary appears to have the general power to pass regulations of this nature, his regulation and his order may be challenged on the grounds that it allows the Secretary to act where there has been a single instance of serious public disorder. Equally, the order could be said to unduly interfere with the convention rights to free speech and assembly, wrongfully delegates too much discretion to the local authorities and the police with respect to policy judgments best decided by the Secretary himself, and fails to provide the applicants with a reasonable opportunity to make representations before the order affects them. Accordingly the court is likely to invalidate both the regulation and the order and the group should seek a quashing order (Certiorari) to that effect.

---

[23]*Bates v Lord Hailsham* [1972] 3 All ER 1019. It is also doubtful that Article 6 of the European Convention is engaged, as the group's 'civil rights' are probably not in dispute.

**What Was Good About This Answer?**

- The student concentrates on the facts in the scenario and builds the answer around the facts.
- Explanation and discussion of general principles are kept to a minimum and are linked to the actual issues arising from the facts.
- The student does not get bogged down in the general law or get too involved in the theoretical and constitutional issues surrounding judicial review.
- The introduction highlights the central issues and contains just enough information on the general legal principles.
- The student has examined the wording of the imaginary Act, regulation and order very carefully and displays very good interpretation skills.
- The student displays a good knowledge and appreciation of the principles of judicial review and uses relevant case and other authority where necessary.
- The student deals with each legal issue in order and explains the relevant law and its application in a clear and structured manner.
- The answer uses useful sub-headings and considers the legality of the regulation and the order in turn.
- The answer considers a range of possible interpretations and conclusions before settling on the most likely result.
- The conclusion is clear and incisive.

**What Is It Worth?**

One would expect the marker to make the following comments:

This is a very good effort to address all the issues raised by the scenario. The structure is good and you deal with each aspect in a logical and constructive manner. You show a very good understanding of the relevant principles and have made a very good attempt to apply those principles to the facts. Very sound interpretative skills displayed, although some of your suggestions are a little far-fetched. Discarding some possible interpretations might have allowed you more time to consider the substantive law in more detail.

Overall, a very good, clear and interesting answer. **70%**

## Part B: A Poor Answer

The following answer is provided as an example of poor problem-solving skills. Try to spot where the student is going wrong and what errors he is making. Then read the commentary and points at the end of the essay.

The purpose of judicial review is to ensure that public authorities who are invested with statutory powers by Parliament carry out those powers lawfully, reasonably and fairly. Thus, the courts have an inherent jurisdiction to ensure that public bodies and inferior courts and tribunals keep within their jurisdiction.[1] This ensures that the rule of law is upheld because public authorities will need to show that they have acted within the law and the courts will be able to invalidate their actions if they have acted beyond their powers.[2] The grounds of judicial review were summarised by Lord Diplock in the famous *GCHQ* case,[3] where it was stated that administrative action could be challenged on grounds of illegality, irrationality or procedural impropriety.

Illegality, according to Lord Diplock consisted of the wrongful interpretation and application of legal powers and would thus cover the situation where the public authority acts in breach of their jurisdiction,[4] takes into account an irrelevant factor (or fails to take into account a relevant one),[5] or where that body acts for an improper purpose or otherwise abuses its powers.[6] On the other hand, irrationality would cover the situation where the person has acted within his or her legal powers but has nevertheless come to a decision which defies all logic, or where it could be said that the decision-maker has taken leave of his political senses. This ground of review is more commonly referred to as *Wednesbury* Unreasonableness.[7] Finally, Lord Diplock referred to 'procedural impropriety,' which covers either a breach of a procedural

---

[1] See Ewing and Bradley, *Constitutional and Administrative Law* (Longman 2003) 13th edition, at page 695.
[2] See for example, *Entick v Carrington*, where the courts held that the Secretary of State was not beyond the law.
[3] *Council of Civil Service Unions v Minister for the Civil Service* [1985] AC 374.
[4] *Anisminic v Foreign Compensation Commission* [1969] 2 AC 147.
[5] *R v Home Secretary, ex parte Venables and Thompson* [1998] AC 407.
[6] *Congreve v Home Office* [1976] 2 QB 629.
[7] From the decision in *Associated Provincial Picture House Ltd v Wednesbury Corporation* [1948] 1 KB 223.

requirement laid down in the parent Act itself, or otherwise involves a breach of the rules of natural justice. Lord Diplock also left open the possibility of the development of the ground of proportionality, which is used by both the European Court of Human Rights and the European Court of Justice in determining whether individual rights have been infringed under both the European Convention on Human Rights and EC law. This ground of review was rejected by the House of Lords in *ex parte Brind*[8] because it might involve the courts in determining the merits of the administrative decision, but the Human Rights Act 1998 now allows the domestic courts to use the doctrine of proportionality and this will subject executive decision-making to a more rigorous challenge.[9]

However, although delegated powers are subject to judicial review, the domestic courts have made it clear that judicial review is concerned with the decision-making process rather than the decision itself.[10] Accordingly, the courts are not allowed to review the merits of the decision itself, but must concern themselves with the process by which that decision was made. In other words, judicial review is concerned with the decision-making process rather than the decision itself, ensuring that the courts keep to their traditional constitutional role of declaring and applying the law, and in this way the courts will respect both the separation of powers (by showing respect to the judgment of the public authority) and the sovereignty of Parliament.[11] Thus, the courts have traditionally held that the doctrine of proportionality cannot be applied in domestic judicial review proceedings (*ex parte Brind*, above) for that would allow the courts to substitute their view for that of the original decision-maker.[12] In this case, therefore, the courts will not be able to strike down the Secretary's regulation or order simply because they do not regard it as effective or wise, for that would be encroaching on the role of the executive and would involve a merits-based review.

For a person to be able to begin judicial review proceedings, they must seek leave for permission from the High Court under the Civil Procedure Rules 1999. This will involve a two-stage process (permission to apply for leave and the actual hearing itself) and to be eligible under the Rules the applicant needs to have sufficient interest in the matter to which the application relates.[13] It has been held that representative groups can have sufficient interest if they are representing the genuine interests of their members,[14] and thus in our case Amnesty International would have sufficient interest to bring an application with respect to the cancelling of their proposed rally. If the person succeeds in their action the courts can award a number of remedies including a quashing order (formerly known as Certiorari), a mandatory order (Mandamus), or a prohibition order (Prohibition). In addition, they can award civil remedies such as a declaration, an injunction and, in appropriate cases, damages. It must be noted, however, that the

---

[8]*R v Home Secretary, ex parte Brind* [1991] AC 696.

[9]*R v Home Secretary, ex parte Daly* [2001] 2 AC 532.

[10]See Lord Brightman in *Chief Constable of North Wales v Evans* [1982] 1 WLR 1155.

[11]See Craig, *Administrative Law* (Sweet and Maxwell 2003), 5th edition, at page 24.

[12]That ground of review is relevant when Convention rights are at issues under the Human Rights Act 1998.

[13]See s. 31(3) Supreme Court Act 1981 and *R v IRC, ex parte National Federation of Self-Employed and Small Businesses* [1982] AC 617.

[14]See *R v Inspector of Pollution, ex parte Greenpeace (No2)* [1992] 4 All ER 329.

private law remedies can only be awarded in judicial review proceedings if the dispute relates to public law.[15]

As stated above, an administrative act may be quashed if it is *ultra vires* the parent Act. Thus, the court must interpret the relevant primary legislation to see whether the public body has acted within their powers. For example, in *Attorney General v Fulham Corporation*[16] it was held that the power to set up baths and washhouses under the Baths and Washhouses Acts 1846–1878 did not give the local authority the power to set up a laundry service. This case illustrates that the courts will interpret statues in the light of constitutional principles to ensure that the public body in question uses its powers both lawfully and reasonably and in the public interest. In addition, the courts will assume that Parliament did not intend to approve of any act which offends certain constitutional principles, such as the denial of access to the courts,[17] or the raising of taxes by bodies other than Parliament.[18] However, local authorities have got a power under s. 111 of the Local Government Act 1972 to do such things which are incidental to their statutory powers.[19]

Turning to the present application, it is clear that the Home Secretary does have the power to make regulations for the protection of the public from serious public disorder. Thus, under s. 2 of the Act the Secretary of State may pass such regulations as he thinks fit for the purpose of protecting the public from serious public disorder and for restoring stability to the community. It is also clear that he passed the regulation in this case for that purpose, because he passed it following a serious disturbance at a Gay Rights meeting in Bognor Regis. Thus, the regulation is clearly *intra vires* the Public Order Act 2005. The regulation would also appear to be reasonable. In the case of *Associated Provincial Picture House Ltd v Wednesbury Corporation* (above) Lord Greene held that a decision could be challenged if it was so unreasonable that no reasonable person would have arrived at that decision. In this case a reasonable Home Secretary would have reacted to the trouble in Bognor Regis by passing the regulation, which is not excessive and attempts to deal with serious public disorder in the a locality. Further, in this case the Home Secretary has sought the assistance of the police and the local authorities in helping him carry out those powers. This appears very reasonable and prudent and will ensure that each situation is dealt with according to the circumstances that prevail in each community.

However, from the facts it is clear that he has not consulted with anyone before issuing the order under the regulation, even though he did consult with the police and the local authorities. One of the grounds of judicial review identified by Lord Diplock in the *GCHQ* case was procedural impropriety, which includes the duty to abide by the rules of natural justice. One principle of natural justice is *audi alterem partem* – that a person is entitled to a fair hearing and has the right to be heard before any decision is made

---

[15]See *O'Reilly v Mackman* [1983] 2 AC 286.
[16][1921] 1 Ch 440.
[17]*Raymond v Honey* [1983] AC 1.
[18]*A-G v Wilts United Dairies* (1931) 37 TLR.
[19]*Attorney-General v Crayford UDC* [1962] 2 All ER 147.

▼

against him. Thus, in *Ridge v Baldwin*[20] it was held that a person had the right to know the charge made against him and should be provided with an opportunity to refute that charge. In that case, therefore, it was held that a police officer who had been dismissed from the police force without being given an opportunity to attend a hearing could challenge that decision, and it was held that the decision was void for want of natural justice. The decision in *Ridge* was important because it applied the rules of natural justice to all decisions which affected the rights of others, whether that decision was judicial, quasi-judicial or purely administrative.

In our case, Amnesty International had not been given the opportunity to make any representations to the Secretary before he made the order. In the case of *Agricultural, Horticultural and Forestry Industry Training Board v Aylesbury Mushrooms*[21] it was held that the applicants should have been consulted before the Minister made a regulation which directly affected them, and that it was not sufficient that the Minister consulted generally with the National Farmer's Union. In the present case, therefore, Amnesty International is affected by the order and should have been consulted, either before the regulation was made or at the very least before the order was issued. In addition, the Secretary may have offended the second rule of natural justice – *nemo judex in causa sua* – which provides protection against bias or the appearance of bias. In this case, therefore, the Secretary has passed his regulation after disturbance at a Gay Rights' meeting. Thus, the Secretary may be biased against gays and have passed the regulation as a consequence of that prejudice.[22]

It could also be argued that the Home Secretary has violated Amnesty International's human rights. Under Article 10 of the European Convention of Human Rights, everyone has the right to freedom of expression, including the right to receive and impart information and ideas without frontiers. This right was described by the European Court in *Handyside v United Kingdom*[23] as one of the essential foundations of a democratic society, applying also to views which might shock and offend the reader. However, according to Article 10(2) of the Convention, this right is conditional and carries with it duties and responsibilities. Accordingly, freedom of expression can be violated provided the restriction is prescribed by law and necessary in a democratic society for achieving some legitimate aim. In this case the right to hold a demonstration is not an absolute right and can be restricted if the Home Secretary does so for the purpose of protecting the public from serious public disorder. In our case the Home Secretary had very good reasons for doing what he did and thus there does not appear to be any ground for suggesting that he has breached their convention rights, either under Article 10, or under Article 11 which guarantees the right to peaceful assembly.

In conclusion, the Home Secretary appears to have acted lawfully, rationally and proportionately in making the regulation and ordering the local authority to interfere with Amnesty Internationals' proposed rally. The regulation was made to protect the public

---

[20][1964] AC 40.
[21][1972] 1 All ER 280.
[22]See *R v Sussex Justices, ex parte McCarthy* [1924] 1 KB 256.
[23](1976) 1 EHRR 737.

HOW TO WRITE BETTER LAW ESSAYS

from serious public disorder, and it does not appear that he has used his powers for an improper purpose or taken into consideration any irrelevant factors. The regulation is one which a reasonable Home Secretary would have made in the circumstances and constitutes a proportionate interference with the group's right to hold their meeting. However, there appears to be a breach of the rules of natural justice and Amnesty International may have been denied the right to a fair hearing under article 6 of the European Convention on Human Rights. This is because the Secretary of State did not consult with it before passing the regulation or telling the local authority and police to ban its meeting.

## What Is Wrong With This Answer?

- The opening paragraphs contain some fair general points on judicial review but do not mention the actual facts of the question or the legal issues arising from those facts. Any introduction to the subject area needs to focus much more on the question and identify the specific problems evident from the facts. This can then be combined with some of the general information contained in this paragraph.

- The student spends a lot of time explaining the purpose of judicial review and the constitutional role of the courts and then provides some history of the ground of proportionality, only to say that it is now an accepted ground of review.

- Paragraph 3 repeats some points already mentioned in paragraph 2 and does not take the reader much further.

- The general information relating to procedure and standing is relevant but could have been mentioned very briefly at the outset. He has misunderstood the rule about representative actions; *Greenpeace* is not relevant, as our group is directly affected. Also, he has missed the point about whether the groups can bring proceedings before the regulation actually affects their rally.

- The information on remedies will be important if the applicants are successful and thus should be given only at the end of the advice. The comment about exclusivity at the end of paragraph 4 is irrelevant as the issue in this case is clearly a public law one.

- He uses the Fulham Corporation case but does not explain why that case was decided in that way. He then provides a list of possible general grounds of challenge without applying them to the facts or indeed explaining whether they are relevant to this case.

- When he addresses the facts and the issues, his conclusions are inflexible and not supported by a proper examination of the words of the statute or the relevant principles. Importantly, he fails to consider the possible interpretations of the Home Secretary' powers and their use (see the good answer in the preceding section). Accordingly, his advice is very vague and subjective, and there is little reasoning to his conclusions; he fails to consider all possibilities and gives a rigid and unconvincing answer.

- He identifies the relevant issue of consultation, but spends too much time discussing procedural impropriety in general, instead of concentrating on the statutory duty to consult.

- He raises the relevant and important case of *Aylesbury* but does not examine the wording of the legislative provision in that case so as to explain the rationale of the decision. Neither does he examine the wording of the 2005 Act so as to consider who should be consulted, and when. Instead he makes a bald assertion that the group should have been consulted, and ignores the fact that the police and the local authority have been consulted.

- He makes a confusing observation about possible bias, which is not supported on the facts and which does not affect the validity of Amnesty International's claim.

- He raises Article 10 of the European Convention, but includes too much general information about the theory and status of freedom of expression and then concludes that the Home Secretary was justified in passing and acting on the regulation without considering the necessity and proportionality of his actions.

- There is no consideration of whether the Home Secretary has wrongfully delegated his powers to the police or the local authority

- The conclusion summarises his findings quite succinctly, but again those findings are not based on any real analysis of the facts and the principles of judicial review, but rather are a product of his own opinion and refusal to examine viable alternatives.

- He introduces Article 6 of the European Convention into his conclusion without discussing it in the main body of his answer, and fails to realise that the article is probably not relevant as there is no 'criminal charge' or 'determination of civil rights' in this case.

Overall, the student found it difficult to engage with the question and was unable to identify the real legal arguments or to resolve them by applying the relevant legal principles or cases. He has a reasonable knowledge of the general principles but has not really appreciated the principles of judicial review or the legal problems raised by the question. His answer is reasonably well written and the structure is fair. There is also evidence of some research. However, most of the content is not particularly relevant and he has thus wasted a great deal of effort by not addressing the issues.

**What Is It Worth?**

The answer would receive the following comments:

---

**Marker's Feedback**

You do include some useful general information and, occasionally, address the question. However, you spend too long on general issues that have little or no bearing on the outcome of a particular dispute and fail to address the specific legal problems raised by the scenario. Your appreciation of the law is rather limited, and you make a number of errors based on a partial understanding of some legal principles such as irrationality, proportionality and the right to a fair trial. You also fail to show a real appreciation of the cases and how and why they were decided in that way. You fail to consider whether the Home Secretary has wrongfully delegated his powers to the police and the local authority. You need to display the necessary interpretation and analytical skills to spot the possible meaning of the statutory provision and to consider the range of possible answers. Your conclusions are unsupported by the facts and are not reasoned. Instead you make bald and often unjustified assertions. Overall, although you have identified some of the general issues, your answer fails to show an appreciation of the question and its various aspects. **42%**

---

# Summary of Problem-solving Skills

After reading this chapter and examining the good and bad answers, you should be able to practice good technique in answering problem questions.

- Always ensure that you can identify the relevant area of law and the specific legal and factual problems that are raised by the scenario.
- Go back to your previous study in the area to ensure that you are confident with the law and the cases. If the area has not been studied before, ensure that you learn it thoroughly before planning your answer.
- Make a plan of your answer, illustrating how you are going to identify and address the issues, and placing them in the order in which you are going to address them.
- Begin your answer by briefly outlining the relevant legal issues and explaining the significance of the outcome of any claim.
- Do not get drawn into long detailed accounts of the law or cases.
- Keep your account of the law and the cases as succinct as possible, concentrating on their application to the facts.
- Write in a clear and structured way, dealing with each issue in turn, applying the law and cases clearly and correctly.
- Read the facts of the question or the wording of any imaginary provision very carefully and consider a number of possible interpretations.
- Do not just explain the law and then state that 'X will win his action if the above law applies.'
- Always keep relating the law to the facts and never lose sight of the main task – to advise the parties.
- Always explain the reasoning behind any findings or conclusions, including whether the advice is conditional on things such as the uncertain state of the law or the lack of factual evidence.
- Always consider every possibility or possible interpretation of the law and the facts.
- Conclude by giving a brief overall summary of your findings, along with any relevant reasoning.
- Consider all possible and reasonable answers before coming to a firm, or the most likely, conclusion.

You can test your skills by carrying out the relevant exercises on the Companion Website (**www.pearsoned.co.uk/foster**)

## Introduction

This chapter examines the skills required of a law student when answering questions in exam conditions. In particular, the chapter includes guidance on the following:

- the expectations of the examiner and the skills that are tested in law exams;
- the difference in technique in answering questions in exam conditions;
- preparation and revision for examinations;
- question spotting;
- identifying the legal areas and the scope of the question;
- planning answers to exam questions;
- using authority in exam conditions;
- answering questions in open-book and seen exams;
- time management in exams.

## General Exam Skills

### What Skills Do Law Exams Test?

Basically, a law examination is going to test your knowledge of a particular subject area, together with your ability to apply that knowledge to different essay or problem questions. In that sense it is little different from coursework assessment (see the following sections). Equally importantly, it will test your ability to use that knowledge in exam conditions, where you are expected to identify the scope and meaning of the question and to write the answers in a limited space of time, often without the aid of materials. Thus, to succeed in examinations you must display:

- a sound overall knowledge of the general subject area and the specific legal areas tested on the examination paper;
- an ability to identify the scope and legal areas covered by the question;
- an ability to identify the specific issues raised by the essay question or the problem scenario and to place those issues in the order in which you are to address them;
- an ability to write clearly and legibly and to provide a structured answer under examination conditions;
- an ability to keep calm in the face of time and other pressures and to manage one's limited time in completing the paper.

## How Do Exam Answers Differ From Coursework Answers?

As mentioned previously, many of the general assessment skills discussed in the preceding chapters with respect to coursework assessment apply to answering examination questions. In particular, you should, as far as possible, employ clear and appropriate writing and grammatical skills, ensure that you are addressing the specific question, and use case and other legal authority constructively and appropriately. In many respects, therefore, your answers in examinations should be smaller versions of answers provided in coursework assessment.

However, given the time constraints and other pressures imposed in examinations, some of the rules applicable for coursework assessments will have to be adjusted.

- You will not be expected to employ the same level of professional style of presentation in an examination. For example, you will not be expected to employ footnotes or to provide full legal citations and references for legal authority.

> **Example**
>
> It is perfectly acceptable to cite a case by using an abbreviated citation and omitting the full reference:
>
> 'This was decided in *Carlill v Carbolic Smoke Ball* (1893),' or even 'This was decided in *Carlill*.'

- The answers will not generally be supported by formal citation of academic authority.

Reference to secondary sources should be fully credited and referenced in coursework assessment, but this is not generally required in an examination.

> **Example**
>
> In an exam you can write:
>
> 'This has been supported by various academic opinions, and Professor Foster believes that the above case law recognises a wide area of judicial discretion in this area.'

Equally, you will not be expected to provide full citations and references for cases and can instead merely identify the case by one name (*Carlill*). If you forget the case name, it is permissible to identify it by its facts, but do not make a habit of this. If you continually use the phrase 'there was a case where . . . ' you will create a poor impression.

Also, in most cases you will not be expected to quote a statutory provision verbatim (unless it is a central provision, such as s. 3 of the Human Rights Act 1998). Try to remember section numbers of the Act, but if you cannot remember it, at least identify the relevant Act.

Note that the situation may be different in an open-book examination, where students *may* be required to use some referencing and citation skills; if you are in doubt, consult the module leader on this matter.

- In the vast majority of cases you will be required to write out your answers and will not be allowed to use a word processor. Thus, you must write in a clear and legible fashion, whilst employing the writing skills expected in law assessments.

- There will be *some* allowance made for spelling and grammatical errors, and you should not have marks deducted for scrappy presentation, for example, crossings out. However, scrappy presentation can be a product of confusion and lack of time management, which will affect your marks.

- You will include your question plans and rough work in the examination script. Ensure that such work is distinct from the formal answer and that the marker can see the difference.

## Why Do Students Find Law Examinations More Difficult?

A great number of students say that they are fine with coursework but that they cannot perform in examinations. Quite often, students are wrong in this respect, and in fact they perform better in examinations. The reason for this might be that the student lacks the enhanced academic and writing skills required for coursework at undergraduate level but nevertheless possesses the basic legal knowledge, and ability to apply that knowledge, to succeed in examination conditions. Such students thus can benefit from a marker's more liberal approach to grammar, spelling and citation and referencing of legal materials. Equally, some students can provide a good concise answer to a question in 1,000 words but then find it difficult to elaborate on that answer so as to complete a 2,000-word essay. Despite this, students may not be suited to examinations for a number of reasons.

### Lacking a Sound Overall Knowledge of the Subject Area

To tackle most examinations, the student needs a sound and broad knowledge of the subject area – for example, the law of contract. Although the student can have relative success in question spotting (see the next section), they are going to require a good grasp of most of the general principles studied in that area. For example, a student studying contract law will need a good appreciation of contract formation, terms, breach of contract and remedies for breach of contract, in addition to some knowledge of a number of specialist areas such as mistake, misrepresentation, undue influence and restraint of trade.

If students lack this foundation knowledge, they will find it difficult to spot the scope and sense of the question (see the next section). Equally, they may be left floundering after answering one or two of the compulsory four (or five) questions, having exhausted their limited knowledge of specific subject areas. This limited knowledge is all too often caused by the following factors:

#### Concentrating Too Heavily on Coursework Assessment Instead of Engaging With the Whole Subject and Obtaining a Broad Knowledge of That Subject

Some students adopt the strategy of putting all their effort into the research and preparation of coursework rather than attending lectures and seminars and fitting the coursework round the teaching programme. This strategy may succeed in the short term because the student may receive a high(er) mark, but inevitably the student is failing to gain an overall understanding of the subject. Thus, in examinations they may struggle to identify and tackle enough exam questions, having acquired a very specific knowledge of the area covered in the coursework (which might not even appear in the exam).

### Otherwise Not Engaging With the Subject Area

This may not be the fault of the student, but those who do not attend lectures and seminars on a regular basis, and who do not undertake regular and consistent study of their texts and other sources, will find it much more difficult to tackle the examination at the end of the term or year. In contrast, students who attend and study regularly will acquire confidence and competence in the area, which should serve them well in the examination.

### Poor Management of the Revision Process

If you start your revision programme too late, or fail to get the right balance between each subject area, you may be left with an inadequate or incomplete knowledge of the legal area for the examination. This problem is often combined with non- or late engagement with the subject area (see the preceding sections), because students may find that some subject areas are more difficult than they imagined when they start researching and studying them. Consequently, students can find themselves with knowledge in too few areas.

### Inability to Think and Write Quickly Enough

This is a genuine concern and problem for some students, even those who are intellectually prepared for the examination. Students can often be galled by the fact that they must write four or five answers in an examination, particularly if the examiner expects those answers to be in the region of four to six sides long. In addition, some students find it difficult to identify and articulate the relevant legal points in time.

1. Practice writing exam answers in longhand, particularly if you have not done this before and you are used to using the word processor.
2. If you are a slow writer, practice point 1 to a greater extent; in addition, try to adopt a crisper, more concise writing style that addresses and deals with the relevant issues as quickly and precisely as possible. For example, do not give yourself the luxury of giving a long account of the facts and decision of cases and concentrate instead on the underlying principles and ratio of such cases. This is sound advice for all students, but particularly so if you are a slow writer.
3. Practice answering questions in examination conditions so that you find it easier to identify and tackle legal issues in the exam. Again, practicing these skills in seminars and throughout your study of the subject will help you in the exam.

### Exam Nerves

All students will experience exam nerves, and to a certain extent this is natural and can even enhance your performance. It also helps to share these nerves with your friends on the course, for then you will see that you are not alone in your anxiety. For those who suffer genuine examination nerves, where this substantially impacts on your performance in the examination, you should seek to undertake your exams under special 'sheltered' conditions. If you *are* overtaken by nerves during the examination, try and take time to calm yourself.

In general, students will feel *less* nervous if they have thoroughly prepared for the examination and are confident with that legal subject. Again, regular and consistent engagement with the subject area in lectures and seminars will help you feel more prepared and less anxious. One reason for anxiety in exams is where the student cannot identify the meaning and scope of the question, and this is less likely to happen where you are conversant with the subject area and have practiced such answers during the academic session. If you panic when finding out that the question on an area that you have revised is obscure, start off by writing some descriptive information; you can then blend that information with your analysis once the panic is gone.

## Exams as a Continuation of the Learning and Assessment Programme

As stressed in the preceding sections, examinations are the culmination of the knowledge and skills that you have acquired on the course during the whole academic session (or semester). Although they test different skills, they should not be seen as a separate entity of your law studies. Many students who get into difficulty with examinations experience these difficulties because they only begin to engage with the subject at revision and exam time. Exams provide the opportunity for you to employ all the skills that you have learnt on the course so far and, equally importantly, they should be related to the rest of the teaching programme.

- The knowledge required to tackle exam questions is generally based on what you have been taught in lectures and/or what you have been directed to study as part the subject area.
- Exam questions will often be based on similar essay and problem questions studied in seminars.
- The general skills necessary to answer exam questions will already have been practiced in coursework and/or seminars.

## ● The Revision Process

### Preparing for Examinations

You should begin your preparation for the examination at the beginning of the academic term. This text stresses that the exam is the culmination of the learning process (see the preceding section) and that by engaging with the module at an early stage, attending lectures and seminars, and acquiring the knowledge and practicing the sort of skills you will need in the exam throughout the course, you will be better prepared for the examination itself. Always be on the lookout for hints and begin storing information for the examination (and for the rest of the course) at the earliest opportunity – for example, the module leader's favourite topic, topical legal subject areas and recent developments.

Thus, the final revision process, as described here, should be the final stage of your preparation for the examination, not the first. The whole examination and revision process will be much easier if you are confident with the subject area and the necessary legal skills before the revision begins.

# Revising for Examinations

Whether you have been able to engage fully with the subject area or not, you will still need to adopt a revision programme in preparation of the examination. Remember, this should be a revision programme, and not an opportunity to learn the law for the first time.

- Ensure that you have all the necessary information and sources to undertake your revision, particularly if you are going to be away from the university until the examinations.
- Make sure there are no gaps in your lecture and seminar notes, that you have the required texts and updates and that you continue to keep up to date with recent developments, at the very least by reading the newspapers and accessing relevant websites.
- Focus on relevant areas and likely sources of questions rather than trying to revise the whole subject area (see the section 'Question Spotting'), but do not expect to answer a specific question.
- If you are reasonably confident with the subject at the start of your revision, then you may be ready to proceed to revision of specific subject areas, but make sure your notes and so on are complete and that there are no major gaps in your knowledge.
- If you have not been able to engage with the subject throughout the year, give yourself a day or so, at least, to acquaint yourself with the subject, and do not attempt intense revision of any areas until you are reasonably confident with the general subject.
- If you have a number of examinations, consult the timetable at an early stage and devise a revision programme that fits that timetable; for example, ensure that you allocate yourself an appropriate number of days for each subject.

## Example

**I have got Contract on 20 May, ELS on 24 May, Constitutional on 28 May and Crime on 4 June.**

I will start my revision programme on April 29, two days after lectures and seminars finish **(You can start earlier if you want to)**. I will go over Crime for about three days to make sure I have all the notes and so on and that I understand it all, because that's my last exam and I won't be looking at it until 29 May. I will also get all my notes in order for ELS and Constitutional and do some revision for those subjects because I am going to concentrate on Contract first. I will begin my Contract revision on 12 May, leaving myself eight days, which should be ample. I will then have four days to do ELS and another four days for Constitutional. I will then have six days to revise for Crime.

- You do not have to allocate your time as in the example. Some students prefer to mix the subjects – one or two days per subject, then change – rather than concentrate on one subject for a fixed number of days.
- If you have an number of examinations over a short period of time – in other words there is not a convenient gap between each examination – accommodate for that and ensure that you start your revision programme a little earlier and that you are prepared for those clashes. Using the preceding example, 'as I have got Constitutional on June 2 and Crime on June 4, I need to adjust my revision programme and I will need to do more earlier revision for those subjects, so that I am in the last stages of revision for them by the time I finish ELS.'

- Start your revision programme in plenty of time so that you do not have to cram information in a short space of time or spend too much of the day and night revising.
- Devise a timetable and try to stick to it, but build in time for rest and to accommodate some interruptions. Below is a typical revision programme. You do not have to, or might not be able to, use this exact programme, and it is quite flexible. In particular, if you do not have seven clear days to revise one module, then spread the programme shown in the example over a wider period. However, keep in mind that the programme in the example contains a good mixture of regime and discipline, rest and relaxation, and variety of revision exercises.

## Example

**Monday**

9.00–12.00 – Offer and acceptance (for a three-hour session perhaps have two hours revision and attempt a practice question); 12.00–14.00 – Lunch and break; 14.00–17.00 – Consideration; 17.00–19.00 – Eat and rest; 19.00–21.00 – Intention (as above); 21.00–23.00 – TV.

**Tuesday**

9.00–12.00 – Terms; 12.00–14.00 – Lunch; 14.00–17.00 – Exclusion clauses; 17.00–20.00 – Play tennis and eat; 20.00–22.30 – Finish off exclusion clauses; 22.30–24.00 – TV.

**Wednesday**

9.00–12.00 – Misrepresentation; 12.00–13.00 – Lunch; 13.00–16.00 – Mistake; 16.00 – Rest of the day off.

**Thursday**

9.00–12.00 – Undue influence; 12.00–14.00 – Lunch; 14.00–17.00 – Breach of contract and performance; 17.00–19.00 – Eat and rest; 19.00–21.00 – Frustration; 21.00–24.00 – TV.

**Friday**

9.00–12.00 – Practice breach and frustration questions; 12.00–14.00 – Lunch; 14.00–17.00 – Remedies; 17.00 – Eat and night out.

**Saturday**

11.00–13.30 – Go over formation of contract and do some more practice questions; 13.30–14.30 – Lunch and go for a walk; 14.30–17.00 – Go over terms and exclusion clauses and do some more practice questions; 17.00–18.00 – Eat and rest; 18.00–23.00 – Go over misrepresentation, mistake and undue influence, doing the same; 23.00–24.00 – Some TV.

**Sunday**

8.00–11.00 – Go over breach and frustration, practicing questions; 11.00–12.00 – break; 12.00–14.00 – Go over remedies, practicing questions; 14.00–16.00 – Eat and rest; 16.00–18.00 – Go through an old exam paper and try a couple of questions under exam conditions; 18.00–19.00 – Eat and rest; 19.00–22.00 – Go through notes and make sure there is nothing you are unsure about; 22.00 – 23.00 TV.

**Monday**

Contract exam at 9.30.

- Try not to work too late into the night, ensure you get a good night's sleep and if you drink alcohol, cut down your normal intake and just drink occasionally and in moderation – it will make you lethargic. Always try to start early in the morning after a decent breakfast.
- On the day of the exam get up at 7.30 and get to the university half an hour before the exam starts. Try not to do any revision in the morning, but have your notes handy to avoid any panic.

## Using Past Papers and Seminar Questions

The university or the module leader should be able to provide you (not always gratis) with past examination papers in the subject area. In addition, many seminar questions, and coursework questions, are often actual, or similar, past exam questions.

- Do not expect the questions on your examination paper to be exactly the same as in previous years. Search for likely subject areas rather than the exact question.
- In many cases, some legal areas will not be examined every year. Check your notes and handouts to see what you have covered in the academic session. This will give you some indication as to which topics are likely to appear, or to be omitted from the examination.
- In addition, some subject areas that regularly appear on examination papers – offer and acceptance, damages, separation of powers, rule of law, juries and access to justice – might appear in a variety of forms; for example, they can sometimes be essays and sometimes problem questions or case studies.
- Practice writing past examination papers under exam conditions, and if the module leader holds a session to go through a past paper, ensure that you attend it.
- Practice answering discussion and problem questions in seminars. Regular attendance and constructive participation in these sessions will provide you with good experience for the examination and will ease the tension of the examination experience.

## Using Question-and-Answer Books

Some staff do not like question-and-answer books because 'they lead the student to believe that there is a perfect answer to the question,' or 'students use them as a substitute for texts and overall revision.'

Used properly, such texts can be of immense help to students preparing for examinations (and courseworks – see Chapter 1). In general, they are much more likely to enhance your performance in examinations than basic revision texts, which serve their purpose in consolidating your knowledge, but which can often dilute legal knowledge and expertise.

- Such texts provide guideline answers to, and advice on the construction of, and the sort of questions that *might* appear in examinations. (Do not assume that you can use the same answers for the question given to you in the exam.)
- They provide you with an overall impression of the way in which you should express yourself in exam answers, how you should plan answers, and how you should incorporate legal materials into answers. They also offer a general guide as to the required length and detail of the answer.
- They provide an opportunity to see how your knowledge and appreciation of the law should be employed in exam conditions.

- They offer a *limited* benefit to revision, as they cover a broad range of legal areas that might appear on the examination.
- However, they should not be treated as a substitute for textbooks or for thorough revision.
- They presuppose that you have a good knowledge of the subject before you read or use them. Use them alongside your texts and other secondary and primary sources to hone your skills in addressing and answering exam questions.

## Question Spotting

It is unrealistic for you to cover the whole legal subject area in detail in your revision programme. You should first ascertain what has been taught on the module over the academic year and then obviously exclude those areas included in the text but not covered on your course. In addition, you should be able to get a reasonable indication of what is likely to come up in the examination by considering factors such as the content of past papers, hints dropped in lectures, seminars and revision sessions and the topicality of the issue (e.g., terrorism and human rights is a 'good banker' on most civil liberties exams for the foreseeable future, as is the reform of the law of homicide on most crime and criminal justice papers).

After considering these factors, you may want to reduce the scope of your revision by predicting certain questions (or rather subject areas) and concentrating on those areas whilst excluding others. This is not too dangerous a tactic provided you follow these rules:

- Do not exclude from your revision an area that is fundamental to the understanding of the whole subject and that might infiltrate other areas of study. For example, the exclusion of the Human Rights Act 1998 from a civil liberties course, or the whole of formation of a contract from a contract course, would be courting disaster.
- Do not exclude too many areas so that you are left with an inadequate knowledge to tackle a whole exam paper. For example, for a constitutional exam, do not exclude the whole of administrative law, civil liberties and Parliament and sovereignty, leaving only constitutions, the nature and sources of the British Constitution, the rule of law and the separation of powers. You are relying on all these four areas coming up in the examination and have nothing to fall back on.
- Ensure that you have one, or a number of, fall-back positions just in case your favourite areas do not appear on the paper. For an exam requiring four answers, you should have at least two other areas in which you could provide a reasonably full answer.
- Even where you exclude a subject area, normally ensure that you have at least a basic understanding of that area because it will help you understand and answer other questions. For example, if you are going to exclude judicial review in your constitutional question ensure you have some knowledge of its rationale because this will help you answer questions on the control of executive government, the rule of law, parliamentary sovereignty, the separation of powers and the constitutional role of the courts.
- Your revision plan should thus identify three subject categories: (1) those that you hope will appear on the paper and which you will revise thoroughly (including your backups); (2) those for which you need a general knowledge because they may appear in questions under item 1 or you might have to do as a last resort; (3) those that you feel are safe to exclude.
- It is only safe to exclude a specific subject area when it is a distinct and separate topic. Thus, for example, it would normally be safe to exclude areas such as restraint

HOW TO WRITE BETTER LAW ESSAYS

of trade in contract, parliamentary privilege in constitutional law or defamation in tort law.

- Be aware that many examiners like to ask mixed questions. For example, a question in a contract law exam could cover offer and acceptance, exemption clauses and damages for breach of contract, and in a tort paper a question could cover negligence, occupiers' liability and/or nuisance, and damages.

- In summary, ensure that you have a sound overall knowledge of the subject, acquired from regular attendance and engagement with the course, and exclude from your overall revision programme only those areas that you feel will not impact on the questions you will answer.

## ● The Examination

### Identifying the Legal Areas and the Scope of the Question

When you first look at the paper, identify the legal areas tested by each question and identify as quickly as possible which questions you are going to tackle. A sound knowledge of the legal subject will allow you to do this fairly quickly, and the broader your knowledge, the more likely you are to spot that some questions cover two or more legal areas. Exam questions can be fairly similar to seminar and coursework questions, so again the scope of the question should be relatively easy to spot.

- If you are given extra reading time in the exam, use that time to look over the whole paper, excluding some questions, identifying your preferences and making a list of relevant legal points covered by each question. This should settle your nerves and prepare you for the start of the examination proper.

- If you spot a favourite topic but think that the question is obscure, do not discard that question. Move on to your other choices and then go back to that question to see whether you could really tackle it. Often the question is not as obscure as you originally thought, and the answer still requires a lot of the information that you have revised. (See the section titled 'Practice 2: The Constitutional Essay')

### Understanding the Question

As with coursework assessment, you must answer the exam question and cannot simply write all you know on that area or rewrite the question. Examine the question very carefully, identifying whether it is a descriptive or analytical question, or both, and what its central features are:

---

**Example Question**

**'The role of the courts is to interpret and apply the law. No more and no less.' Do you agree with this statement?**

This question is about the role of the courts in a constitutional and legal system, and you need to know how courts resolve disputes and, specifically, how they interpret statutes and develop the common law. However, the question is really about whether *in practice* they simply carry out that role, and whether they *should or should not* go further and actually make the law.

▼

A student who simply talks about the rules of statutory interpretation, the development of the common law and the doctrine of precedent will not be addressing the central thrust of the question.

## Planning the Answer to Exam Questions

Use the reading time and then an extra few minutes to draw a plan of your proposed answer. List the points in order, according to the structure of the question, and include any relevant case or other authority. Thus the plan to the question above could look something like this:

### Example

- Explanation of the general and traditional role of the courts in a legal and constitutional system, including the relationship between the courts and Parliament and the executive.

- Examples of the traditional approach, using hypothetical and case examples in illustration.

- Examination of alternative approaches and views, using specific examples to illustrate how the courts have departed from their traditional role.

- Consideration of academic and personal views on the appropriate role of the courts.

- Conclusion.

## Structuring Your Answers

As with coursework assessment, adopt a structured approach; deal with each point in order and explain the law and the relevant cases and other authority clearly.

Begin by identifying the legal and factual issues raised by the question, and then deal with those issues in turn, adding any necessary analysis and authority. You can then include a (brief) conclusion summarising the points that you have made.

In exam conditions you will obviously make some errors in this respect and may need to revisit some of the issues if you suddenly remember a point that you have omitted in the answer. Leave a small gap between each paragraph and at the end of your answer so that you can insert additional information at a later time:

### Example

'A contract is a legally binding agreement and must contain an offer and acceptance (the basics of any agreement or consensus ad idem), consideration and an intention to create legal relations. If one of those essential elements is missing, then the agreement will not be legally binding and cannot be enforced in a court of law.

Every contract must have a definite offer . . .'

If you now remember that you should have mentioned the requirements of legality and legal capacity, you can include that information at the end of the relevant paragraph, instead of including it at the end of the answer marked by an asterisk and giving a (or a number of) complicated instructions to the examiner on where to find the additional information and where it should be placed.

## Writing Clearly, Simply and Legibly

Examiners will make some allowance for grammatical and other writing errors in the examination, and you will not be expected to write with the same degree of fluency and professionalism that you displayed in coursework for (in which you have had weeks to prepare and check your answer). However, in general, you should follow the basic rues relating to grammar, style and clarity that you employed for coursework assessment.

In particular, write legibly and keep crossings-out and amendments to a minimum. Always leave time at the end to check your work for grammar and sense, as well as for completeness.

## Tackling Problem Questions in Exam Conditions

Adopt the guidance given in Chapter 4 of this text when answering problem questions. The difference is that you must identify the relevant issues, and plan and structure your answer to such questions, in a short space of time. Practice the general skill in seminars and throughout the course, and in particular, practice doing it under exam conditions during your revision programme.

As time is of the essence, keep your introduction and comments on the general state of the law to a minimum and proceed directly to the relevant legal point and its application to the facts. Avoid the following style:

### Example

'This problem question is concerned with the law of mistake and whether a party who has ostensibly entered into a contract can claim that the agreement is void because of such a mistake. As all contracts are based on a *consensus ad idem* – a meeting of the minds – the common law may refuse to enforce a contract which is based on a fundamental mistake of one or both a parties to the apparent contract. According to Professor Foster, the basis of the court's intervention in this type of case is that the parties negotiate on the implied assumption that . . . .'

Instead, get straight to the legal point raised by the scenario and begin addressing and answering that point:

### Example

'The first issue is whether X can claim that his contract with Y is void for unilateral mistake when he was unaware that the painting was not a Picasso, and Y was aware of his misunderstanding. A unilateral mistake is . . . .'

## Answering Skills Exercises in Exams

Many Legal System, Legal Method and Legal Skills exams test students' ability to interpret legal materials (imaginary and real) and to see if they can apply the basic rules of statutory interpretation or case analysis to a specific setting. Below is a typical example of such an exercise. The examiner wants you to identify any potential ambiguities and to apply your knowledge and understanding of statutory interpretation to identify which words of the statute are engaged and then to provide a logical solution to that ambiguity. You will not get any or many marks if you simply say, for example, 'In this case there are three rules of interpretation and it depends which one the court favours' (even if you give general authority for the rules).

### Example Question

In 2005 Grandchester County Council made the following (imaginary) bylaw:

> "It is an offence for any person to place an advertisement on council property without the consent of the council."

The word 'advertisement' is defined in the bylaw as 'any written material publicising any event or cause.'

Using your knowledge of the established rules of statutory interpretation, explain whether an offence has been committed in the following cases:

A.  Billy, a local councillor, places an advertisement on the doors of the council's town hall, inviting people to attend a forthcoming council meeting on housing issues.
B.  Karl, the chairman of the local communist party, drapes a banner on the steps of the town hall, lamenting the fall of communism in Eastern Europe in the past 20 years.
C.  Sally, a child minder registered with the local authority, attaches a number of leaflets publicising Children's Week, having received permission to do so from two local councillors.

You should proceed directly to situation A. and identify the relevant words of the bylaw in dispute and what the potential ambiguities are. In other words, is a councillor 'any person' and has this advert been placed 'on council property without the consent of the local council' if it has in fact been placed there by a councillor, and to publicise council business? You should now use the relevant principles and case law to consider a number of possible interpretations.

You then do the same for situation B. Is the banner an advert ('written material'), and does the bylaw apply to political and public interest speech (taking into account the Human Rights Act 1998 and applying s. 3 of that Act, along with any relevant case law). Finally, consider situation C. and whether Sally is 'any person' (as she is registered with the council), and whether she has the 'consent of the council' because she received permission from two councillors.

## Open-Book Exams

Although many students like open book examinations, if you are allowed to bring in your books or notes to an examination you must adjust your examination technique from that adopted in the closed book exam.

- The purpose of this concession is to avoid the exam being a pure memory test and to put the student at ease in this respect. All you need to do now is apply the law you have before you to the questions that have been asked.

- Expect the questions to be more challenging and for you to be required to show much more analysis and application. You can not expect questions such as 'Explain the main requirements of a legally binding contract' if you have the textbook in front of you, because you can then simply copy out the answer from the book. The questions will, therefore, be in the form of problem questions, or essay questions requiring an analysis of that legal area; for example, 'Critically analyse the extent to which the separation of powers is adhered to in the British constitution. Are any exceptions truly breaches of the doctrine?'

- Do not use this concession as an excuse not to do any revision for the examination. You must be ready to apply the information before you to the question and if you have not revised you will not be able to identify the question and will simply end up writing chunks out of the textbook in the hope that it is relevant.

- Thus, do not simply write out of the book or your notes, ignoring the question and failing to use those analytical and application skills. Use the text to get the basic principles, but concentrate on how that information can be used to answer the question. Unlike the closed-book exam, you will get very little, if any, credit for supplying general information from the text because you haven't even used your knowledge and memory to provide that information.

- It is best to use the text as a safety net, just in case you get stuck, and to rely on it for definitions, case names, quotes and so on.

## Seen Examinations

Some examination questions are seen by the students in advance, and students simply turn up on the day to provide the answer. In such a case, you will probably not be allowed to take in notes and texts, but this type of exam can put students at their ease and will allow them to research thoroughly and to rehearse a prepared answer to the question.

Some such examinations are not quite so seen, and the student may be simply informed that the exam question(s) will be on a particular topic, without revealing the specific question. Another method employed by some universities is to provide a case study and to tell the students that they must expect a series of questions on that case in the examination.

- If the question is entirely seen, examine the scope and meaning of the question very closely and ensure that your rehearsed answer is relevant and as comprehensive as possible within the time limit.

- Practice writing out the answer in exam type conditions to see that your answer is feasible with respect to the time you are to be allocated.

- If you are simply given the topic area, research that area thoroughly and expect a variety of questions, essays or problems. Because you have been allowed this concession, expect the question to be demanding and for you to display strong analytical skills. Check on questions asked in previous exams, but do not expect the same question.

- If the seen exam is in the form of a case study, study the case and the relevant legal areas very closely and be prepared to answer all manner of questions on it.

## Time Management in Exams

This is a common problem with students. Always try to manage your time effectively so that you do not run out of time. Try to be strict with yourself and give yourself an allocated time in which to answer each question.

If you start a three-hour, four-question exam at 14.00, plan to have question 1 done by 14.50 (you will spend more time on the first question because it will take a while for you to get going, the first question is usually your favourite, and you will have spent time looking at the paper, choosing questions and making plans). You can then plan to finish question 2 by 15.35, and question 3 by 16.20, leaving you about 40 minutes to tackle the final question and to check all your answers at the end.

- Do not rely on one or two very full and good answers at the expense of providing four sound answers. In most cases, the marks awarded for the first two answers will not compensate for the other poor and incomplete answers.
- Avoid the temptation to spend much more time on the first answer, even though you feel confident and competent in this area.
- It is easier to acquire the first 40 or 50 marks for an answer than it is to get the next 20 or 30 marks, so try to ensure that each answer is of reasonable length and depth.

## Running Out of Time

If you fail to follow the time management rules laid out in the preceding section, and you do run out of time, you must have a strategy to obtain the maximum marks for a short or incomplete answer. Examiners can very often distribute quite respectable marks for short or incomplete answers, and they are usually more generous towards these answers if you have already provided sound answers to the previous questions.

The guidance on this issue will be based on the answer to the following question on misrepresentation:

On 14 July, 2005, Barry was discussing the possible sale of his record shop in Heavington to Harry. During the negotiations, Harry asked Barry what sort of turnover the shop had, to which Barry replied, 'Since I have been manager we have never fallen short of £200,000 a year.' Harry also asked about local competition, and Barry replied that 'apart from the mega stores in Boventry (10 miles away), we are the only record shop in the area. As Harry was leaving, Barry told Harry that Heavington was the trendiest place within 50 miles and that the local youth would always spend their money on records and clothes.

After that meeting Harry agreed to buy the business and placed the matter into the hands of his solicitor. A contract was drawn up, which made no mention of the matters stated in the previous conversation, and when Harry's solicitor asked Harry whether he wanted him to investigate the takings of the shop, Harry replied, 'No, I don't think I can go wrong in Heavington.'

Harry concluded the contract for the sale of the shop for £120,000 in October 2005 and after seven months he has recorded a turnover of just £40,000 with a projected turnover of £75,000. He has also discovered that the shop's previous turnovers were all below £90,000, that Barry was only manager (as opposed to just the owner) for one year, and that the year in which the turnover was £200,000 coincided with a month-long national music festival held in Heavington. Finally, he has just discovered that a competing shop will open next week, having received permission to open in September 2005.

Advise Harry as to whether he can sue for misrepresentation and any remedy he may receive if he is successful.

If, for example, you are left with 15 minutes to complete your final answer, follow these rules:

- Do *not* waste time by explaining to the examiner that you are running out of time!

### Example

'Please accept my apologies, but I have run out of time and cannot complete this question. As a result I have made a brief list of issues which I believe are relevant to the question. I know this is my fault, but I hope you can take this into consideration when marking my paper.'

- Do *not* waste time providing an academic introduction to the question or taking generally about the question.

### Example

'This (problem) question is concerned with misrepresentation, where one party has been induced to enter into a contract because of a false statement of fact. Professor Foster has defined a misrepresentation as . . . and notes that the law is currently in a state of flux, particularly with respect to the award of damages for misrepresentation. In this question I will examine the facts to see whether X made a false statement of fact and whether Y was induced to enter into the contract because of that statement. I will then consider whether Y will have any remedy in misrepresentation.'

As you only have 15 minutes, you need to proceed *immediately* to the factual and legal issues. By providing a general introduction you are not displaying much general legal knowledge, and you are failing to show whether you can or could answer the question.

- Do not simply make a general list of points, covering basic ground. You will get some, limited, marks for this (provided they are basically relevant) but the following list does not display any real awareness of the actual question and its scope. Only adopt this approach if you genuinely have no more time (in other words, you only have 30 seconds!); even then make sure the points are directly relevant to the problem.

- Definition of misrepresentation

- Statement of fact, not of intention (*Edgington*) or opinion (*Bisset*)

- Inducement (*Heilbut Symons, Redgrave v Hurd*)

- Remedies – rescission, damages, Misrepresentation Act 1967

- Do *not* spend all your time dealing with one point in detail, leaving the other points untouched.

The first issue to consider is whether the statement about the turnover of the shop was a statement of fact and, most importantly, whether it was untrue. For a misrepresentation to be actionable the statement must be untrue and the general rule is that the representor is under no liability to provide the representee with factual information, in other words silence will not normally amount to misrepresentation. This was established in the case of Smith v Hughes. In that case . . . and it was held that there had been no misrepresentation simply because the defendant had remained silent, Blackburn J commenting that '. . . ' Thus, on the facts the representation made by Barry does not appear to be untrue as the year he was manager the shop did in fact have a turnover of £200,000, even though Harry may have been misled by the way that information was presented to him.

However, silence may amount a misrepresentation in a number of circumstances. One such situation is where the representation constitutes a half-truth and thus misleads the representee. In this situation there may be a duty on the representor to break his silence and to provide fuller information to the other party. For example, if when applying for a job I tell my employer that I studied law at Oxford, I would have a duty to qualify that statement by stressing that I failed my first year and never completed the degree programme. Otherwise I am misleading the employer by this half truth. Thus, in Nottingham Patent Brick Co Ltd v Butler it was held that there had been a misrepresentation when the defendants stated, truthfully, that they knew of no covenant on the land, neglecting to say that they had failed to make appropriate investigations into the matter. In our case, therefore, there appears to be an actionable misrepresentation because Barry neglects to provide Harry with the full facts, viz that he has not always been manager and the large turnover was exceptional because of the holding of the musical festival.

Sorry, ran out of time . . .

This answer is really quite good, but only as far as it goes. The writing style is good and the point is dealt with fully and clearly, displaying good logical skills. But the student only deals with one of the many issues raised by the problem. There is a limit to how many marks an examiner can give in this case, and the student would have been better advised to deal with this and other issues in less detail, thus showing a greater appreciation of the whole question.

- Try to provide a mini-answer, outlining all the relevant issues and omitting detail on cases and your full arguments. The following answer would only take up a page or so of the exam book, but it covers the essential issues and displays some understanding of those issues and their potential application to the facts.

The first issue concerns Barry's statement about the previous profits. Although it appears literally true, and his silence does not normally amount to misrepresentation (*Smith v Hughes*), it may constitute a half truth (*Notts Patent Brick*) and thus impose on Barry a duty to clarify the original statement by giving Harry information about the music festival and to clarify his position as manager.

Secondly, although the statement about the competitors was true at the time, again Barry may have a duty to notify Harry of the change of circumstances regarding the competitor, applying the principle in *With v O'Flannagan*.

Thirdly, Barry's statement about the youth of Heavington appears at first sight to be a statement of opinion (*Bisset v Wilkinson*). However, it may be argued that the statement suggested that he had the expertise to back that statement up with facts (*Esso v Mardon*), in which case it could amount to a misrep or a negligent misstatement at common law if it was clearly not a true assessment of the spending power of the youth in that area.

Next, was Harry induced by any of the statements, and were any of them material factors in making him sign the contract? The factors do not have to be the only reason for concluding the contract (*Edgington v Fitzmaurice*), and he is not under a duty to investigate the truth of the statements (*Redgrave v Hurd*). However, if he relied on his own investigations and judgement ('can't go wrong in *Heavington'*), he will not be able to sue (*Attwood v Small* and *Heilbut Symons v Buckleton*).

It appears he has been induced by Barry's statements and should seek rescission, either as of right in the tort of deceit or at the court's discretion under s. 2(2) Misrep Act if it was not fraudulent. – in this case it would not appear to be inequitable to deny rescission and award damages in lieu. Finally, on the question of damages he can either sue in the tort of deceit for all actual loss (*Derry v Peek*), flowing from the representation, or under s. 2(1) if it was non-fraudulent.

The examiner may award a low pass mark, or more, as this answer provides a basic answer to the question and indicates understanding and thought from the student.

- If you haven't got time to provide even a mini-answer in prose style (as in the preceding example), make a list of relevant points, ensuring that the examiner gets the gist of the arguments that you would have presented:

- Was Barry's statement about the previous profits true, and has he a duty to break his silence (*Smith v Hughes*)?

- Did it constitute a half truth (*Notts Patent Brick*) and thus did Barry have a duty to clarify the original statement by giving Harry information about the music festival and to clarify his position as manager?

▼

- Did Barry have a duty to notify Harry of the change of circumstances regarding the competitor? (*With v O'Flannagan*)

- Was Barry's statement about the youth of Heavington a statement of opinion (*Bisset v Wilkinson*) or a mere advertising puff, or did it suggest that he has the expertise to back that statement up with facts? (*Esso v Mardon*)

- Was Barry induced by any of the statements – were any of them material factors in making him sign the contract? (*Edgington v Fitzmaurice*)

- Is he under a duty to investigate the truth of the statements? (*Redgrave v Hurd*)

- Did he rely on his own investigations and judgment? (*Attwood v Small* and *Heilbut Symons v Buckleton*)

- Can he rescind the contract in this case? (depends on whether it is fraudulent or falls under s. 2(2) Misrep Act)

- What damages would he receive? – depends on whether it is fraudulent (*Derry v Peek*) or non-fraudulent (s. 2 Misrep Act – would it be inequitable to allow rescission – no!)

This list of points should earn you some marks. The points are all relevant to the factual scenario (not just to the area of misrepresentation). They also deal with the issues raised in the scenario in a logical order. Furthermore, the student has provided appropriate legal authority of all the points. Most importantly, the list suggests that the student has understood the factual and legal issues arising from the scenario and would have been in a position to give a full and intelligent answer to these questions.

## Re-sit Examinations

If you have failed the initial examination, or could not sit if for a valid reason, you may be eligible for a re-sit in that examination. This re-sit will normally take place at the end of the summer vacation and will normally be similar to the initial examination. However, re-sit students should note the following:

- As you will normally revise for this exam in the vacation, you will not have the luxury of regular contact with either the module leader or your fellow students.

- Try to contact the module leader, preferably before the summer vacation begins, to discuss the re-sit paper and its likely content and format. In addition, try to keep in contact with fellow students so as to discuss the subject and the forthcoming examination.

- Ensure that you retain or get a copy of the first examination, either to work through the answers again or to see what sort of questions you missed first time round

- If you have failed the first paper, try to find out, if you can, why you failed. Often the university will not discuss specific papers, but try to discover what was basically wrong with your paper.

- If you have failed because you did not engage with the module during the year (by reason of illness or otherwise), your revision (or learning) programme will be more intensive, and you must begin that programme in good time so that you can become familiar with the subject area. Do not expect to digest and understand that subject easily simply by looking at the texts and other materials.

- In such a case, you must go back to your basic texts and notes and familiarise yourself with the subject. In addition, you should go through the seminar and other exercises that you missed during the academic session.
- Do not expect the re-sit paper to be exactly the same as the first paper. It may contain questions on different areas, or different types of questions on the same areas.

## ● Examples of Exam Answers

The chapter is now going to use some typical examination questions to provide guidance on examination technique and to provide the reader with appropriate answers to those questions. The author does not represent them as perfect or model answers, but nevertheless the answers do employ sound legal and writing skills, address the issues raised by the question and use case and other materials in an appropriate way.

## ● Practice 1: The Contract Problem

This problem question tests the student's knowledge of a number of areas of contract law – intention to create legal relations, consideration, implied terms, classification of terms, breach of contract and damages. An examiner will often make such a question compulsory, in an effort to see that the student has learnt a number of basic contractual principles during the course. To answer it, students need a good overall grasp of contractual principles and the law of contract. In addition, in an exam environment, they will need to be able quickly identify those various areas and deal with them speedily and effectively.

### Example Question

George intended to celebrate his 30th birthday party at his home on December 20, 2005. He contacts his friend, Harold, who plays in a group, and asked whether the group could play at his party. Harold agreed that the group will play two 2-hour sets for a fee of £400, some £200 below their normal fee. Two days later, George telephones Harold and reminds him that the band will be playing at a family party and that they must play a range of music that will keep everyone happy. Harold replies, 'Don't worry, we won't play anything too heavy.' George also contacted Barry, a professional children's entertainer, and asked whether he could perform for the children between 8 and 9 o'clock. Barry agreed and after George stated that Barry must be finished by 9 o'clock, because the children are due to leave the party at that time, a price of £120 was agreed upon.

On the night Harold and his band played two sets, but George received constant complaints from the older guests that the music was too loud. Harold and the band refused to turn the volume down, saying that some younger guests had asked for the volume to be turned up. Harold also received some complaints after the party had finished that the band had played too many Robbie Williams records and had refused to play several requests.

Barry turned up at 8.45 but stated that he could go straight on and be finished by 9.45. George was annoyed at this stage and despite the children's and parent's pleas to allow

Barry to perform, George said that it was now too late and sent Barry away without payment. Advise George, who believes that the whole night was a disaster, whether he can sue Harold for breach of contract, and, if so, what remedy he would claim. Also, advise Barry whether he can sue Harold for breach of contract for non-payment of his fee.

Your plan of the answer should look something like this:

- Did George and Harold possess the intention to create legal relations in order to enter into a legally binding contract?
- What terms have been agreed between the parties?
- Specifically, was the request to play a range of music a term of the contract?
- Did Harold and the band breach any contractual duties?
- If so, can George sue for damages and what loss can he recover?
- Was the term that Barry is finished by 9.00 a condition of the contract? Or rather was it an 'inominate' term?
- If it was inominate, was George deprived of the contract's substantial benefit?
- Can Barry sue for the contract sum?

**The Answer**

**Answer**

### The Dispute Between George and Harold

The first issue to consider is whether there was a legally binding contract between George and Harold. Although both parties appear to provide consideration, and there has been an exchange of promises, it could be argued that given the relationship between George and Harold, neither party intended the agreement to be legally binding. The parties to a legally binding contract must have an intention to create legal relations from that agreement, and in the case of a social or domestic agreement (*Balfour v Balfour*) there will be a presumption that the parties did not intend such relations. Thus, in *Jones v Padvatton* it was held that a promise made by a mother to her daughter to pay her maintenance for returning to the country was not legally enforceable. This presumption can be rebutted on the facts and in *Simpkins v Pays* it was held that an arrangement between friends to share a competition prize was enforceable because of the prospective sum involved as well as the continuity of the arrangement.

In our case although George and Harold are friends, and the band are to play at a social occasion for the benefit of George, Harold and his band appear to be a professional outfit and have charged George a reasonably substantial amount of money for the performance. Thus, it could be argued that the arrangement constitutes a business arrangement, where the legal presumption is that parties do intend to be legally bound (*Rose and Frank Co Ltd v Crompton and Bros Ltd*). This is despite Harold making a concession on the normal charge, and the fixed terms of the agreement suggest an intention to enter into a clear and binding agreement. It is submitted therefore that both parties did contemplate legal relations, however remote the possibility of legal action may have been at the outset.

The next question is what terms were contractually agreed between George and Harold. It is clear that at the initial meeting the parties agreed the essential terms relating to the fee and the length of performance. However it is not clear whether George's insistence that they play a range of music and the assurance that 'we will not play anything too heavy' are of any contractual significance. This discussion and Harold's assurance appear to come after the conclusion of the contract and thus it could be argued that George's consideration for any such assurance had already been spent on the original concluded contract and thus amounts to past consideration (*Re McCardle*).

On the other hand, George might argue that the negotiations taking place two days after the contract was concluded merely re-affirmed Harold's obligations under that contract. Hence, it could be argued that the band's duties to play a range of music and not to play anything 'too heavy' were already implied into the contract. A term may be implied in fact if it is so obvious that both parties would have agreed to such a term had it been mentioned expressly *(Shirlaw v Southern Foundries)*.

Alternatively, the courts may imply a term if it is necessary to give that contract business, as must have been intended by both parties to the contract (*The Moorcock*). In our case, as Harold knows that he was playing at a birthday party, and should have suspected that there would be a range of family members and friends at the party, we could imply a term that he plays at least a reasonable range of music which would satisfy the broad tastes of those who will be present. In addition, if Harold has entered into the contract in the course of a business, statute will imply that he performs his undertakings with reasonable care and skill (Section 13 of the Supply of Goods and Services Act 1982).

If such a term could be implied into the contract, the next issue is whether that term has been broken. We are told that George received constant complaints that the music was too loud and that the band refused to accede to several request to turn the sound down. Although any duty to play a reasonable range of music, and perhaps a duty to control the noise so as not to disturb specific sectors at the party, would be a flexible one, it could be argued that by deliberately ignoring the requests of the older members, Harold and the group have broken the implied term to ensure, as far as is reasonably practicable, that they play a range and type of music that would be to the general satisfaction of the people in attendance at the party.

However, as other sections of the party had asked for the music to be turned up, it would be difficult to prove that Harold and the band had broken this very general term. In addition, the complaint that the band played too many Robbie Williams songs would appear to be too specific and subjective to indicate that they were in breach of the duty to play a range of music. Finally, the refusal to play several requests would not amount to a breach of contract unless the band were capable of playing those numbers and, for example, deliberately refused to play them so as to annoy the guests. In the absence of any clear intention to depart from this duty, therefore, it is submitted that the band would not be in breach of contract and that George would not be able to sue for damages.

However, *if* the court was satisfied that the term had been broken and Harold and the band are in breach of contract, we must consider George's remedies. We are not told whether George has paid the band in advance, but if he hasn't he would be able to refuse to pay that contractual sum if Harold and the band had failed to provide

▼

substantial performance of the contract (*Bolton v Mahadeva*). That would depend on whether the broken term was a condition, or, if it was inominate, whether the breach deprived George of the substantial benefit of the contract, and in this case, despite the complaints, the band appeared to have provided the essential purpose of the contract.

*If* Harold was in breach, George would be able to sue Harold for damages for failing to perform their obligations. Under general rules an innocent party can sue for all loss that was in the reasonable contemplation of the parties when the contract was concluded, or which arises naturally from that breach (*Hadley v Baxendale*). This may include damages representing the disappointment suffered by George because of the complaints received about the band's performance. In *Jarvis v Swan Tours* it was held that damages to reflect the disappointment resulting from the contractual breach could be recovered where the express or implied terms of the contract promised enjoyment, in other words, where the purpose of the contract or a specific term is to provide enjoyment and or freedom from distress. Thus, in that case, the plaintiff was entitled to sue for damages reflecting his disappointment and distress when the holiday fell short of the quality and facilities he was promised in the contractual brochure. In our case, a contract for entertainment would fall squarely into that type of contract, and George would be able to recover damages to compensate him for the contemplated loss of enjoyment and the anxiety caused by any breach. These damages can also reflect the loss of enjoyment suffered by the guests because of any breach by Harold and the band (*Jackson v Horizon Holidays*), particularly as that loss exacerbated George's personal distress and disappointment.

### The Dispute Between George and Barry

Whether Barry can sue for the contract price depends initially on whether the agreed term that Barry finish by 9 o'clock was a condition of the contract. Traditionally, contract terms were divided into either conditions – important terms which allowed the innocent party to terminate the contract on its breach – or warranties – less important terms which merely entitled the innocent party to claim for damages, whilst not allowing termination. In the absence of statutory classification (see, for example, the Sale of Goods Act 1979, ss. 13-15), whether a term is a condition or not can be determined by looking at the intention of the parties when the contract was formed (*Schuler v Wickman Tools*). In our case the requirement to finish by 9 o'clock appears to be a condition of the contract and thus a condition subsequent of Barry's entitlement to the contract sum. This is because George specifically stresses the finishing time to Barry and states the reason for such timing (the children leaving the party). In addition, the contract and the contract sum were not agreed until after that term was agreed. If that is the case, then the term would be a condition of Barry's entitlement to payment, even though on the night Barry's lateness does not appear fatal to the contract's performance.

Alternatively, the courts might regard the term as neither a condition nor a warranty, but instead an 'inominate' (intermediary) term (*Hong Kong Fir Shipping v Kaishen Kaisha*). In such a case the court will wait and see if the breach of such a term deprives the innocent party of substantially the whole benefit of the agreement, that it was the intention of both parties he should receive under the contract. In this case, therefore, it could be argued that Barry was still able to deliver the essential aim of the contract despite arriving late, as the parents and children were willing to stay and watch the

HOW TO WRITE BETTER LAW ESSAYS

performance. Had the agreement been a purely commercial one, the courts would almost certainly classify the term as a condition, but given the relative informality of the arrangement in our case the courts *may* be willing to treat the term as inominate, perhaps by implying a term to the effect that the term would cease to be important if the circumstances originally envisaged changed, as they did in this case. In that case Barry would be entitled to his payment as he was ready and willing to perform the essential element under the contract, less any damages George could prove for late or defective performance, which on the facts would be very nominal.

Despite this argument, however, it is submitted that the term relating to the starting and finishing of Barry's performance was a strict condition of the contract when it was concluded. Barry is, presumably, a seasoned performer, and should have known that the starting and ending time of the act was of the essence. He should thus fail in his action for the contract price. Although in this case George is not suing for damages, any such claim *might* be reduced because claimants must take reasonable steps to reduce their loss, in this case by accepting a reasonable alternative performance (*Payzu v Saunders*).

### What Is It Worth?

The preceding answer is very competent and deals with all the salient issues raised in the question. It does not contain a detailed examination of the law and the cases, but covers the whole range of issues and is a sound attempt to apply those principles to the facts. Most importantly, it displays a sound knowledge of the basic rules on contract and of the variety of issues tested in this 'mixed' question. Perhaps falling short of a first-class answer, it would receive the following comments on the student's script:

| Marker's Feedback |
| --- |
| 'A good effort to answer all the legal issues and some interesting application of those principles to the facts. You omit some detail on some of the cases, but overall a very good and clear effort.<br><br>66% |

## ● Practice 2: The Constitutional Law Essay

The following essay question might appear daunting to the student at first sight because it does not allow students to write everything they know about the British Constitution, but instead asks them to consider the British Constitution in the context of the rather abstract concept of constitutionalism. This is a common problem faced by students in exams, because questions rarely say 'write all you know about.'

| Example Question |
| --- |
| **To what extent are the features of the British Constitution consistent with constitutionalism?** |

Some students will shy away from answering this question because they feel it will not allow them to employ their general knowledge of the British Constitution and its sources and characteristics and because the question is too theoretical to be attempted. Others will press on regardless, and tell the examiner everything they know about the British Constitution, failing to address the concept of constitutionalism and thus not answering the question. As shown in the example, provided students appreciate the general meaning of constitutionalism, and provided they keep referring to the central feature of the question, this question can be successfully attempted by most students.

A competent law student with no special interest or expertise in constitutional theory wrote the following answer. Despite the lack of expertise, the student appreciates the basic principles of that concept and is able to use his basic knowledge of the sources of the British constitution to answer the question.

Your plan of the answer should look something like this:

- Definition of constitutionalism and the importance of that doctrine in constitutional theory.
- Examination of the nature and features of the British Constitution as they impact on the concept of constitutionalism, including the unwritten nature of the constitution, a lack of entrenched constitutional rules, parliamentary sovereignty, the flexible approach to the separation of powers and the rule of law, and the protection of fundamental rights.
- Conclusions on the compatibility of the British Constitution with the doctrine of constitutionalism.

**The Answer**

Answer

One of the essential purposes of a constitution is that it maintains an effective control over government. This involves ensuring that those who operate government do so within the boundaries of the law and the limits of the constitution. This should also ensure that there is a reasonable balance of power between the government and the citizen and that the organs of government do not exercise excessive or arbitrary power. The doctrine of constitutionalism demands that government act within the remit and rules of the constitution; the government derives its power from the constitution and must act in accordance with its provisions and remit. In addition, as constitutions should control arbitrary power, every constitution, and the doctrine of constitutionalism, insists that the rules of the constitution must adhere to basic principles of constitutional fair play, such as the separation of powers, the rule of law and the protection of individual liberty. A constitution that does not uphold these values, therefore, could be said to be inconsistent with constitutionalism.

One of the essential features of the British Constitution is that it is unwritten. This means that, unlike the majority of constitutions throughout the world, there is no written document containing the essential rules of the constitution. Instead, as Bolingbroke stated, the constitution consists of an assemblage of laws and customs by which the community has agreed that the country is governed. This fact in itself should not be used to deny the existence of the British Constitution, or its compatibility with constitutionalism. Written constitutions do not guarantee constitutional behaviour on behalf of government and may expressly provide for the use of arbitrary power. However, the fact that the British constitution is flexible and lacks, in theory at least, any entrenched constitutional rules, does call into question its ability to effectively control governmental power. As most constitutions entrench certain constitutional values, making it impossible for them to be changed, or requiring their amendment via a special constitutional procedure, the lack of any such entrenchment in the British Constitution suggests that the government are not restricted in its power to change or depart from fundamental constitutional principles. Thus the domestic courts do not accept any restriction on the manner in which constitutional legislation can be created by parliament (*Manuel v Attorney General*), and accept that such legislation can depart form established constitutional conventions (*Madzimbamuto v Lardner Burke*), leaving the court no choice but to recognise and uphold such legislation.

This flexibility illustrates that the British Constitution lacks the fundamental and supreme status of most constitutions. Thus, in most jurisdictions, the constitution, and the state's constitutional law, is the fundamental law of the land, constituting a basic law, and possessing its own constitutional status and method of creation and amendment. In the United Kingdom, on the other hand, we have no such basic law, and there is no separate legal source of the constitution; all laws, including the majority of constitutional rules, derive from traditional sources such as Acts of Parliament and case law, which are created by a normal legal procedure and which are not subject to special amendment (*Manuel*, above). So too, unlike other constitutions, the constitution cannot be regarded as a supreme or higher law, restricting the government's power to pass legislation or to otherwise act incompatibly with the constitution. The domestic courts are thus powerless to strike down an Act of Parliament (*Chenney v Conn*), or executive or other acts which are clearly authorised by Parliament (*R v Home Secretary, ex parte Brind*), and this contrast with the US Supreme Court's powers to invalidate unconstitutional legislation (*Roe v Wade*). It is this, the lack of entrenched constitutional rules, and a legal constitutional power on behalf of the courts to overrule the legislative edicts of Parliament, that casts doubt on the effectiveness of the British Constitution, rather than its unwritten status.

In the absence of a rigid, formal and entrenched constitution, parliamentary sovereignty and parliamentary supremacy lie at the heart of the British Constitution. Under the former principle, an Act of Parliament passed by parliament is regarded as legally sovereign, and no court of law can strike down an act that has been passed by parliament and which has received the royal assent (*Chenney v Conn* and *Pickin British Rail Board*). Thus, Parliament, at least in theory, can legislate on any matter it chooses, whether such legislation is regarded as unconstitutional or not. For example, the War Damages Act 1965 retrospectively overturned a constitutional pronouncement of the courts with respect to government liability to pay compensation (*Burmah Oil v Lord Advocate*) and the courts were powerless to strike down the Southern Rhodesia Act 1965, which overturned the constitutional convention that parliament would not legislate for its dominions (*Madzimbamuto*, above). In addition, each parliament is sovereign and one parliament cannot bind its successors (*Vauxhall Estates*), even to the extent of insisting that fundamental constitutional principles are not abrogated. This doctrine has been limited by the passing of the European Communities Act 1972, which gives EU Law supremacy over domestic law in that area, and by the passing of the Human Rights Act 1998, which allows the courts to declare legislation incompatible with the European Convention on Human

▼

Rights. However, both acts could, in theory, be repealed, and under the Human Rights Act parliament could refuse to amend legislation that has been declared incompatible under the Act. Parliamentary sovereignty exists side by side with the notion of parliamentary supremacy, whereby parliament is regarded as supreme over executive government and, by convention, the town. As parliament is elected democratically and regularly, this should ensure that parliamentary sovereignty becomes in reality the sovereignty of the people, although executive dominance in Parliament is said to undermine such a notion (Lord Hailsham, 'The Elective Dictatorship').

Despite the absence of a rigid and formal mechanism for ensuring constitutionalism, the British Constitution does adhere to the basic principles of both the rule of law and the separation of powers. These concepts, which insist, respectively, that government acts by and within the law, and that power is not concentrated in one organ of government, are recognised as fundamental to the British Constitution and good government, and have received judicial recognition (See, for example, Lord Donaldson in *M v Home Office*, where his Lordship held that it would be divisive of the rule of law if a government minister could ignore a judicial ruling, and Lord Diplock in *Duport Steels v Sirs*, where it was stated that the courts' role was to interpret the law made by Parliament and not to create justice outside the law). Thus, the courts have always insisted that government act with the support of formal law (*Entick v Carrington*), and remedies such as judicial review ensure that executive government acts lawfully, rationally and in accordance with the principles of procedural propriety (*the 'GCHQ'* case). Equally, the domestic courts have declared executive sentencing as incompatible with human right law (*R v Home Secretary, ex parte Anderson and Taylor*). The constitution is also founded on the basis that each government power is separated, insisting, in theory, that no one organ carries out more than one governmental power. However, the flexibility of the constitution and the sovereignty of parliament allow both doctrines to be violated. Thus various breaches of the separation of powers are evidenced within the constitution: the role of the Lord Chancellor (soon to be rectified under the Constitutional Reform Act 2005), and the sovereign parliament can sanction the passing of delegated legislation by executive government (albeit under parliamentary and judicial control). More significantly, the existence of a parliamentary executive, whereby the majority of executive government reside within a sovereign parliament, means that the courts' power to control the government is limited.

Every modern constitution should have some machinery to protect the human rights of its citizens from arbitrary interference from government. This assists constitutionalism as it ensures that fundamental rights are beyond the reach of legislative and executive interference, thus placing a limit on government power. The British Constitution has lacked, and still does lack, a formal bill of rights, which protects those rights and allows the domestic courts to overrule legislative and executive acts that are inconsistent with their enjoyment. Nevertheless, such rights have always enjoyed the protection of the domestic courts, which have controlled arbitrary interference with legal rights (*Entick*, above) and have presumed that Parliament did do not intend to interfere with fundamental rights such as access to the courts (*Chester v Bateson*) and the presumption of innocence (*Khaawaja v Home Secretary*). Such protection has been re-enforced by the passing of the Human Rights Act 1998, which gives effect to the rights in the European Convention on Human Rights, and which gives the courts

HOW TO WRITE BETTER LAW ESSAYS

greater powers to interpret legislation in line with human rights (s. 3) and provides the higher courts with the power to declare primary and secondary legislation incompatible with Convention rights (s. 4). For example, in the recent case of *A v Home Secretary*, concerning the detention of foreign terrorist suspects, the House of Lords found that such detention was incompatible with the right to liberty of the person, and declared that it was their constitutional and, since the passing of the Human Rights Act, statutory duty to safeguard such rights in a rights-based democracy. However, it must be stressed that the courts have no power to strike down such inconsistent legislation, and thus parliamentary sovereignty is preserved, even to the extent of allowing parliament to repeal, or derogate from, the 1998 Act.

In conclusion, the British Constitution lacks the formal qualities and features of many other constitutions and, in theory at least, the basic means to secure constitutionalism. Parliamentary sovereignty, the lack of any basic or supreme constitutional law and the limited role of the courts in declaring unconstitutional actions legally unlawful, appear to offer little or no protection against the will of Parliament and the actions of arbitrary government. However, a general adherence to the notions of the rule of law and limited government, including a basic, although limited, respect for the separation of powers, provides some evidence of the constitution's consistency with the principles of constitutionalism. In addition, the democratic features of the constitution, including the supremacy of parliament and the holding of free and regular elections offer some support for the doctrine in the absence of more formal and entrenched constitutional arrangements.

**What Is It Worth?**

This answer displays confidence and competence in the area, without showing any specialist knowledge and appreciation of complex constitutional theory. Many examiners would have expected the student to give more detail on the theories of constitutionalism and to examine some individual theorists in this area. Nevertheless, the answer combined the student's sound knowledge of the features of the British Constitution with the broad principles of the concept. Importantly, the student has not been fazed by the question and has been able to weave his general knowledge in the area into this apparently obscure and difficult question. In addition, it was written clearly and was well structured. It would attract the following type of comment from the examiner:

**Marker's Feedback**

'Well written and structured and including some interesting examples. Explore the definition, scope and theory of constitutionalism in greater depth. Overall, a very sound effort.' 67%

## Summary of Examination Skills

At the end of this chapter students should be able to:

- appreciate the benefits of consistent engagement with the subject and the course, and in particular of regular practice in identifying the scope and meaning of law assessments;

- be able to devise and carry out a suitable revision programme, balancing constructive and consistent revision with relaxation;
- make use of a variety of sources during the revision process, including past papers and question and answer books;
- bring out the best of their knowledge and other legal skills under examination conditions;
- identify the scope and meaning of examination questions and to apply their existing knowledge and skills to those questions;
- adjust their skills in order to answer open book and seen examinations;
- make effective and simple plans before answering exam questions;
- write in a clear, crisp and effective style under exam conditions;
- manage their time effectively under exam conditions, including when they are running out of time;
- prepare for re-sit or deferred examinations.

You can test your skills by carrying out the relevant exercises on the Companion Website (**www.pearsoned.co.uk/foster**)

## 6 — Tackling Extended Essays and Projects

# Tackling Extended Essays and Projects

## ● Introduction

The purpose of this chapter is to allow students to acquire and practise the skills necessary to research and present written work both on the advanced stages (years two, three and four) of their law programmes, and to provide some basic advice on tackling assessment on postgraduate courses. Earlier chapters concentrate on basic essay writing and legal skills, and whilst these skills must be practised beyond year one of your undergraduate studies, coursework and project work in these later stages of your law study will impose further demands on your research and writing skills. In particular this chapter will give guidance on:

- writing extended and advanced essays on your undergraduate programme;
- researching and presenting undergraduate dissertations;
- researching and writing assessments on postgraduate programmes.

This chapter does not provide detailed information on how to research and present these assessments. Instead it will provide some basic advice on matters such as style, depth of research and employment of academic writing skills. A website accompanying this text (www.pearsoned.co.uk/foster) contains examples of undergraduate and postgraduate essays as well as an example dissertation, which can be used to inform you with respect to style, layout and the employment of relevant academic skills. **Please note** that the substantive law in these examples may well be out of date, and in any case students should not use such for the purpose of submitting work on their courses.

## ● Extended and Advanced Essays at Undergraduate Level

### The Skills Required for Extended and Advanced Essays

When you are on the second and third year of your law degree you will be required to write longer and more advanced pieces of coursework. Not only will the word limits of such coursework be increased (from perhaps 1,500 words to 2,000–3,000 words or more), but the marker will have greater expectations of both your essay writing skills and your substantive and theoretical knowledge. This will be reflected in the type of work you will be set and the research and other skills needed to complete the task. You must, therefore, adjust to these new demands if you are going to succeed at these stages of the course.

### Writing Longer Essays

Writing longer pieces of work is not in itself more difficult than tackling the shorter pieces you were given in year one. Students often have problems keeping within, for example, a 1,500-word limit, and might welcome a 2,500-word limit. However, students cannot simply use the extended word limit to pad out their answers with yet more substantive and descriptive material. You will be expected to use the word limit to display both the writing skills which should have improved since the beginning of your studies, and your enhanced substantive and theoretical knowledge.

Thus, essays at this level, and of longer word limits, at the very least test your ability to sustain your legal skills and arguments over a longer period. They also test other skills, such as deeper and more careful research, enhanced powers of analysis and critical reasoning, and skilful use and referencing of legal sources.

## Tackling More Theoretical and Demanding Questions

The work set on years two and three of your programme will inevitably be more demanding. You will notice a shift away from largely descriptive and basic essay questions, to questions which test the student's ability to critically analyse the law, its application, and, in some cases, its social, economic or political impact.

### Theoretical and Conceptual Questions

In year one, when studying constitutional law, you may be asked 'What are the principal grounds of judicial review?' What is the constitutional purpose of such review? You will be given approximately 1,750 words in which to answer the question. The first part of the question requires a fairly descriptive answer and the whole question could be answered by looking at the main text, the central cases and perhaps an article or two.

On years two or three, if you were studying a specialist administrative law course, any question in this area would be more complex and challenging.

### Example Question

'The grounds of judicial review ensure the maintenance of the rule of law and government accountability, and the observance by the courts of their proper democratic mandate.

Examine that statement in the light of the modern law of judicial review.' (2,500 words)

This question requires a strong theoretical appreciation of judicial review and a deep awareness of its constitutional significance, as well as a sound knowledge of the legal principles and case law. There will be little room for purely descriptive material and the student will be expected to research and present a variety of academic theories in this area, some of which will be politico-legal. This in turn will impact on the amount and type of research students must undertake – more articles and specialist texts and the need to look at some cases in great detail, extracting relevant extracts from the judgment. Much of these differences are reflected in the word limit, the question allowing the student to undertake and include more research and to incorporate more complex arguments.

### Critical Legal Questions

In addition, you may get more questions which require your opinion on the acceptability of the current law, possibly with a mandate to suggest possible reforms.

As you can see, the examiner's expectations of you as an academic lawyer have changed since the first year, and (s) he now requires you to show an in-depth knowledge and appreciation of the law and of its application and impact.

However, this type of question is not as daunting as it seems. You will not be expected to lead academic opinion and to come up with startling new proposals. This sort of task will require you to rely on sources other than your trusty textbook (See the section titled 'Undertaking Greater Research'), but in turn those sources will provide you with the leading opinion in this field, which you can then incorporate and discuss in your essay.

#### Coursework on Unstudied Areas of Law

Many questions on years two and three will test your ability to research and write in an area not covered in lectures and seminars. This will test your advanced research skills, see below, but importantly the student will not have the comfort of testing their appreciation of the legal areas in formal classes. In other words, it is testing your ability to study the law, rather than be taught it. Again, this sort of task should not prove too difficult in practice, provided you display the research and other skills identified subsequently (and those identified generally in chapter two of the text), and you engage with your course from the outset.

You will also notice the difference in the difficulty of problem questions. On year one the scenario will raise fairly familiar issues and problems, and the student should readily recognise them from their previous study and from established cases. However, on years two and three the scenario will raise more and varied issues, including some points which have not been judicially settled – the examiner is setting the question to address one or more 'moot' points. This will require the student to display enhanced skills in advising the parties, because the answer will not be settled and the student will need to skilfully evaluate and distinguish previous authority.

## Demonstrating Enhanced Writing and Legal Skills

Chapters 1 and 2 stress the need to display sound writing and legal skills – good grammar and spelling, a clear crisp writing style, sound referencing and citation skills and so on. You must continue employing these skills throughout the course, and markers will now be less tolerant of any lapses in these areas, deducting marks for poor practice.

In addition, they will expect you to have **refined** those basic skills by showing **enhanced** writing skills:

- There should be no lapses in your citation and referencing skills. Full and proper citations will be expected; for example, *Carlill v Carbolic Smoke Ball* (1893) might be overlooked in year one, but in year two the marker will expect the full citation.
- By this stage you will be expected to use footnotes effectively and professionally, including the use of Latin abbreviations, such as *ibid, op cit* and so on.
- Your writing style should now be mirroring the legalistic and professional style adopted in respectable texts and journals. Some casual phrases and colloquialisms might not be penalised too harshly in year one, but in years two and three they will be, which will be reflected in the marks you receive
- Bibliographies should be constructed appropriately and expertly – to cite the lecture notes in your bibliography in the first year might be forgiven, but to do so in year two (or worse) in year three displays an ignorance of legal skills and/or an unwillingness to learn.

## In-Depth Research

The key to writing more advanced, and longer, coursework is the ability to undertake in-depth research and to use such research in the presentation of the piece. Coursework in the second and third year will test your ability to cover either a specific aspect, or a substantial amount of, the subject area, and this will test your ability to find and explain relevant and varied sources and to convey that material in an appropriate, analytical and critical style.

In particular, advanced essays will require you to:

- undertake advanced, careful and selective research;
- research and understand new and developed areas of law;
- research and then condense bulky legal information;
- research and discover recent legal developments in the form of new cases, statutory developments and proposals, and academic opinion.

## Undertaking Greater Research

The essays that you will be set in years two and three cannot be answered simply by relying on your notes and the standard textbook. These sources will still be essential to your basic understanding of the relevant subject area, but you will need to go beyond them to get the sort of information required to tackle advanced coursework.

- Unless your set text or notes do not cover the areas tested in the coursework, always begin your research with these basic sources. You must ensure that you are competent and confident in the area and these sources will provide you with at least a basic knowledge of the essential principles and primary cases and so on.
- In addition, a good textbook will have explored many of the most controversial and interesting issues surrounding the relevant legal areas. This will allow you to appreciate the legal rules and their impact and will begin to equip you in tackling the question.

- Lecture handouts are useful if the subject area of the work has been, or will be covered, in lectures. They will provide you with a basic structure, an indication of what the lecturer feels are the most interesting and controversial points, and, often, a useful essential and additional reading list.

- Good textbooks (and in particular cases and materials texts) will provide you with references to further reading, which you can then explore as part of your research. Look at the references used by the author in footnotes and further reading lists at the end of the chapter or the text. This should not be used as alternative to full research, but if an expert has compiled a list of useful sources, make use of her research.

- You should now be in a position to move on to advanced sources – articles, specialist texts, additional cases and so on. Do *not* 'jump in at the deep end' by starting your research here. You should build up your knowledge and appreciation of the subject and the relevant issues, but if you begin with specialist material and advanced arguments you and your answer will become confused and unconvincing.

- There is no golden rule about how many texts, articles and primary sources you should use in advanced essays. Your research and bibliography should be thorough and reasonably extensive, but remember you are not writing a project. You should show research beyond the basic texts, but avoid researching and using an inordinate amount of materials.

---

**Example Question**

Critically assess the impact of the Human Rights Act 1998 on the power of the police to detain and question suspected criminals. (3,000 words)

---

This, question, to be found on a criminal justice or human rights course, requires a reasonably detailed analysis of the legal area and thus will require fairly detailed research.

Students should begin with the relevant chapter in their set text (either their human rights or criminal justice text). They can then read similar chapters in one or two other main texts to see what views and ideas those authors have on the topic. This will identify the central issues and the main statutory provisions and cases.

Students can now consult chapters in more specialist texts in areas such as police powers, human rights and criminal justice and the European Convention on Human Rights. More specifically, students will need to find and use a number of articles (say four) dealing with this specific topic and which will allow them to address the question in a critical fashion.

In this case, therefore, the student has used approximately ten secondary sources, which should, generally, be more than adequate to provide a suitably detailed and analytical answer (along, of course, with a proper analysis of any relevant statues, cases and so on).

## Keeping Up to Date With Recent Developments

One of the skills expected of students presenting advanced essays is the incorporation of recent legal developments. The set text will be at least six months out of date, and thus reliance on textbooks will lead to the omission of recent cases, statutory developments and new secondary sources. Failure to keep up to date may result in students making legal errors in their work, or, at the very least, providing an incomplete answer to their work. Not only will students be penalised for omitting this information, markers will be impressed by the inclusion of it, particularly if it appears that students have taken the initiative in this respect.It is vital therefore to have a regime for keeping up to date

- Get into the habit of checking daily and weekly updates on law websites. These will provide you with references to new cases, statutory law, proposals for reform, articles (including newspaper articles) and, sometimes, books. The sites may also allow you to access the specific source and to print it off.

- Get into the habit of looking at the most recent journal issues and law reports housed in your library. The websites mentioned in the preceding point may not refer to all journals and cases, particularly overseas journals, so this is a good way of ensuring that you don't miss any relevant developments.

- Consult the monthly publication *Current Law*. It contains reference to recent developments, both primary and secondary (including forthcoming books) under specific legal headings, such as Human Rights, Tax, Sale of Goods and so on. Note that its references to secondary sources is not as expansive as most law websites (mentioned previously).

- Always listen in lectures and seminars for information on new cases. Very often the lecturer will notify the students of a new case or development, covering it in the lecture and alerting the student to academic opinion on it. Understandably, the lecturer will be disappointed if the student shows ignorance of it in their assessed work.

- Make use of websites that accompany textbooks. These very often provide updates on the law as they affect the content of the textbook.

## Finding and Using Appropriately Advanced Sources

By employing your basic research skills (learnt in year one and covered in chapter 2 of the text), and by following the advice given in the preceding section with respect to undertaking greater research and finding recent developments, you will be able to locate the type of sources required to answer advance essays.

Specifically, you need to know how to make the most of these advanced sources in order to show off your research skills and to enhance the quality of your work

- Use your research skills and your knowledge of the subject area to find *appropriate* journals and texts.

  In addition to researching mainstream journals, such as the *Modern Law Review, Law Quarterly Review*, which contain articles and case notes on all manner of legal areas, you will need to identify and consult the leading journals in specific subject areas. These journals are subject specific and will need to be used by students studying particular subjects – Human Rights (*European Human Rights Law Review, Human Rights Law Review*), Commercial Law (*Business Law Review, Journal of Business* Law), Criminal Law and Justice (*Criminal Law Review, Howard Journal of Criminal Justice*) and European Union Law (*Common Market Law Review, European Law Review*).

  Students may also need to consult overseas journals, whether their content is general (*Harvard Law Review, Yale Law Review*), or subject specific (*Netherlands Human Rights Quarterly*). Many of these journals contain articles on English law, especially

Commonwealth journals, and many overseas journals contain articles on European and international law.

Search your library catalogue, and the library catalogues of other libraries, for books in a specialised field. These texts are also often referred to in more general textbooks in footnotes and bibliographies.

- Show a wide reading in the area by using a variety of texts and journals – basic and specialised, domestic and overseas, academic and 'trade' journals.

  In particular, ensure that you refer to appropriately detailed and respected journals and avoid the overuse of 'trade' journals. For example, do not just use articles from the *New Law Journal* and *Law Society Gazette* when tackling an advanced essay. These journals provide an invaluable source of information on recent developments and include some excellent, yet brief, analyses of legal issues. However, some of them are written by, and for, practitioners and might not be suitable for essay purposes. Students should use them alongside more respected and weightier journals if they are going to tackle the issues raised by advanced essays fully and effectively.

- Use your skills to refer to and cite these journals and texts properly – *Current Law* (mentioned previously) has a glossary of article abbreviations at the front of each issue, and you can learn how to cite specific journals by looking on their website or the inside cover of the journal.

- Do not cite or refer to journals or texts that you have not read. It is not a competition to put as many books and articles in your bibliography as you can, and you should not try to mislead the marker in this respect. Do not try to use academic opinion unless you understand the author's views and try to avoid over complicated and esoteric sources.

- Ensure that you understand the source so that you can explain the meaning and significance of views expressed in them and add your own views, see the section titled 'Adopting a Critical and Analytical Approach.'

## Writing in a Professional and Academic, Critical and Analytical Style

At this stage, students should be able to write in a reasonably professional and academic style, imitating the style (as opposed to the exact words) of academic writers.

Importantly, students must be able to incorporate all their research and a variety of legal materials into their work in an expert fashion. Examine the style adopted in the following passage (an introduction on a commercial law question relating to sales by a nonowner) and notice how the piece is constructed and how it uses a mixture of secondary sources and personal reflection.

### Example

When a nonowner sells goods to an unsuspecting purchaser, two strong claims are in conflict – the right of the true owner to assert his title if another person lays claim to those goods, and the right of the innocent third party who has paid for the goods in good

▼

faith to keep those goods as his own.[1] Somehow the law has to reconcile these rights and determine 'Who is the owner?'[2] The answer is vital because, although the person who is held not to be the owner will, in theory, have a remedy against the unauthorised seller,[3] that seller will probably be a 'rogue' who has disappeared, and, if he can be found, may be penniless and any unsuccessful (and innocent) party will lose out financially. The starting point in law is that the true owner's rights are paramount, although many exceptions have been created to this rule by both common law and statute.[4] This has created an unsatisfactory situation, with the law being developed in a piecemeal fashion and being interpreted restrictively, and often inconsistently, by the courts.[5]

---

[1]See Davis, I, 'Transferability and sale of goods' (1987) LS 1, where the author explores the property rights of the true owner and the claims of bona fide purchasers.

[2]In many cases a number of innocent parties may be involved, as where a rogue sells the true owner's goods to X, who then sells them to Y. See Dobson, *Sale of Goods and Consumer Credit* (Sweet and Maxwell 2000), at pages 72-73.

[3]By virtue of s. 12 of the Sale of Goods Act 1979.

[4]Under ss. 21-27 of the Sale of Goods Act 1979.

[5]See Bridge, M., *The Sale of Goods* (OUP 1977), at page 410.

## Adopting a Critical and Analytical Approach

As indicated here, advanced coursework will require you to do more than provide descriptive material. The marker will expect you to analyse the area and the cases, to criticise, and to draw your own rational and supported conclusions. The skill here is to merge established academic opinion with your own understanding and arguments. In other words, draw on academic opinion in this area as the basis of your critical examination of the question and then show that you critically understand those views.

Look at the following section, where the student begins to examine the possible reform of the rule relating to sales by nonowners. Note how she uses her research of primary and secondary sources and adds her own reflections and views.

### Example

Given the complexity of the legal rules, their potential for unfairness and the continual problem of nonowners selling and pledging goods to innocent purchasers, it is surprising that this area has resulted in little proposal for reform and even less actual law reform. In 1966 the Law Reform Committee looked into the area,[6] and in 1994 the Department of Trade and Industry published a Consultation Paper, proposing reforms to the nemo dat principles, which resulted only in the removal of the 'market overt' rule.[7] Whatever proposals, if any, are introduced, the present general rule combined with its exceptions cannot be described as satisfactory. The cases discussed in the earlier part of this essay show that the rules are technical and that the rights of the innocent parties are often determined by complex and often inconsistent application of commercial legal rules. For example, Thornely refers to a system of complicated and duplicated provisions that require a thorough overhaul.[8] It is essential therefore, that other possibilities of reform are addressed.

---

[6]Law Reform Committee: Twelfth Report on the Transfer of Title to Chattels (Cmnd. 2958, April 1966). For a discussion on the Committee's findings, see Diamond (1966) MLR 413.

[7]Transfer of Title: Sections 21 to 26 of the Sale of Goods Act 1979 (January 20 1994).

[8]Thornely, Thieves, Rogues, Innocent Purchasers and Legislative Tangles [1988] CLJ 15, at page 18.

## ● Undergraduate Projects

### Introductory Points

Whilst on your law course, you may be given an opportunity to submit a project (or dissertation as they are commonly known) as part of your programme. Indeed, on some law courses it is compulsory to undertake a dissertation. This normally occurs in the final year of your course and will take the form of a 12,000- to 15,000-word piece on a legal topic of your choice, which you will need to get approval for from the dissertations tutor.

Undertaking a project will provide several benefits. It will allow you to research and study a legal area of your choice and interest in detail. This will enhance your research and writing skills and will equip you for further academic study on postgraduate courses and research degrees. In addition, it is often useful to include details of individual research in letters of application for both academic and professional courses and for employment.

### Choosing to Do a Project

If the dissertation is optional, you must think very carefully before choosing to embark on a dissertation instead of studying another taught subject.

- Be guided by interest, not just by the desire to avoid exams.

  Many students think that the dissertation will be a 'soft option' because there is no examination and it is only a 'large coursework.' As shown subsequently, nothing could be further from the truth, but the cardinal rule is this: Do not undertake a project unless you have the interest to start and finish it. Unless you are interested in the topic area, and can maintain that interest throughout the whole academic session, you will not succeed in the dissertation.

- Ensure that you have got the necessary skills to embark on a dissertation.

  Some students think they are better at coursework than examinations, but the evidence does not always bear that out. To finish a dissertation you need patience, good intellectual and academic ability, and very good writing and academic skills. If you are receiving regular negative comments in courseworks about your writing style and your coursework skills, the dissertation is probably not for you. If that is the case and the dissertation is compulsory, then you need to work on acquiring those skills by the time you reach your final year.

- Expect the dissertation to be demanding and be prepared to research thoroughly.

  The dissertation will involve a tremendous amount of in-depth research, discovery, comprehension and collation of legal materials, writing and rewriting and extensive proofreading. Unless your heart is in it, it is best to choose a taught subject. However, if your interest in the subject and the project is maintained, you will find the dissertation an enjoyable and stimulating experience. It gives you an opportunity to acquire a specialist knowledge and appreciation of the law, but it does come at a price.

- Be prepared to meet deadlines and to practise self-discipline.

  This is often the most difficult aspect involved with a dissertation. You must settle on your area and title at an early stage, present the supervisor with a viable plan well in advance of starting the dissertation (usually in the early summer preceding the final academic year), meet with your supervisor at regular intervals and take into account any advice and recommendations, present individual chapters throughout the academic year for checking and amendment, and leave ample time to write, rewrite and proofread your work.

An effective way of meeting deadlines (for the completion of chapters and the final project) is to make proper use of your supervisor and to follow the instructions on seeking their advice. Always attend the meetings with supervisors and ensure that you have the necessary work for them to check. If you submit drafts in good time, supervisors will generally look at that work and make recommendations. However, you cannot expect them to do this if you have not kept your appointments through the year and then suddenly hand them a 12,000-word project to look over in the three days remaining before the submission date. Always incorporate the changes recommended by the supervisor and ensure that you understand what the recommendations are and how to execute them.

In short, you need the following skills to undertake a project:

- ability to write extended assessments and to sustain research and other skills over a long period of time;
- ability to learn new areas of law and to grasp a variety of complex legal theories and arguments;
- ability to undertake in-depth, selective and specialised research;
- ability to cover a substantive amount of a chosen subject area and to condense bulky legal and other information;
- ability to practise advanced writing skills and to convey the information in an appropriate style;
- ability to time manage the dissertation with the remainder of your law studies.

### Choosing a Legal Area and Title

You will be given a fairly wide choice and remit with respect to choosing your area and title, although you will need to get this ratified by the supervisor, who may reject it because the title and plan is too vague or not viable, because it covers too specialised an area or because there is insufficient legal content.

Although students might welcome choosing their own title, after years of being forced to answer other people's questions, choosing an area and an appropriate title has its difficulties. Your supervisor will help you out in this respect, but you should follow this guidance.

#### Ensure That the Area of Law Is Interesting, Suits Your Skills and Is Reasonably Familiar

As you are going to be working on this project for a number of months, it is essential that you choose an area that is of interest to you and that will sustain your interest over that time. You should choose an area that you will look forward to researching and studying. This might not necessarily be a topical or generally controversial social or other issue. In fact, there is often a danger of choosing something simply because it has received wide media coverage (see the next section). However, it should be an area in which there are plenty of unresolved and academically interesting issues. You will not be allowed to write a project describing entirely established substantive law; there will need to be some 'edge' to the project.

Also, ensure that the subject area suits your knowledge and skills. It is usually a good idea to choose an area that will allow you to display your existing skills. For example, you may be better at legal theory rather than 'black letter' law, or better in the commercial law subjects rather than subjects such as human rights or criminal justice.

Although you will need to research new aspects of the law and a variety of new sources, you should choose an area that is reasonably familiar to you.

For example, a student who chooses to look at the legal and social implications of domestic immigration law without the benefit of any previous study in this area might run into subsequent difficulties with respect to researching and understanding this complex area of law. In contrast, if that student has studied (or will be studying) administrative law and/or human rights, it would be feasible to undertake a project on the impact of judicial review/human rights law in that area. At least the student is aware of the underlying principles of judicial review/human rights and can now undertake research on immigration law in the context of that understanding.

Similarly, students should not attempt projects on, say, the US law on copyright unless they have studied intellectual property and even then intend to examine the US law as a comparator with the domestic law.

### Ensure That the Topic and Title Have Sufficient Legal Substance

Some topic areas appear very interesting and controversial yet do not raise sufficient (current) legal issues. For example, basing a project idea on a recent event like the proposed ban of smoking in public places or the resignation of a government minister over a national scandal, may appear to be an interesting basis for study, but if there are insufficient legal issues to examine, the project will end up as a general discussion on a matter of social interest.

Similarly, a project on, for example, the interference with literary speech by domestic obscenity laws was a very topical area in the 1960s and 1970s but is now largely academic. In this case the student needs to change the focus of the project to study a live legal issue relating to obscenity, such as the control of child pornography or obscenity laws and the Internet.

Equally, where the area does raise a number of legal issues, the student's title and aims and objectives must focus on those issues. For example, the recent controversy surrounding the publication of blasphemous cartoons in Denmark, causing offence to Muslims and leading to violent protest, is a suitable topic for a project, but only if the student is made aware of the relevant domestic and international rules on blasphemy laws, freedom of speech and the protection of religious observance.

Study the following project plan, proposing to look at the controversial area of terrorism and public safety.

---

**Example**

#### 'Terrorism and the Protection of the State'

The aim of this project is to study the evils of terrorism and how the state may take steps to control it. It will be argued that in the light of the atrocious events in New York and London that Parliament and the courts require additional powers to control terrorism and that the normal safeguard of due process and civil liberties should not be available to terrorists.

---

The proposal has several flaws. First, the title is too wide and vague – it does not suggest that the student is going to research the legal issues involved in the law against terrorism. Second, the aims are vague and there is little indication what the focus of the project will be, including which laws are going to be studied. Third, the language used in the aims is too subjective and passionate, indicating that the project will simply include the views of the author on 'what we should do with terrorists'!

In this case, the student needs some assistance in focusing on the legal issues – the relevant legislation, its compatibility with domestic and international law, and the compatibility of recent proposals with human rights norms.

## Ensure That You Can Access Sufficient Information on the Subject Quickly and Easily

You will be expected to choose something novel and interesting, but you must ensure that you will be able to find and access the sources necessary to complete your project. There is no point choosing an area that, although exciting and controversial, will pose too many problems in accessing the necessary information. For example, if you choose to study the law of another jurisdiction, you may run into difficulties when you attempt to access relevant texts, articles and cases.

Many projects will require you to go beyond sources available in your own library (or available on legal websites), but at least initially, check whether the information is available at these points. If they aren't, then you can identify that early on and explore other possibilities.

Specifically, if your project is going to involve empirical research or questionnaires, check whether you are likely to be allowed access to this information. Always have a backup just in case these sources or information do not materialise. For example, if you intend to do a project on prisoners' rights, and intend to interview prisoners and prison officers, always have a library-based project to fall back on if your interviewees let you down. The key is to start your research early, just in case it does not go as expected.

As with any coursework, get to the library early and never underestimate the benefit of early research. Although photocopying is not the same as research, it is often a good idea to get paper copies of relevant articles as soon as possible. That way, at least you know that you have your copy and you will not be competing with others for that source at a more vital time.

## Devise an Appropriate and Interesting Title

Students often find it difficult to devise an appropriate title for their project, but it is an essential part of the whole exercise.

- Your title should clearly reflect the focus of your project and provide the reader with a clear idea as to its content. For example, 'The protection of the right to celebrity privacy in English law' identifies the legal area and the focus of the study, implying that the central thrust of the project is the inquiry into whether the law provides adequate protection of this right. Although there will be much discussion on press freedom and the public right to know, if there is too much emphasis on this aspect, then the content of the piece will not reflect the title, and vice versa.

- Do not choose a title that looks like an essay question. Students are used to essay questions and often use similar questions for their projects. For example, it would not be appropriate to title your project 'The existing laws on privacy protection are inadequate and incoherent. Discuss.'

- Make your title snappy and informative. You can always add a subtitle for fuller description – 'Protecting Celebrity Privacy: An Examination of Domestic Privacy Laws on the Protection of the Private Lives of Public Figures.'

- You can choose an eye-catching title, provided it is not too sensational or frivolous – 'An Insult to Humanity or Plain Free Speech? The Acceptability of Criminal Laws for Denying the Holocaust' is acceptable, but 'Political Correctness and Denying the Holocaust – Is Austria the New Fascist State?' is not.

### Set Yourself a Realistic and Clear Remit

Make sure you choose a realistic area of study and set yourself a realistic and attainable remit. Whilst you want to choose something sufficiently novel and controversial, you should not choose something that is going to be too technical or complex to research, digest and explain. 'A Study of Blasphemy Laws in Central and South Eastern Asia' would require an inordinate amount of research and is more suited to a doctoral thesis than an undergraduate project. It would also require you to undertake very comprehensive and difficult research and to digest quite complex individual laws and theories.

Equally, ensure your aims are clear, both to you and your supervisor. Plan the aims and content of the project so that you can get a picture of the end product and how it is to be divided, and avoid submitting vague and unfocussed proposals.

---

**Example**

#### Freedom of Expression

The aim of this project is to explore the juristic and philosophical basis of the fundamental right to free speech. The project will begin with a theoretical exploration of the notion of free speech and its values. I will then identify the possible justifications for its control, detailing the case law of both domestic and international courts in the specific areas of press freedom, censorship and obscenity and indecency laws. Finally the project will make a study of Article 10 of the European Convention to examine the extent to which the Convention and the European Court of Human Rights upholds freedom of speech.

---

This proposal is far too extensive, and it would not be realistic for the author to cover that much ground, unless he did so very superficially and mechanically. The proposal contains about five separate project areas, and the author has simply copied the contents of a book on freedom of speech and used it as his proposal.

## Preparation and Research for Your Dissertation

### Settle on Your Area and Its Scope at an Early Stage

You should start thinking about whether you wish to do a project and the topic area in the middle or at the end of your second year. By that time, you should be aware of your best skills and your favourite legal areas and will have encountered enough substantive law and legal issues to make an informed decision about what sort of area you would like to research.

You will then (late in the third term) be able to approach your tutor or dissertations supervisor with a coherent and viable idea, and get his or her advice on the scope and direction of the piece.

Although the direction of the project may change slightly during the next few months, you should have a general idea of:

- what you are going to cover;
- how it might be broken into chapters;
- what angle the piece is going to take;
- whether it is going to be largely substantive law or legal theory;
- whether it will require solely library based-research or empirical study.

### Get to Know the Area Involved

It is essential that before you launch into full research of the topic that you acquaint yourself with the basics of the legal area. You may have acquired this foundation knowledge as part of your previous or concurrent law study, but it is vital that you are comfortable with the basic principles and conversant with any relevant institutions or theories. For example, if you are embarking on a project with a comparative element (e.g., USA), you must acquaint yourself with the basic framework of their legal and/or constitutional system. Similarly, if your project will require a study of international law and institutions, you will need to get some grounding in those areas before you start looking at detailed areas of your project topic.

Before you make a final decision on your topic, spend a couple of weeks reading around the subject and seeing if it is interesting and understandable. Then, conduct some basic research and learn the general principles, the statutory framework and the essential case law. You are now in better position to make a final choice of title and this preliminary reading and the knowledge you acquire from it will aid your subsequent research and understanding.

### Researching for Your Project

As you will be looking at a specialist area and will be writing a 12,000- to 15,000-word project, you will need to undertake quite extensive research. Principally you will have to find all sources – primary and secondary – that are relevant to your project, and you should not leave any substantial gaps in this respect.

- Your preliminary reading (as mentioned previously) should have uncovered a good number of sources and in turn these sources will identify further reading, cases and so on.
- You must conduct a thorough search in your, and other, law library catalogues to find both basic and specialist texts in the area, and if your project involves the study of another jurisdiction, you must conduct a proper research on relevant academic and general websites. Conduct this search early, because you may have to order these texts or visit other libraries.
- You need to do a similarly thorough research for articles, statutory law and cases on law websites, and these searches should be conducted on a regular basis throughout the academic term to ensure that you remain up to date.
- You must become familiar with specialist journals in the relevant legal area and conduct a regular search of their content to see if any relevant articles have been published.

HOW TO WRITE BETTER LAW ESSAYS

You will also need to research overseas journals to see if anything relevant has been written in them, especially if you are making a comparative study.

- You will need to consult a number of websites that have relevance to your legal area. The websites of specialist bodies, such as human rights groups, commercial organisations and governmental agencies will provide you with invaluable information on their work, recent developments and proposals and access to reports. In addition, they will have helpful links to other legal and nonlegal websites.

- You need to check whether the items you have found are actually relevant to your project. In this respect, if your aims and objectives are vague, you will find it difficult to distinguish the relevant from the irrelevant. If you have a clear idea of what you are looking for, you will be able to identify relevant sources by simply looking at the abstract provided by the website.

- You need to check daily and weekly updates on a regular basis. You will be expected to be completely up to date, and new cases or academic opinion must be incorporated into your project. Also, you should check quality newspapers every day for relevant and useful articles and points of discussion.

## Presentation

The presentation of your dissertation is of great importance. You have been working on this piece for the whole academic session, and the supervisors and markers will expect a high standard of presentation.

Your university will have guidelines and instructions about font size, spacing and layout, and you must make yourself aware of these rules and follow them. Normally you must get at least one copy of the dissertation bound within the university, with the university markings on it.

### The Abstract

Your abstract, anything between 200 and 800 words, should provide a brief explanation of the topic area, its topicality, why you have chosen the area, how you researched it and a general indication of the project's content and conclusions. One of the purposes of the abstract is to provide the reader with a clear explanation of the area, and to demystify what might be a complex or specialist area. Thus, it can be written in a reasonably informal manner, and generally it does not need to be supported by legal citations and references. The content of the abstract can differ depending on the nature of the project and the individual university, but below is a typical abstract, in this case relating to a project on the changing status of nonexecutive directors in English companies.

> **Example**
>
> The subject of this dissertation was chosen due to its topicality and relevance to modern company law. The concept of corporate governance has become a byword for corporate responsibility and accountability. Criticisms of "fat cat" directors and other unconscionable corporate practices have fuelled both public and legal debate and have led to a number of reports and reviews to consider these aspects. In particular, there have been

▼

many recommendations in respect to the traditional role of company directors and suggestions regarding the increased role of nonexecutive directors in company regulation.

This dissertation looks at the role of the nonexecutive director in corporate governance and details the various committees and their recommendations with respect to these officers. The research for the dissertation did not follow a traditional academic pattern, the information not being contained in the weightier academic journals. This led me to research in practical and trade journals that concentrated on the practical aspects of the law and its possible reform, as well as, of course, considering in-depth the Higgs Report. The dissertation was also informed by high-profile corporate activities.

Great thought was given to the approach and layout of the dissertation, in particular whether to consider the material on an issue basis or, in the alternative, in a chronological manner, the latter approach being adopted. This was primarily because the material lends itself to some repetition and considering each report in turn was a mechanism to avoid undue repetition and to provide the reader with a clear understanding of the historical treatment of these issues.

I would like to thank (my supervisor) for all her assistance during the supervision of this dissertation.

## The Introduction

After your abstract, you will need to provide an introduction. This can be a separate chapter before your main chapters or can be included as part of your first main chapter. The purpose of the introduction is to provide the reader with essential background information to the legal issue that you are going to cover in the project. Thus, the introduction should provide an explanation of any legal dilemmas that the project area might cover, some explanation of the basic legal principles or an historical account of the legal area, and some indication of how the remainder of the project will deal with the relevant issues.

Examine the following introduction (or at least extracts from the introduction) and see how it introduces the reader to the nature of the legal concept to be discussed in the project (the nonexecutive director), how that concept has been the subject of proposals for reform and how each part of the project will cover those issues.

### Example

During the 1990s new life was breathed into the role of nonexecutive directors and as a consequence their role on the board has gone through a dramatic change. The increase in profile is due to the valuable part most commentators feel they can play in corporate governance and particularly since the Cadbury[9] and Higgs[10] reviews, nonexecutive directors are now seen as the mainstay of good corporate governance, the governance debate emphasising the distinctive contribution of outsiders in helping to ensure that

---

[9] *Report of the Committee on The Financial Aspects of Corporate Governance* (Cadbury Report 1992), hereafter called the Cadbury Report.

[10] *The Higgs Review of the Role and Effectiveness of Non-Executive Directors* (January 2003), hereafter called the Higgs Review.

managers act in the interests of shareholders.[11] The Cadbury Report emphasised the contribution that independent nonexecutive directors could make, opining that the calibre of the nonexecutive members of the board is of special importance in setting and maintaining standards of corporate governance.[12] Similarly, the Higgs review stated that a board is strengthened significantly by having a strong group of nonexecutive directors with no other connection with the company as these individuals bring a dispassionate objectivity that directors with a closer relationship to the company cannot provide.[13] We shall see during this dissertation how the role of the nonexecutive director is becoming critical for not only the transparency and accountability of companies, but also for their capability and business credibility. This in turn has raised questions concerning how nonexecutive directors are selected, how their independence is assured, what their functions are and how their effectiveness may be assessed. . . .

To fully appreciate how the role of the nonexecutive director has changed it is necessary to spend a little time detailing their role prior to examination of the Higgs review. Therefore Chapter one will consider the role of the "old-style" nonexecutive director and the reports commissioned prior to the Higgs review. This is necessary, as although the Higgs review was the most specific report concerning the role of the nonexecutive director it cannot be considered in isolation, otherwise an incomplete picture of how the report came about and the ideas behind its recommendations would be produced. Chapter two is devoted to the Higgs review, its recommendations and its shortcomings. Chapter three will deal with the post-Higgs situation, in particular the new revised combined code, recent legislative proposals and the "new-style" nonexecutive director. Finally conclusions will be drawn in Chapter four.

---

[11]Beekes, Pope and Young, 'The Link Between Earnings Timeliness, Earnings Conservatism and Board Composition: evidence from the UK' (2004) Corp Gov. 12(1), 47–59, at page 47.
[12]The Cadbury Report, paragraph 4.10.
[13]The Higgs Review, paragraph 9.5.

## Laying Out Chapters

It is essential that you have some idea of how you are to split the project up into chapters, even before your meeting with the supervisor, although the supervisor will help you refine or redraft those initial ideas.

The chapters should cover the issues that you have identified in the title, your aims and objectives and your abstract. Thus if your title is 'Protecting Celebrity Privacy,' and your aims were to critically examine the legal protection of private life of public figures against press intrusion, your chapter headings might be as follows:

| Example |
| --- |
| **Chapter 1** - The protection of privacy interests in domestic law |
| **Chapter 2** - Privacy protection and self-regulation |
| **Chapter 3** - Privacy protection and the European Convention on Human Rights |
| **Chapter 4** - Privacy v Freedom of the Press; getting the right balance |

## Quality Word-Processed Work

The quality of the presentation of your dissertation is vital. The work should be professionally presented, and the quality of your word-processing and style are very important. If you are not very proficient at word-processing, then get someone to type it up for you; it will be worth it in the end because you are likely to lose marks for a poorly presented dissertation.

## Clear, Coherent and Professional Writing Style

As with advanced essays, you should employ an academically professional style when writing your dissertation. This style must be maintained throughout the whole work, so you must take great care in how you present your research and with your style of writing. Always write clearly and maintain a critical and analytical style. Examine the following extract and notice how the style is clear, and shows a confidence with the subject matter and the various sources:

### Example

The Higgs review recognised and addressed this concern, providing what may be regarded as a "comply or explain" approach with respect to independence. Thus the definition, above, allows boards to regard a director as independent, even if he or she would not be so regarded by following the strict wording of the definition; there remains, therefore, scope for interpretation.[14] Interestingly, research conducted for the Review suggests that amongst board members independence can simply have the meaning of being able, as an outsider, to see things differently. If interpreted in this way, the characteristic of independence essentially amounts to a nonexecutive director's ability to retain an "independence of mind" that allows him or her to test and challenge the thinking of executive directors on the basis of the nonexecutive director's experience elsewhere. In short, amongst directors, "independence of mind" was felt to be the key characteristic of nonexecutive directors.[15] Therefore a weakness of the review is that it allows companies to say who is independent or not without any additional, external scrutiny.[16]

---

[14] Indeed, it would seem that the essential issue is to ensure that the directors, who decide whether a director is to be regarded as independent, are accountable to shareholders and take decisions in their interests.
[15] Hans-Christoph Hirt, *supra*, note 6.
[16] Lowry & Dignam, *op cit*, note 5, at pages 383–385.

## Advanced Citation and Referencing Skills

Your university will provide specific guidance on citation and referencing of sources, and it is essential that your skills are very strong in this respect. You will be expected to display expertise in this area, and it is advisable to consult (good) previous projects before submitting your project.

- Check whether the university prefers the Harvard or Oxford style of referencing, and follow that style rigorously. (See Chapter 2 of the text for details and examples.)
- Ensure that you are conversant with the appropriate citations and abbreviations of specialist journals, statutory provisions and cases (particularly if those sources are overseas).

- Ensure you are conversant with the appropriate use of Latin phrases, such as *op cit, supra, ibid* and so on. (See Chapter 2 of the text for details and examples.)

## Appropriate, True and Properly Cited Bibliography

Your bibliography, appearing at the end of the project on separate pages, is a reflection of the research that you have conducted for the project. It must be expertly constructed but must also provide the reader with a favourable impression regarding your research and understanding of the subject area.

- Follow the rules about construction of bibliographies (see Chapter 2 of the text) and in particular any advice provided by the university in this respect.
- Again, it is important that you know which style of referencing and citation is expected (Harvard or Oxford).
- Ensure that your bibliography reflects a thorough research of the subject, including appropriately specialist secondary sources, and does not include inappropriate sources (e.g., too many basic texts, too many trade journal articles). The inclusion of a nutshell text or other basic material could be fatal at this level.
- Your bibliography should contain everything that you have read in preparation of writing your project. The source does not have to be referred to in your project; you may, for example, have read a (good) basic text(s) to gain a background or foundation knowledge, and these can be included in your bibliography even though they do not appear in the main body of the project or footnotes.
- Do not include sources that you have not read or sources you do not know the content and gist of. Although you do not have to refer to every source in your project, you must have at least read that source for it to be included in your project. If your bibliography has 100 entries, and only 20 of them have been referred to, the marker will get the impression that your bibliography is not a true one and that you have not read the majority of those sources.
- Try to find room in the project for the majority of your sources, even if they are merely cited in footnotes. In such a case, prove that you have read the source by making some reference to the content of the source – 'for further commentary on the impact of the Act on prisoners' rights, see Foster' . . . Alternatively, 'See Foster, Prisoners' Rights and the Human Rights Act 1998 [2005] PL 333, where he argues that such rights have been extended since the passing of the Act (at page 346).'
- You should split your bibliography into primary and secondary sources. If you wish you can create subheadings; for example, under 'Secondary Sources,' you can have subheadings of texts, journal articles, newspaper articles, and websites.

## Reading Over Your Work Before Submission

The quality of your presentation is a vital factor in gaining a high mark for your project. In particular, ensure that you:

- Take great care with the proof reading of your project and ensure that it as free as possible of typographical and spelling mistakes, poor grammar, and vague or inappropriate phrases.

- Leave ample time (at least one week) before the submission date to check these fine details. It will be worth it in the end, as a project with countless errors will create an impression of hurried work and a lack of care and pride in the work.
- Get someone else to check for style and grammar and to proofread for you after you have looked at it several times. Unnoticed mistakes can often be spotted by carrying out this exercise.
- Before you take it for binding, make sure the page numbers are in order and that the piece looks cohesive; for example, ensure that headings are not placed at the bottom of the page with the text on the next page.

# ● Postgraduate Assignments

## Introduction

This section of the chapter provides some basic advice with respect to the submission of postgraduate assignments. It is not intended to provide any detailed guidance to post-graduate students on matters such as research and presentation, but instead to provide some idea of the skills expected of postgraduate students. In particular, it offers some guide to those present undergraduates who are contemplating postgraduate (Master's) courses and who want to know what will be expected of them.

## Displaying Postgraduate Skills

As a postgraduate student you will be expected to display enhanced and quite sophisti-cated writing and legal skills. Most of these skills will build on those taught and learnt on your first degree, and it is essential that you possess and practise those skills whilst on your postgraduate study.

At the very least, course leaders, module leaders and external examiners will expect you to display sound skills with respect to researching the law, the use of legal materials in your assessment, citation and referencing of sources, academic writing, and professional pre-sentation and proofreading of your work. Although these skills are expected of undergradu-ate students, markers (including external markers) will expect you to have enhanced skills, and they will not be at all tolerant of lapses in these areas. Thus, if you have not acquired all or any of these skills by the time you enrol on the postgraduate programme, learn them as soon as possible so that you can practise them in your assignments.

## Tackling Postgraduate Type Assessment

Even though some postgraduate courses use examinations, case studies and presentations, many such courses assess students via extended coursework and the submission of a disser-tation at the end of the course. It is these assessments that most test the students' enhanced writing skills, and you should expect to adjust and refine your previous practises in this respect.

## The Longer Essay

The word limit for postgraduate coursework will be in the region of 4,000–6,000 words. This will test your ability to sustain legal arguments and a sound legal style throughout the whole extended work. Although it is not difficult to write 6,000 words on a legal area, to do so in a critical and analytical style in response to a searching question requires very sound skills indeed. Work of this length and standard will also require you to undertake extensive and very selective research, and to come to constructive and quite sophisticated conclusions. Expect the titles for such work to be very searching, testing analytical and critical legal skills to the full. The following question is fairly typical of the type and level of question you would receive.

This sort of question requires more than a thorough knowledge of the 1998 Act and its case law; it also requires a very sound appreciation of international human rights law and, specifically, the state's obligation under various human rights treaties to provide effective protection of human rights at the domestic level. These are quite complex areas, and the answer will require very careful and through research and a very sound appreciation of a variety of principles and substantive law.

You should undertake your research for these extended essays at an early stage, and it is vital that you build up a sound knowledge of the area by attending and preparing for relevant seminars and by undertaking the required reading for the subject on a regular basis. This way, undertaking the intensive research for the work will be less daunting and onerous.

### The Shorter, Formative Coursework

In addition to the longer essay, you may be given a smaller piece of work to submit, of approximately 2,000 words, and often used as a formative exercise – to test your knowledge and writing skills and to give the markers an indication of your ability – before the submission of the major piece(s) of work.

These smaller pieces usually test your understanding of some of the basic principles of the legal area that you are studying and may not be that demanding. However, they will test various skills such as your ability to understand and explain central concepts and rules in a concise but academically appropriate style. In addition, they provide you with an opportunity to employ your general research and writing skills and in particular become familiar with the sort of materials that you will be using throughout the course.

Although the pieces are relatively short, you should not expect descriptive questions. The questions will invariably require you to come to grips with quite wide and complex concepts and principles, and answering such questions within a short word limit is not without its difficulties.

**Example Question**

What are the fundamental characteristics and principles of public international law? (1,500 words)

The question does not require a detailed knowledge of the subject area, and such a question could be tackled quite comfortably by most undergraduate students. However, as a postgraduate student, you will not only be expected to display a sound knowledge of these basic principles and to provide a competent answer to the question; you will also be expected to provide an answer that is consistent with the skills associated with a postgraduate student. In particular you would be expected to:

- Explain the principles in a particularly structured, logical and confident manner.
- Consult a wide range of primary and secondary sources, despite the word limit. Students will not be able to get the answer from a basic textbook, but instead must show that they have consulted a number of expert views on this topic.
- Digest and utilise complex and specialist secondary sources within this word limit. The skill here is to refer, briefly, to a variety of sources and to illustrate that you have read and understood these sources despite not having space to include them in any detail in the coursework. The student should use footnotes expertly in this respect, referring to various sources and alluding to the detailed arguments contained in them. For example, 'Foster claims that the universality of international law is a myth created for the purpose of legitimising international treaties that were drafted by powerful Western states.'[25]
- Display a sound appreciation of those sources and arguments and to contribute logical and informed opinion in that area and the issues raised by the question.

### The Case Analysis or Case Note

The case analysis or case note is a popular method of assessment on postgraduate courses. You may be asked to critically analyse a central case in a particular legal area and assess its impact on that area of law.

---

**Example Question**

Explain the significance of the House of Lords' decision in Attorney-General's Reference (2004) with respect to compatibility of the reverse burden of proof in English law. (5,000 words)

---

To tackle this assessment you will need to display a number of enhanced research and writing skills.

- Consult the case notes section of a number of academic journals for guidance on format and style. As the word limit is 5,000 words, you need to consult those journals that include extensive case notes of about that length; *The Modern Law Review* is perhaps the best example, but other examples are *Public Law, International and Comparative Law Quarterly* and *Industrial Law Journal*. Other journals (*Cambridge Law Journal* and *Law Quarterly Review*) contain shorter case notes but can be cited as sound legal authority. The academic and critical style used in those journals will also

---

[25]See also the views of Foster-Harrison, in 'The Myth of Public International Law' [2004] ICLQ 200, at 228. But contrast the opinion of Foster-Jones in 'Finding Conformity in International Law' (2005) OJLS 100, at 129, where the author claims that there is sufficient international consensus to warrant the use of the label' public *international*' law (author's italics).

be consistent with the level of your assignment, where you will need to display sound postgraduate skills.

- Avoid adopting the style used for case notes in trade journals. Although these notes can often be useful, and can be expertly written, they tend to lack the appropriate detail and analysis of the previously mentioned journals.

- If the case has already been noted in an academic journal (or a number of journals), be careful not to copy that note or its style. You may, however, use the existing note as a secondary source and as an indication of modern academic opinion on the subject area and the case.

- You can employ headings to break down your case note – for example, Introduction, Facts and Decision, Analysis, Conclusions or the like. Any case note should have an introductory section (explaining the legal issues raised by the case and the specific dilemma faced by the court in the case), a clear account of the facts, an analytical account of the decision, and a critical analysis of the decision and its impact (including your conclusions).

- Do not spend too much time on the facts of the case; one paragraph will generally be adequate. Your account should be clear and contain enough information to allow the reader to appreciate the context in which the legal dispute arose and to appreciate the court's reasoning and decision.

- Your analysis of the decision should not be too descriptive. Whilst detailing the exact decision of the judge(s), the account should take the opportunity to evaluate why the judge came to that decision, what authority they applied/distinguished/overruled, and whether that decision was flawed in any respect. At this stage you can add references (in footnotes) to inform the reader of your knowledge of existing principles and case law, and to draw attention to any possible errors that you feel the judge has made in coming to the decision.

- A substantial part of the case note should be dedicated to the commentary on and critical analysis of the case. You do not, of course, have to disagree with the decision, but you should at this point highlight the approach taken by the judge, consider whether the approach and decision is consistent with previous authority or sound legal principle, and explain the impact this approach and the decision might have in this legal area.

- A case note in assessment provides you with an opportunity to explain how a decision impacts on your study of a legal area. The style is, therefore, slightly different from the one adopted in case notes in journals because, unlike the author of a case note, you are addressing a set question.

## Avoiding Basic Errors and Displaying Knowledge of the Basics

Although you will not be set coursework that tests your basic understanding of a legal area, it is essential that you possess a sound knowledge of that area. You must avoid making basic errors on the law; otherwise markers and externals will begin to question whether your work is capable of passing at postgraduate level.

- These errors can be made quite easily if you do not have a solid background in the legal area. In addition, postgraduate students often do not have the benefit of lectures or lecture handouts. It is, therefore, relatively easy to make a basic error on, say, international law, if you have not studied the subject before your postgraduate course. In particular, legal mistakes are easy to make if you have studied law in another jurisdiction.

- If you have not studied the subject before, make sure you do some preliminary reading on it before coming on to the course. In addition, although you will be referred to a number of specialist books and articles throughout the course, purchase a standard text that you can use as a companion and in order to learn the essentials of the subject.

- You do not need to cite this basic text in your bibliography or during your work if it would be inappropriate to do so – for example, to cite a very basic text on constitutional law when undertaking an extended essay on the impact of the Human Rights Act. If the text is well respected, then it may be placed in your bibliography and mentioned in your footnotes as suggested reading – "For an introduction on the British Constitution and its fundamental sources, see Bradley and Ewing, *Constitutional and Administrative Law . . .*" If you do cite the text, ensure that you are placing reliance on other, more specialist texts for your understanding and analysis of the issues.

## Enhanced Research Skills

The advice given with respect to advanced research for undergraduate dissertations applies to researching postgraduate assessments. In particular, the postgraduate student will need to make use of certain advanced sources that may not be used extensively on undergraduate programmes.

- Specialist texts – You must not rely too heavily on basic or set texts. They are there to provide the student with a grounding in the subject area, not to allow them to acquire detailed information and analysis on specialised areas.

- Quality journals – The rules about using reputed journals apply particularly to postgraduate assessments. At this level you will be expected to research, engage with and explain the most respected and complex academic views.

- Government reports and official documentation – Especially at this level, you need to be aware of any White or Green Papers, consultation documents, commissioned reports and so on, and to be able to access, use and cite them appropriately.

- Comparative materials – You will often be expected to use foreign cases and statutory provisions, international treaties and overseas academic journals in your work. Ensure you know how to access these materials – law websites sometimes have an international or European section – and cite and use them appropriately in your work.

## Enhanced Writing and Referencing Skills

You will be expected to employ enhanced and quite sophisticated writing skills. Equally, your referencing and citation of authority should be of a similarly high standard. These skills have been explained previously with respect to project writing, but on a postgraduate course the skills will need to be enhanced further to reflect the higher standard of your sources and the complexity of the question.

These skills can often be acquired and/or enhanced by regular reading of appropriate academic texts and journals. You will be given a large number of quality secondary sources to read throughout the course in order to prepare for seminars and workshops, and the more you consult these sources, and the style adopted in them, the more comfortable you will become in writing in that style. So too, your referencing and citation skills will flourish by constant reference to quality academic sources where that style is always employed.

Examine the following extract, from a 6,000-word postgraduate essay on sales by nonowners. Notice how the author uses quality texts in support of her essay and employs expert referencing and citation skills. She also adopts a professionally academic and analytical style, even when explaining the basic legal principles, spending the majority of her time examining the principles and themes, and relegating the essential facts of the case to footnotes.

---

### Example

#### Sale Under a Voidable Title

A *voidable* contract is one that may be avoided on the grounds of fraud, misrepresentation, non-disclosure, equitable mistake,[17] or duress or undue influence, as opposed to *void* contracts for mistaken identity, a lack of coincidence between the terms of the offer and the acceptance, and where goods have been stolen.[18] Under s. 23 of the Act a purchaser may be able to obtain a perfect title to goods out of an imperfect title where the rogue has sold the goods on to an innocent buyer, who buys them in good faith and without notice of the seller's defect in title.[19] This protects the innocent purchaser's rights by placing them above the true owner in cases of fraud, but the success of the innocent purchaser in such cases depends on the timing of the true owner's rescission; the law allowing the true owner to assert his ownership rights provided he does so before the purchaser buys the goods. This rule is not without controversy and in *Car and Universal Finance Ltd v Caldwell*[20] the Court of Appeal held that it was possible to avoid the contract without either telling the fraudulent person or retaking possession of the goods; in this case by informing the police and relevant motoring authorities. It has been proposed that notice to the rogue should be a prerequisite in this respect[21] and the case was not followed in Scotland on virtually identical facts.[22]

---

[17] The scope of this principle is now severely limited by the recent decision in *Great Peace Shipping v Tsvarliris Salvaging Ltd* [2003] QB 679.

[18] Benjamin, *op cit* note 9, at 7-021.

[19] 'When the seller of goods has a voidable title to them, but his title has not been avoided at the time of sale, the buyer acquires a good title to the goods, provided he buys them in good faith and without notice of the seller's defect of title'. This may not be a true exception to the *nemo dat* rule as the voidable title is still a good title until avoided. See Goode, *op cit*, note 13, at page 462.

[20] [1965] 1 QB 525. In this case a car owner had sold his car to a rogue and received a worthless cheque in return. On discovering that the cheque was worthless the next morning he immediately informed the police and motoring organisations.

[21] Twelfth Report of the Law Reform Committee (1966), Cmnd. 2958.

[22] *McLeod v Kerr* [1965] SC 253. See also See Furmston, M, *op cit* note 12, at pages 75-76.

## Summary of Advanced Essay Skills

At the end of this chapter you should be able to:

- identify and practise the skills necessary to undertake extended and advanced essays on the final years of your undergraduate programme;
- in particular, practise enhanced research, writing and referencing skills required of a student at that stage of their degree;
- adopt a more critical and analytical approach to your work, as expected of students at that stage of their study;
- make an informed decision as to whether to undertake a dissertation and to devise a realistic and appropriate title and area for such study;
- practice sound organisational skills necessary to sustain your work on the dissertation;
- acquire appropriately enhanced research, writing and referencing skills expected of a student who undertakes such work;
- acquire the necessary presentational skills to present dissertation work;
- identify the research and writing skills expected of a student who embarks on post-graduate study;
- be familiar with the variety and characteristics of postgraduate work and the expectations of internal and external markers of such work.

You can test your skills by carrying out the relevant exercises on the Companion Website (**www.pearsoned.co.uk/foster**)

# Further Reading

The advice given in this book on preparing and writing law assessments is intended to complement your law studies and your study of legal skills. In addition to reading this text, it is necessary that you consult a number of other texts that provide assistance in acquiring and practising general and specific legal skills. The texts listed here should help in this respect.

There are a number of very good texts on how to study law and how to acquire the skills necessary to survive on a law course. These texts will include some advice on how to research and write essays, but contain more general information on matters such as reading cases, interpreting statutes and employing critical and analytical skills:

Bradney, A, et al. *How to Study Law* (Sweet & Maxwell 2005) 5th ed.

Fox, M, and Bell, C. *Learning Legal Skills* (Oxford 1999), 3rd ed.

Hanson, S. *Legal Method and Reasoning* (Cavendish 2003), 2nd ed.

Holland, J, and Webb, J. *Learning Legal Rules: A Student's Guide to Legal Method and Reasoning* (Oxford 2006), 6th ed.

Kenny, P. *Studying Law* (Oxford 2003), 5th ed.

Rivlin, G. *Understanding the Law* (Oxford 2004), 3rd ed.

Stychin, C, and Mulachy, L. *Legal Method: Text and Materials* (Sweet & Maxwell 2003), 2nd ed.

In addition, there are more specialist texts on matters such as how to how to conduct advanced research, how to use a law library, how to use legal language and how to cite and reference legal authorities:

Clinch, P. *Using a Law Library: A Student's Guide to Legal Research Skills* (Oxford 2001).

Knowles, J, and Thomas, P. *Effective Legal Research* (Sweet & Maxwell 2006).

French, D. *How to Cite Legal Authorities* (Blackstone Press 1996).

Haigh, R. *Legal English* (Cavendish 2004).

Manchester, C, and Salter, D. *Exploring the Law* (Sweet & Maxwell 2006), 3rd ed.

Murray, R. *How to Write a Thesis* (Open University Press 2002).

Salter, P, and Mason, J. *Researching and Writing Legal Dissertations* (Longman 2007).

Stein,. *Law on the Web: A Guide for Students and Practitioners* (Pearson/Prentice Hall 2003).

# Index

## N

Nerve(s), exam, 153-4
*New Law Journal*, 45, 60, 185
Newspapers, scanning of, 45-6

## O

Open-book exams, 162-3
Opinion
    uninformed, 10
    unsupported, 10
*Oxford Journal of Legal Studies*, 61
Oxford method
    in citing books, 71
    in legal case citation, 66

## P

Paragraph(s), clear and structured, 10-12
Past examinations, in exam preparation, 157
Plagarism
    avoiding, 12-14
    copying from other students, 13
    defined, 12-13
    forms of, 12
    how to avoid, 14
    reading over your answer in, 17-18
    reasons for, 13-14
    reasons for avoiding, 13
    using someone's words or ideas without
        crediting them, 12-13
    wrongness of, 13
Postgraduate assignments, 198-203
    avoiding basic errors and displaying
        knowledge of basics in, 201-2
    displaying postgraduate skills
        in, 198
    enhanced research skills in, 202
    enhanced writing and referencing skills
        in, 202-3
    introduction to, 198
    longer essay in, 198-201
    tackling postgraduate type assessment
        in, 198
Preparation, in essay writing, 5
Primary source, *vs.* secondary source, 36-7
Problem question(s), 21, 26, 161. *See also*
        Problem question answers
    always read facts carefully, 122
    answering of, 117-49
    contract formation problem, 124-33
    defined, 117
    essay questions *vs.*, 118-19
    identifying legal areas in, 119-20
    reasons for setting, 117-18
    statutory interpretation/judicial review
        problem in, 133-49
    tackling of, 119-24
    understanding of, 117-19

Problem question answers. *See also* Problem
        question(s)
    case use in, 42
    consider all options in, 122-23
    do no just state law in, 121
    do not give vague and open advice
        in, 121-2
    do not invent facts in, 123
    do not repeat facts in, 122
    ensure that your conclusions are as clear
        and full as possible in, 123-4
    giving clear, simple, but full advice in, 120-1
    use only relevant cases and statutes in, 121
Proper citation, in law assessments, 15
*Public Law*, 62, 200

## Q

Queen's Bench Reports (QB), 46
Question(s)
    analytical, 26-8
    case use in answering, 49-50
    choice of, 24-5
    components of, 19-20
    conceptual, 180
    demanding, 180-1
    descriptive, 26-8
    difficulty with, 28-30
    do not select your own, 18
    essay, 26, 118-9
    exam, 150-78. *See also* Answering
        exam questions
    in law assessments, 18-33. *See also*
        Answering questions
    legal, 181
    on legal theory, concepts, and institutions
        or substantive law, 25-6
    problem, 21, 26, 161. *See also* Problem
        question(s)
    seminar, 157
    theoretical, 180-1
    types of, 25-8
    understanding of, 159-60
Question spotting, in exam preparation,
        158-9
Question-and-answer books, in exam
        preparation, 157-8

## R

Reading over your answer, in law
        assessments, 17-18
Recent legal developments, in essays, 183-4
Reference(s)
    in essay writing, 72-3
    multiple, 46-7
Referencing of sources
    in law assessments, 15
    legal, 65-72

Referencing skills
    advanced, 196-197
    enhanced, 202-203
Relevant sources, in question answering, 31
Report(s)
    journal, 45-6
    law, 44-5
Research
    for dissertation, 191-3
    in essay writing, 5
    greater, 182-3
    in-depth, 182-3
    of law assessments, 6-7
Research skills, enhanced, 202
Re-sit exams, 168-9
Respect, for module and module
    leader, 3-4
Revision process, in exam preparation, 154-9.
    *See also* Exam preparation


**S**

Secondary sources, 36-40
    credit for, 39-40
    within secondary sources, 39
Seen exams, 163
Seminar questions, in exam preparation, 157
Skills
    in question answering, 30
    tested on law exams, 150
*Solicitor's Journal,* 45, 60
Source(s)
    advanced, 184-5
    in essay writing, 36-40
    primary, 36-7
    proper citation and referencing of, 15
    in question answering, 31
    secondary, 36-40
    use of relevant cases in, 54-5
Spelling errors, in law assessments, 8
State of law, explaining and criticising of, 32
Statutory instruments, citing of, 68
Statutory interpretation/judicial review
    problem, 133-49
Statutory materials, citing of, 67-9
Statutory materials use
    convey correct gist of provision in
        paraphrasing in, 58
    ensure that statutory provision is not out
        of date and has not been repealed or
        amended, 59
    in essay writing, 56-60
    indications for, 56-60
    learn to extract relevant words of statute
        in, 57-8

quote relevant section or subsection and
    year of act or regulation in, 56-7
Submission of work, reading over prior to,
    197-8
Substantive legal topics, questions on, 25


**T**

Teaching staff, respect for, 3-4
Theoretical and demanding questions, 180-181
Time management
    in essay writing, 3
    in exams, 164
Treaty(ies), international, 68-9
Typographical errors, in law assessments, 8


**U**

Undergraduate courses, law assessments of, 1-2
Undergraduate level, extended essays
    at, 179-86
Undergraduate projects, 187-98
    abstract in, 193-4
    advanced citation and referencing skills
        in, 196-7
    appropriate, true, and properly cited biblio-
        graphy in, 197
    choosing legal area and title in, 188-91
    clear, coherent, and professional writing
        style in, 196
    introduction in, 194-5
    introductory points in, 187
    laying out chapters in, 195
    preparation and research for dissertation
        in, 191-3
    presentation of, 193-8
    quantity word-processed work in, 196
    reading over your work before submission
        in, 197-8
    selection of, 187-91
Understanding, individual, 31
Uninformed opinion, in law assessments, 10
Unsupported opinion, in law assessments, 10


**W**

Website(s)
    citing of, 72
    in essay writing, 64-5
Weekly Law Reports (WLR), 46
WESTLAW, 46, 61
WLR. *See* Weekly Law Reports (WLR)
Word-processed work, 7-8
Writing, enhanced, 181-2
Writing skills, enhanced, 202-3
Writing style, clear and coherent, 8-10

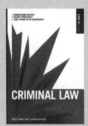